The

PRODIGAL SON
PROPHECY

God's Amazing Plan for the Restoration of the Two
Hebrew Houses and the Salvation of the Gentiles

By Dr. Scott Lively

THE PRODIGAL SON PROPHECY
First Century Bible Church Press,
PO Box 2373, Springfield, Massachusetts, 01101
With assistance from The Old Paths Publishing,
142 Gold Flume Way, Cleveland, GA 30528

Throughout this book we have used the King James for accuracy and NASB or BSB for clarity in modern English, which usage falls within "fair use" guidelines.

Unless otherwise noted, photos and graphics are public domain or the property of the author.

For readability, long quotations from Scripture are not indented but long non-Scriptural quotations are indented.

DEDICATION

This book is dedicated to Marian Oxana,
whose comments over dinner, in the company of her husband Vitalie,
in Chisnau, Moldova in late February of 2011,
launched me on the intensive study of prophecy
that the book is based upon.

TABLE OF CONTENTS

PRELIMINARIES

SECTION ONE

SECTION TWO

SECTION THREE

LIST OF ILLUSTRATIONS

Note: A larger sized version of some of these charts and graphs may be found at the back of this book for those who have difficulty reading the text in the smaller sized version.

Front cover: *Pharoah honors Joseph* by Sir Edward John Poynter, Dalziels' Bible Gallery, 1881.

Back cover: The Menorah of Zechariah's Vision, Jewish Cervera Bible 1299–1300AD.

PRELIMINARIES

INTRODUCTION: WHOLE-BIBLE CHRISTIANITY

I love the Living Word of God, the Bible. Of course, God also speaks to us through His wondrous Creation, and in the still, small voice of His Holy Spirit, who literally dwells in those who have accepted Christ as Savior. But His Bible is our complete, detailed instruction manual in all things that pertain to this life and the one to come. It is a resource of inestimable value whose counsel and decrees overwhelmingly trump every human authority on every possible question. To believe that and act accordingly is the essence of what it means to have a "Biblical worldview."

Much of the church of the modern western world has lost that Biblical worldview. Biblical literacy has plummeted, worldly "wisdom" has supplanted Biblical authority in the minds of average Christians on any number of issues, and most disturbingly, the church as a whole has developed what I characterize as "New Testament Myopia:" the nearly exclusive emphasis on the New Testament in preaching and teaching. The Old Testament is regarded as "Jewish stuff," largely irrelevant to Christianity except in small doses to illustrate some point of New Testament doctrine.

However, when Paul wrote in 2 Timothy 3:16 that "*All Scripture is given by inspiration of God, and is profitable for doctrine, for reproof, for correction, for instruction in righteousness*" he used the Greek word *graphe*, meaning the Old Testament. He undoubtedly meant to include in his definition of scripture what we know today as "New Testament" writings, but when Paul wrote 2 Timothy, the various scattered pieces of the New Testament had not yet been assembled, and 2 Peter, Hebrews, Jude, Revelation and the Gospel and Epistles of John had not even been written. Before He had supplanted the Mosaic law by His death and resurrection, Jesus Himself told His disciples in Matthew 23:2-3: "*The scribes and Pharisees sit in Moses' seat. So practice and observe everything they tell you. But do not do what they do, for they do not practice what they preach.*"

God gave Christians the whole Bible, and all of its books are His Living Word. Jesus didn't bring the New Covenant to "correct the mistakes" of the Father or apologize for His "excesses." He said "*I and the Father are One,*" and built directly upon the foundation of the Old Covenant, teaching emphatically that "*until heaven and earth pass away, not the smallest letter or stroke shall pass from the Law until all is accomplished.*" His teachings augment and elevate the Old Testament, but as He Himself made clear, they don't abolish it (Matthew 5:17-19).

In contrast to and correction of "New Testament Myopia" is what I call Whole Bible Christianity, which I define as embracing and following the whole counsel of God's Word. Here in America, from the time of the Pilgrim's landing till just a few decades ago, Christians read, trusted and followed the whole Bible, and not just the New Testament. Our government was designed on principles drawn largely from the Old Testament, such as Isaiah 33:22 "*For the LORD is our judge, the LORD is our lawgiver, the LORD is our king; he will save us.*" That scripture is the basis for our tripartite governmental structure and constitutional separation of powers. Until relatively recently our courts followed the "Common Law," drawn primarily from Old Testament, and the whole Bible – from Genesis to Revelation -- was America's favorite public school textbook.

We have been greatly impoverished by losing our whole-Bible perspective and many if not most of our social ills are the direct consequence. It is one thing to affirm the New Testament truth that Christians are not bound to the letter of the law or the rituals. It's an entirely different and unscriptural matter to treat the law, the rituals, the feasts, the history and the prophecies of the Old Testament as discarded relics of the past and to replace them with human-created alternatives.

As Jesus taught in the Beatitudes, Christians are actually held to a higher standard than the written law, in being subject to it's underlying spirit and intention (e.g hate is murder, lust is adultery). So while in His grace we can exercise freedom in HOW we keep the law, and we are assured that the penalty for our sins was paid by His blood, we nevertheless remain subject to its underlying principles, and not granted a license to sin in any aspect of it. The Olive Tree into which we are grafted is still rooted in Old Testament soil (Romans 11).

Whole Bible Christianity is thus compatible in many ways with the emerging Messianic Judaism movement which accepts Jesus as the Messiah and attempts to realign the beliefs and practices of modern Judaism to Him. However, just as it is true that the "whole Bible" Christians of the very early years of the church closely fellowshipped with Jews on the Sabbath (Saturday) in the synagogues, their separate worship of Christ was done on the first day of the week (Sunday). And Paul, the former "Pharisee of Pharisees," was even then strongly cautioning believers not to trade their freedom in Christ for the legalism of ritual Judaism (see especially Galatians 3), as some in Messianic Judaism have done.

Importantly, the form of Judaism influencing many of today's Messianic Jews is not primarily the temple-centered Torah-based Judaism of the apostles' era, which was still debating whether Jesus was the Messiah, but the Jesus-rejecting second century (and following) Babylonian Talmudic form observed in the Jewish Diaspora after the final Roman expulsion of the Jews from the Holy Land in 135 AD.

Let me clarify that I believe Bible-faithful Messianic Judaism will be the religion of the Millennial Kingdom, practiced by the human beings living on earth during the coming thousand year physical reign of Christ. And I think its emergence in this generation is a Holy Spirit phenomenon, representing the front edge of the cusp of the reunification of the two Hebrew houses that will be completed in the Millennial Kingdom. Thus, Christians should embrace and facilitate its development by exhorting Messianic Jews to anchor firmly in the Bible and not the Talmud. And we should welcome with eagerness the wealth of knowledge that Messianic Jews can share with us about the Hebrew roots of Christianity.

Whole-Bible Christianity is then a place of common ground – a theologically "safe space" – for the traditional branches of Christianity to interface with Messianic Judaism for mutual enrichment.

It is upon that common ground that the foundations for this book are laid, because nowhere are the Hebrew roots of Christianity more essential than in the field of prophecy. And indeed, I suggest that it is not possible to correctly discern the plan of God for our future without a firm grasp of the Hebrew cultural perspective of the prophets and the apostles. To that thesis, this book is offered as evidence.

FOREWORD: MY PERSONAL GROUND RULES FOR PROPHECY STUDY

1. Be Humble

There have been many spectacular failures in the field of prophecy, most of which involve setting dates for the return of Christ or some other key end-times milestone. From William Miller in the mid-1800s to Hal Lindsey and Harold Camping in more recent decades, the trail is littered with examples of what we might charitably call bad guesses -- except most of these "guessers" spoke with certainty about their predictions.

I want to avoid that pitfall. While I am diligent in my research and know that God has gifted me with a good analytical mind, I freely confess that I do not have all the answers, and that I could be wrong on any number of facts or speculations.

But neither do I want to run with the mob that bashes "date setters" as heretics as is so fashionable today. In my reading of Scripture I find no Biblical prohibition on speculating about the timing of the second coming or other future events, so long as one doesn't make the deadly mistake of falsely claiming to speak for the Lord (Deuteronomy 18:20). If in this study I venture to make educated guesses about future events I will endeavor to clarify the speculative nature of my conclusions and show the steps in my deductive reasoning.

Furthermore, unlike most prophecy teachers I have encountered, I readily admit that most of what I know is based on others' work. Sometimes I have original ideas by the prompting of the Holy Spirit (these are moments of great excitement) but, like everyone else, I learned most of what I know from other people. I will endeavor to give them credit where it is due.

Importantly, I am not in complete agreement with any of the prophecy teachers I have read. Indeed, I believe some of them are wrong in most of what they teach. However, I always intend to accept truth where I find it and never to "throw out the baby with the bathwater."

"For the word of God is quick, and powerful, and sharper than any two-edged sword, piercing even to the dividing asunder of soul and spirit, and of the joints and marrow, and is a discerner of the thoughts and intents of the heart" (Hebrews 4:12).

The biblically-minded scholar should carry the two-edged sword of Hebrews 4:12 into every intellectual pursuit: dividing truth from error with precision, always preserving and honoring what is true. And conversely, rejecting what is false, no matter how eminent the person asserting it. God is not a respecter of persons (Acts 10:34) and neither should we be.

2. Think Like a Judge, Not a Lawyer

"Do not show partiality in judging; hear both small and great alike. Do not be afraid of anyone, for judgment belongs to God" (Deuteronomy 1:17).

I happen to be a lawyer in addition to being a pastor. Lawyers are often paid big money for their skills in advocating for their clients. In other words, we specialize in championing one point of view against all opposing views.

Judges on the other hand have an ethical duty to be impartial and to hear all the evidence before rendering an opinion on a matter.

In studying prophecy we should not only think like judges -- holding our conclusions lightly and remaining open-minded as we go -- but we should also be very hesitant to draw firm conclusions because so much of the evidence before us is necessarily speculative. How could it be otherwise when many of the prophetic events we're considering haven't happened yet?

Unfortunately, many Christians tend to think and act like lawyers on matters of doctrine, including eschatology (the study of end-times theology). It is a problem that is in fact worsened by the phenomenon of denominationalism in which churches tend to train members exclusively in their own perspective of Scripture, rather than teaching a holistic biblical worldview and critical thinking skills with which to understand the Bible for themselves.

Denominationally-bound believers typically hear one perspective on prophecy and then start advocating for it without any real understanding of other views. Look at the comments sections under prophecy-oriented news stories on the Internet and you'll see lots of these folks battling it out like armchair quarterbacks after a Superbowl game.

In this book I will make arguments for what I believe to be the correct conclusions but also acknowledge opposing views, especially regarding matters of which I am less confident.

3. Stay Biblically Grounded

I believe in the absolute authority of the Bible in all matters of doctrine and theology and in a contextual interpretation of its meaning within the totality of all the Scripture. This study will therefore rest on a foundation of Scripture. Most of my key assertions will include citations to the scriptural references I rely upon.

One glaring fault shared by many prophecy teachers today is the problem of selective editing of the Bible. Beware of teachers who rely heavily on scriptures which support their theories and ignore or dismiss passages contradictory to them.

I strongly believe that if a person can't reconcile the apparent contradictions in the text of the Bible -- in a manner that flows smoothly and naturally -- then that person doesn't yet understand the truth being conveyed.

In my view, the Word of God is perfectly harmonious and I will work to present a natural reading of it in this study.

4. Follow a Hebrew rather than a Hellenic Perspective

"Beloved, while I was making every effort to write you about our common salvation, I felt the necessity to write to you appealing that you contend earnestly for <u>the faith which was once for all handed down to the saints</u>" (Jude 1:3).

Every word of the Holy Bible was written down before the end of the first century by those who either received the teaching of the Judean Messiah, Jesus Christ, personally or secondhand via one of His Hebrew disciples. The *"faith which was once for all handed down to the saints*, is thus best understood from the Hebrew cultural perspective they shared, not the Hellenic (Greek) perspective of the generations that followed.

As Paul emphasized, the Gospel of Christ was only a *"stumbling block"* to the Jews (our spiritual first cousins) but was *"to the Greeks, foolishness"* (1 Corinthians 1:23). "Greeks" in this context refer to all the various enthicities and nationalities of the Roman Empire, whose culture was adopted from the Greek Empire it had conquered and supplanted. The presuppositions of the "Greeks" regarding God specifically and spiritual matters generally, were far different from those of Jews and Christians.

Likewise, the study of prophecy is a minefield for those who study it from a Greek perspective, and they are invariably forced to "spiritualize" (and thus confuse) concepts, symbols and events that make perfect literal sense from a Torah-literate Hebrew perspective.

This is not, however, a Catholic or Orthodox v. Reformed issue, because nearly every Christian denomination since Constantine follows a Greek perspective regarding prophecy.

Neither does "Hebrew perspective" in this context mean "Jewish perspective" since modern Talmudic Judaism does not necessarily hold the Hebrew perspective of the first century, which was based on the Torah (what Jesus called *"the law and the prophets"* in Matthew 5:17). In contrast, the earliest portions of the Talmud were written in Babylon starting around 200 AD. Thus, the legitimacy of the various Jewish sources today must be measured by their faithfulness to the Torah, not the Talmud, just as Christian sources must be measured by their faithfulness to the Bible, not denominational leaders or doctrines.

Importantly, contrary to the false claims of some critics of the Hebrew Roots movement, seeking the Hebrew perspective as a guide to deeper understanding of Scripture does not mean that Christians should go back under the law of Moses. Paul warns against that very clearly in his epistles, writing, for example:

"Christ hath redeemed us from the curse of the law, being made a curse for us: for it is written, Cursed is every one that hangeth on a tree: That the blessing of Abraham might come on the Gentiles through Jesus Christ; that we might receive the promise of the Spirit through faith" (Galatians 3:13-14).

Yet former Pharisee Paul, God's choice to be the Apostle to the Gentiles, revealed the perfect balance of law and grace in his Hebrew Roots teachings, tempering Galatians 3 with such passages as Romans 11 (where the Hebrew Roots theme originates), and Hebrews 5:11-6:20, where he sharply rebukes those who lack a Hebrew perspective of Scripture regarding God's promises to Abraham.

To clarify, then, I define "Hebrew perspective" as "The New Testament interpreted primarily through the teachings of the Old-Testament-as-read-literally, supplemented by the writings of the first century disciples of the Apostles, who may be presumed to know better than anyone else what Jesus and the Apostles meant by the things they said, and for whom the subtleties and nuances of the parables, metaphors and symbols employed in Scripture were understood as present-day cultural references."

After I began studying prophecy from a Hebrew perspective, I was forced to reconsider many of the things I thought I already knew about prophecy.

5. How to Get the Most Out of This Study

First, wipe the slate clean and resolve to re-study prophecy, letting go of whatever you may have already been taught. Be ready to reclaim those beliefs that you can confirm by your own Berean-style study and to leave behind or modify those that you discover are false or flawed.

Second, buy a new Bible exclusively for prophecy study and mark it up with highlighting and margin notes, and insert additional note pages in key sections. It will be very helpful to have all the key passages flagged.

Third, start re-reading the Old Testament with a prophetic eye and a literalist's mind, from Genesis 1:1, examining every scripture for its end-time implications, as if the entire Bible was written for the last days as much or more than for ages past (as I am convinced it was). Read voraciously.

Lastly, stay in fellowship with Bible-grounded believers. The last days are upon us and the world as we have known it is crumbling apace. Let us take joy in the fellowship of the remnant and seek value in these relationships rather than in the darkening material world. Let us also search evangelistically and diligently for others to join us in this lifeboat.

6. How this Book is Organized

This book has three distinct sections.

The first section, **A Fresh Look at End-Time Prophecy**, is an attempt to identify and explicate the fundamentals of end-time prophecy from a first-century Christian perspective, as if none of the various existing prophecy assumptions being taught by the various denominations had been written. Many "mainstream" Christians will be unfamiliar with the facts presented in this section but will likely find them very interesting and illuminating. Some of the analysis and conjecture in this section is original to the author, while most is a compilation, re-phrasing and reorganization of the teachings of various competent teachers and scholars.

The second section, **The Two House Prophecy**, is a reinterpretation and revalidation of the so-called Two House Teaching that was well known to many nineteenth-and early twentieth-century Christian believers but rejected by later generations after it was co-opted and corrupted by various cultic and racist organizations.

In its original, uncorrupted form, this astonishingly powerful and enriching Bible teaching, which is not in the least racist or antisemitic in its original form, opens a dimension of Bible knowledge that can be likened to putting on spiritual 3-D eyeglasses. Once enlightened, the student will begin to recognize the Two House teaching interwoven throughout the entire Bible, with profound theological implications.

I implore the reader who has previously encountered this teaching in any form not to prejudge this section as if you already know its assertions and arguments. In my experience <u>very few</u> Christians have encountered the original pristine form of the teaching that is presented here. Please give me a chance to walk you through the facts as the Bible presents them, uncorrupted by the human agendas that have tainted nearly every variation of this teaching that has emerged over the past century.

The third section, **What Happens Next?**, is a discussion on the Law of Cumulative Sin relative to the prophecies of a last-days apostasy and an assessment of the extent to which apostasy has manifested in the United States (as a representative of the world system). It offers insights and analysis of the factors most central to the rise of apostasy, and makes predictions about what is most likely to occur next based upon past and current events.

A Short Summary of the Prodigal Son Prophecy

Like so many of the teachings of Jesus, an apparently simple message unlocks a door to profound understanding of the things of God...but only for those who have eyes to see. Jesus said that He taught in parables intentionally to hide the deeper truths of His teachings from the less diligent, so that "*seeing they might not see, and hearing they might not understand*" (Luke 8:10).

One way to see but not see the teaching of the Parable of the Prodigal Son is to interpret the message at its most superficial level -- that God joyfully welcomes sinners who repent. How many sermons have we all heard (or, like me, preached) in mainstream Christian churches on that theme?

That teaching is, of course, true, but it's not the main point or purpose of the parable.

The Parable of the Prodigal Son is a teaching by Jesus on the restoration and reunion of the House of Judah and the House of Israel in the last days. He was expounding it to fellow Hebrews who should all have been intimately familiar with the prophecies of Isaiah, Hosea, Jeremiah, Ezekiel and others that addressed the division of the twelve tribes of the House of Jacob and their eventual reunification in the Millennial Kingdom. Many of the then-current Jewish leaders -- being Herodians (Edomite converts to Judaism aligned with Edomite King Herod) or being Judaic hyper-legalists (whose extra-Biblical theology supplanted the Bible) -- were less likely to know these prophecies.

Only people with an authentic *Hebrew* Biblical worldview could actually see what Jesus wanted them to see. And that remains true to this day. Only competent knowledge of the Scripture *from an Apostolic-era Hebrew perspective* unlocks the Parable of the Prodigal Son.

Very simply, the father in the parable is God. The older son is Judah, and the younger (prodigal) son is Joseph. These are the two sons of Jacob's wives Leah and Rachel, respectively (the human roots of the two houses and later two kingdoms of Judah and Israel). Joseph, who is represented by his son Ephraim among the twelve tribes (as the head of the House of Israel), led his house into idolatrous rebellion against God so egregiously that God "divorced" the House of Israel and sent him/them away to live among the Gentiles. God then made a way for Israel to be restored that simultaneously opened the door to salvation for the Gentiles. To allay any doubt of His intended meaning to the alert Hebrew listeners, Jesus used the symbolism of the ring, the robe and the sandals to clearly link the restoration of the "Prodigal Son" to the story of Joseph's restoration from prison to high position by the Egyptian Pharaoh in Genesis 41.

That, in its most simplistic form, is the deeper and more profound meaning of the parable, hidden in plain sight from Christians (like myself) who had always looked at the Old Testament as "Jewish stuff" only marginally relevant to Christians.

If these ideas seem foreign to you, prepare to be shocked at how foundational they are to prophecy as it is actually written in the Old Testament. You will find that these aren't mere speculation, but the plain, literal teaching of prophets, when seen through the proper contemporary Hebrew cultural perspective.

This summary is just to whet your appetite. The deep and detailed scriptural support for this summary is explained in Chapter 7 for those who would like to read ahead, though it would be best to approach this study systematically, reading the book in the sequence in which it is written. We've constructed this book carefully, precept upon precept, line upon line, to make clear and simple what might otherwise seem complex and obtuse if approached piecemeal.

Importantly, while the parable (the key) can be unpacked and explained in a few pages, the far more valuable treasure lies behind the door that it unlocks: the Hebrew cultural perspective of the Word that can (with diligent study) illuminate ALL of the rest of the Bible to the initiated, including the Two House teaching that is so central to history and prophecy. That door is now open to the reader who grasps the premise. The astounding implications of it will become increasingly more obvious as you proceed.

What we mean by Whole Bible perspective is the study of Scripture as it would have been understood by first century Christians in the Hebrew cultural milieu that the Apostles and their disciples shared throughout their entire lives, as distinct from the Hellenic (Greek) perspective of the church in later centuries. The latter is a perspective which persists even to this day, recognized in such things as the keeping of Christianized pagan holidays (e.g., Christmas and Easter) to the exclusion or outright ignorance of the actual Biblical holidays established by God in Leviticus 23 (e.g. Passover, Tabernacles). We should celebrate Christmas and Easter but also remember the biblical holidays.

Again, we feel it necessary to distinguish Whole Bible Christianity from the Hebrew Roots movement, which has been mischaracterized by critics as a collection of Judaizing cults drawing Christians back under the law of Moses, when in reality the movement includes a broad spectrum of Hebrew-oriented organizations and individuals who simply seek to explore and understand the Hebrew perspective on New Testament teachings -- from otherwise thoroughly mainstream Christian churches which have a nominal interest in the Hebrew perspective, to full-fledged "Messianic Jewish" groups and individuals who accept Christ as Messiah but also study and attempt to follow the Mosaic law.

By defining our approach as Whole Bible Christianity we seek to show that holding a Hebrew cultural perspective of the Scripture does not equate to trading freedom in Christ for Jewish legalism, though some in the Hebrew Roots movement do that. Remember that it was Paul who showed the healthy balance between law and grace in his writings, warning against Judaizers on the one hand, while exhorting Christian believers to retain the Hebrew cultural perspective of Scripture on the other.

In Hebrews 5:11-6:3 Paul sternly rebukes the Christian believers for their lack of understanding of the Hebrew perspective:

"We have much to say about this [the nature and history of the Hebrew priesthood], but it is hard to explain, because you are dull of hearing. Although by this time you ought to be teachers, you need someone to re-teach you the basic principles of God's word. [To your shame] you need milk, not solid food! Everyone who lives on milk is still an infant, inexperienced in the message of righteousness. **But solid food is for the mature,** *who by constant use have trained their sensibilities to distinguish good from evil [and no longer have to be exhorted continually in matters of morals and ethics].* **Therefore let us leave the elementary teachings about Christ and go on to maturity,** **NOT** *laying again the foundation of* repentance from dead works, *and of* faith in God, *instruction about* baptisms, *the* laying on of hands, *the* resurrection of the dead, *and* eternal judgment. *And this [moving past these kindergarten lessons] we will do, if God permits."* [Bracketed comments here and throughout this book are mine for clarification and/or interpretation relevant to this study.]

Consider the implications for typical Christian churches in this exhortation. If you took away the weekly sermons directly or indirectly based on these topics what would be left? Not much in many churches. And that's just among the more conservative Bible-centered churches. In these days of loose pop-culture morality and "seeker sensitivity" these "milky" subjects are considered *too* substantial and "fundamentalist" in many less faithful churches.

However, for those wanting to press on to spiritual maturity, Paul provides clues about what might be considered "meat" in contrast to the "milk." We've noted that the immediate context suggests that learning and teaching the Hebrew perspective is "meat," generally speaking, but he also makes a specific doctrinal point in his transition from chastisement back to the substance of his lesson:

"When God made His promise to Abraham, since He had no one greater to swear by, He swore by Himself, saying, 'I will surely **[1] bless you** *and* **[2] multiply your descendants'** *And so Abraham, after waiting patiently, obtained the promise. Men swear by someone greater than themselves, and their oath serves as a confirmation to end all argument. So when* **God wanted to make the unchanging nature of His purpose very clear to the heirs of the promise,** *He guaranteed it with an oath.* **Thus by** two unchangeable things *[these* **promises]** **in which it is impossible for God to lie,** *we who have fled to take hold of the hope set before us may be strongly encouraged"* (Hebrews 6:13-18).

As we will clearly show in this book, God's promises to Abraham are at the heart of the Two House teaching. These two separate but parallel promises were held as one package by Abraham, Isaac and Jacob in turn, but divided between the two houses of Jacob's family: Leah's son Judah receiving the first promise, and Rachel's son Joseph receiving the second promise as their inheritance from their father.

There is certainly more that Paul would consider "meat" suitable for the spiritually maturing Christian, but understanding the Hebrew roots of the gospel is the example that he used, and is the very study in which we are engaged. So let's get on with it.

THE HEBREW ROOTS MOVEMENT AS A MANIFESTATION OF THE SPIRIT OF ELIJAH

Presumably many readers of a prophecy-themed book such as this likely agree with this writer that ours is probably the last generation before the Millennial Kingdom. But that is by no means a prerequisite to the study of the Hebrew roots of the New Testament and there is much to learn from this book that is unrelated to one's eschatology. Nevertheless, the facts and deductions we will examine support the last-days assumption.

One matter that is speculative on this writer's part is the notion that the Hebrew Roots movement we will now explore is in a spiritual sense a partial fulfillment of Malachi Chapter 4:1-5:

"For behold, the day is coming, burning like an oven, when all the arrogant and all evildoers will be stubble. The day that is coming shall set them ablaze, says the LORD of hosts, so that it will leave them neither root nor branch. But for you who fear my name, the sun of righteousness shall rise with healing in its wings. You shall go out leaping like calves from the stall. And you shall tread down the wicked, for they will be ashes under the soles of your feet, on the day when I act, says the LORD of hosts. Remember the law of my servant Moses, the statutes and rules that I commanded him at Horeb for all Israel. **Behold, I will send you Elijah the prophet before the great and awesome day of the LORD comes. And <u>he will turn the hearts of fathers to their children and the hearts of children to their fathers</u>,** *lest I come and strike the land with a decree of utter destruction."*

Letting the Bible interpret the Bible, the "fathers" are almost certainly the patriarchs, Abraham, Isaac and Jacob (Romans 9:5), and the children are believers in God through faith (Romans 9:7-8).

As with the first advent of Christ, there may be a physical Elijah figure (a last-days equivalent to John the Baptist) preceding His second coming as some believe. But in a broader spiritual sense the Spirit of Elijah (2 Kings 2:15) seem to already be operating through Christian believers of the Hebrew Roots movement, whose function and purpose is to awaken believers to their Hebrew spiritual heritage: turning the hearts of the children to the fathers.

SECTION ONE

A FRESH LOOK AT
END-TIME PROPHECY

A Christian Lawyer and Pastor Examines the End-Time Prophecies of the Bible *De Novo* from the Hebrew Cultural Perspective of the First Century Church

CHAPTER ONE:

WHAT JESUS TAUGHT THE APOSTLES ABOUT THE LAST DAYS

"And I saw a strong angel proclaiming with a loud voice, "Who is worthy to open the book and to break its seals?" And no one in heaven or on the earth or under the earth was able to open the book or to look into it. Then I began to weep greatly because no one was found worthy to open the book or to look into it; and one of the elders said to me, "Stop weeping; behold, the Lion that is from the tribe of Judah, the Root of David, has overcome so as to open the book and its seven seals" (Revelation 5:2-5).

Prophecy of the end times is a complex topic that is interwoven throughout the entire Bible. Where should we begin the process of unraveling its mysteries?

Not the Old Testament. Why? Because we are disciples of Christ, following in the footsteps of His Apostles. While it is impossible in my view to understand prophecy at anything more than a superficial level without also studying the Old Testament, a Christian's first and primary guide must be Jesus, not Moses, Daniel, Ezekiel or any other Old Testament figure.

Not the Book of Revelation. Why? Because Revelation was delivered to and written by the Apostle John in about 95 AD, long after the rest of the Apostles had passed on the teachings of Jesus to their disciples (including His teaching on the end times) and most of them had passed on to glory. Importantly, as we will see, the Book of Revelation is in large part a supplement to and best interpreted in light of what Jesus had already taught.

We Should Begin with "The Olivet Discourse."

The most logical starting point for the study of the end times is the instruction given by Jesus (whose Hebrew name is Yeshua) to the disciples in response to their direct question, *"When will this happen, and what will be the sign of your coming and of the end of the age?"* (Matthew 24:3)

His answer, called the Olivet Discourse, or "The Lecture on the Mount of Olives," is (in a natural reading of the text), a point-by-point chronological summary of end-time events which is repeated with only slight variation in the Gospels of Matthew (Chapter 24), Mark (Chapter 13) and Luke (Chapter 21), and reiterated in an expanded and annotated fashion in the Book of Revelation by the Apostle John, who also authored the fourth gospel. Matthew, Mark and Luke are known as the "synoptic" (meaning "summary form") gospels, as opposed to John's which is said to be more topical.

Interestingly, the Gospel of John is very closely aligned with the Biblical feast days and their symbolic significance (a little-recognized fact which we will explore later in this book).

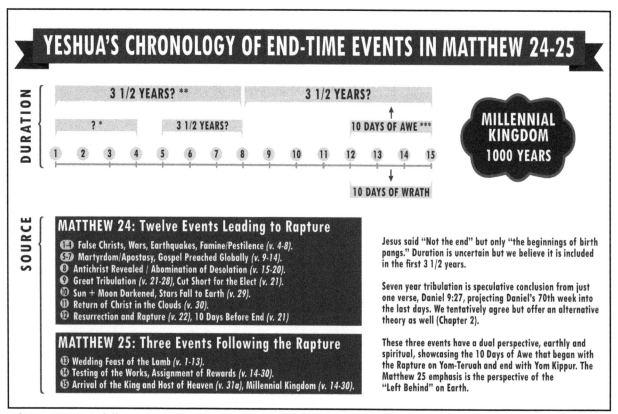

YESHUA'S CHRONOLOGY OF END-TIME EVENTS IN MATTHEW 24-25

DURATION

3 1/2 YEARS? **

3 1/2 YEARS?

? *

3 1/2 YEARS?

10 DAYS OF AWE ***

1 2 3 4 5 6 7 8 9 10 11 12 13 14 15

10 DAYS OF WRATH

MILLENNIAL KINGDOM 1000 YEARS

SOURCE

MATTHEW 24: Twelve Events Leading to Rapture

1-4 False Christs, Wars, Earthquakes, Famine/Pestilence *(v. 4-8)*.
5-7 Martyrdom/Apostasy, Gospel Preached Globally *(v. 9-14)*.
8 Antichrist Revealed / Abomination of Desolation *(v. 15-20)*.
9 Great Tribulation *(v. 21-28)*, Cut Short for the Elect *(v. 21)*.
10 Sun + Moon Darkened, Stars Fall to Earth *(v. 29)*.
11 Return of Christ in the Clouds *(v. 30)*.
12 Resurrection and Rapture *(v. 22)*, 10 Days Before End *(v. 21)*.

MATTHEW 25: Three Events Following the Rapture

13 Wedding Feast of the Lamb *(v. 1-13)*.
14 Testing of the Works, Assignment of Rewards *(v. 14-30)*.
15 Arrival of the King and Host of Heaven *(v. 31a)*, Millennial Kingdom *(v. 14-30)*.

Jesus said "Not the end" but only "the beginnings of birth pangs." Duration is uncertain but we believe it is included in the first 3 1/2 years.

Seven year tribulation is speculative conclusion from just one verse, Daniel 9:27, projecting Daniel's 70th week into the last days. We tentatively agree but offer an alternative theory as well (Chapter 2).

These three events have a dual perspective, earthly and spiritual, showcasing the 10 Days of Awe that began with the Rapture on Yom-Teruah and end with Yom Kippur. The Matthew 25 emphasis is the perspective of the "Left Behind" on Earth.

Editors Note: A full page version of most charts may be found at the back of the book.

YESHUA'S CHRONOLOGY OF END-TIME EVENTS IN MATTHEW 24-25

For the purpose our analysis, Matthew's account is most helpful, because the chronological nature of Jesus' teaching continues through Chapter 25, ending with a glimpse at the Millennial Kingdom.

Importantly, Chapters 24-25 are clearly identified by Matthew as a single package, opening with the disciples' query about the end times (24:3) and closing with Matthew's segue of 26:1: "...*when Jesus had finished all these sayings...*"

"*All of these sayings*" that we read between the bookends of Matthew 24:2 and 26:1 should thus be viewed as a set of lessons delivered together, explaining the events of the last days in a manner most relevant to His disciples. He is in essence saying, "This is what my followers will see with their own eyes and what they must watch for during the last days."

In order of occurrence, Jesus listed twelve events or landmarks leading to and including the rapture that are recorded in the three synoptic Gospels, followed by three post-rapture events leading to the Millennial Kingdom that are found in Matthew 25.

The Matthew 24 events are all seen from the physical, earthly perspective as they would be visible to humans in the material world.

In contrast, the Matthew 25 events have a dual nature, being experienced in the spiritual realm by the redeemed and glorified Bride of Christ, but with an earthly parallel experienced by those who are "left behind" at the rapture. The descriptions in Matthew 25 emphasize the earthly perspective while merely acknowledging the spiritual one.

Following is a list of all 15 events, divided by chapter:

From Matthew 24:

1. False Christs.
2. Wars and Rumors of Wars.
3. Earthquakes (natural disasters).
4. Famines/Pestilence.
5. Martyrdom.
6. Apostasy.
7. Gospel Preached to the Whole world.
8. Antichrist Revealed/Abomination of Desolation.
9. Great Tribulation.
10. Sun and Moon Darkened (*after* the tribulation).
11. Return of Christ (in the clouds).
12. Resurrection/Rapture.

From Matthew 25:

13. Wedding Feast of the Lamb.
14. Testing of the Works.
15. The King's Return and Final Preparations for His Millennial Kingdom.

THE RAPTURE AND THE RETURN OF THE KING

Having now touched the "third rail" of eschatology, the timing of the resurrection and rapture, we must pause to explain our position. This necessitates a discussion of the "Ten Days of Awe" which we will address below.

First, the word "rapture" does not appear in Scripture, but it is a convenient and biblically accurate term to describe the "calling up" and concurrent glorification of the members of the Bride of Christ, both living and dead, at the second coming of Christ. We prefer the phrase "resurrection and rapture" to emphasize the dual nature of the event, but sometimes use "rapture" as shorthand for both. [For our answer to the post-millennial view see our discussions on Daniel's seventy weeks and the phenomenon of repeating patterns in Chapter Two.]

Regarding the timing of the rapture in prophecy, a natural reading of the Olivet Discourse does not support the majority pre-tribulation view. Although numerous passages can be made to fit the external theological framework of its proponents, the passages themselves don't naturally lead the diligent researcher to the same conclusions absent that external framework. The shortcomings of pre-tribulation doctrine (rooted in Hellenic assumptions) and the intensity of internecine conflict they frequently engender with believers of other viewpoints are among the reasons we chose to approach this prophecy study *de novo* (from scratch).

In contrast, consider the natural reading of the text.

Jesus said " *Immediately __after__ the tribulation of those days shall the sun be darkened, and the moon shall not give her light, and the stars shall fall from heaven, and the powers of the heavens shall be shaken: And then shall appear the sign of the Son of man in heaven: and then shall all the tribes of the earth mourn, and they shall see the Son of man coming in the clouds of heaven with power and great glory. And he shall send his angels with a great sound of a trumpet, and they shall gather together his elect from the four winds, from one end of heaven to the other*" (Matthew 24:29-31). [Simply read 1 Thessalonians 4:16-17 and 1 Corinthians 15:51-52 with this passage in mind to see proof that Jesus is telling us exactly when "the rapture" occurs.]

This passage lends greater weight to the classic post-tribulation view, but that view has its own shortcomings because it shares some misleading Hellenistic presuppositions and resulting flaws with its pre-tribulation counterpart. Tellingly, both camps rely on selective use of proof texts and intellectual gymnastics to harmonize passages that clearly conflict when viewed through their common "Greek" lens.

Starting with a clean slate from a first-century Hebrew cultural perspective, the key to unraveling the timing of end-time events lies in Leviticus 23 and 25, the instructions on God's timekeeping system and His seven annual feasts.[1] This approach harmonizes all passages quite naturally.

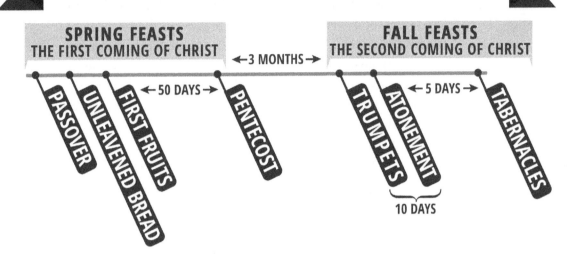

LEVITICUS 23: THE FEASTS OF THE LORD

SPRING FEASTS
THE FIRST COMING OF CHRIST

← 3 MONTHS →

FALL FEASTS
THE SECOND COMING OF CHRIST

PASSOVER
UNLEAVENED BREAD
FIRST FRUITS

← 50 DAYS →

PENTECOST

TRUMPETS
ATONEMENT

← 5 DAYS →

TABERNACLES

10 DAYS

Same Holy Day, Different Names:
The first three holidays are collectively known as The Feast of Unleavened Bread, Pentecost is also known as
The Feast of Weeks and Shavuot, The Feast of Trumpets is also known as Yom Teruah and Rosh Hashana.
The Day of Atonement is also known as Yom Kippur. The Feast of Tabernacles is also known as Sukkot.
We use these names interchangeably in this book.

THE FEASTS OF THE LORD

"And the LORD spake unto Moses, saying, Speak unto the children of Israel, and say unto them, Concerning the feasts of the LORD [Moedim] which ye shall proclaim to be holy convocations [Miqra], even these are my feasts [Moedim]" (Leviticus 23:1-2).

The Hebrew word *moed* (plural *moedim*) means an appointed day or time. The word *Miqra* means rehearsal. The Feasts of the Lord are therefore not simply ritual holidays but times established by God for rehearsing and preparing for a prophetic calendar of events, specifically the first and second coming of Christ. The emergence of Messianic Judaism has made this teaching increasingly familiar in the American church over the past decade, but it is still not well known, so we will address it in detail here.

Each of the feasts has its own role and symbolic significance related both to Hebrew culture and to Christianity. The Passover lamb is the symbol of substitutionary atonement. Unleavened Bread is a symbol of sinlessness. First Fruits is symbolized by the Spring barley harvest. (What is "waved before the Lord" in that ritual is the harvest of the first barley plant to have emerged from the soil, having been marked upon its appearance with a scarlet thread by the farmer). The Feast of Weeks, or Pentecost, celebrates the giving of the Torah when God appeared in the form of fire on the head of Mt. Sinai and is thus symbolized by fire, but also by wheat, since it celebrates the spring wheat harvest.

The Feast of Trumpets is represented by the ram's horn (shofar), symbolic both of the metaphorical "resurrection" of Isaac (Hebrews 11:17-19) and of the celebration of the birthday of Creation (Job 38:4-7), but is also symbolized by wheat, since it celebrates the fall wheat harvest. The Day of Atonement is symbolized by both goats and grapes – symbols of rebellion and the sins that must be atoned for by the High Priest. It also celebrates the grape harvest, and the crushing of the grapes (the wicked) in the winepress of God. Finally, the Feast of Tabernacles is symbolized by "booths" or tents, representing the time of God dwelling among men.

These seven feasts were times of the year when the Hebrews were expected to make pilgrimage to Jerusalem (Exodus 23:14-17; 34:18-23), and for that purpose were divided into three groups. Importantly, the Hebrew calendar begins in the fall with Rosh Hashana (New Year's Day) much as the Hebrew "day" begins in the evening rather than the morning. The Biblical name of Rosh Hashana is *Yom Teruah*, or the Feast of Trumpets.

- Pilgrimage 1: The fall Feast of Tabernacles Pilgrimage includes the Feast of Trumpets, the Day of Atonement and the Feast of Tabernacles.

- Pilgrimage 2: The spring Feast of Unleavened Bread Pilgrimage includes Passover, the Feast of Unleavened Bread, and the Feast of First Fruits.

- Pilgrimage 3: The one-day late spring/early summer Feast of Pentecost Pilgrimage includes just Pentecost itself, which literally means "fiftieth day" and falls fifty days after the conclusion of Passover. That first day after Passover is also the first day of the Feast of Unleavened Bread. Importantly, the Feast of Unleavened Bread it is also known as the Feast of Weeks – seven weeks of seven literal days each followed by a feast day, which is the same pattern as the Jubilee Calendar of seven "weeks" of years, followed by the Jubilee year (the fiftieth year).

More importantly to the prophetic calendar is the separation of the seven feasts into the spring and fall seasons representing events aligned with the first and second coming of the Messiah.

The four spring feasts of Passover, Unleavened Bread, First Fruits and Pentecost and are deemed to have been fulfilled at His first coming. Jesus was the "Lamb of God" who died on Passover (John 1:29), whom the grave could not hold because He was sinless (without leaven) (Acts 2:24), and who rose from the dead on First Fruits, the first fruits from the grave (1 Corinthians 15:20). He, being the triune God, appeared in the form of the Holy Spirit on Pentecost, as "tongues of fire" on the heads of the disciples (John 14:26). Each prophetic event was literally fulfilled by Christ on the actual day it fell on the holiday calendar.

The clear logical deduction is that the remaining three fall feasts -- Trumpets, the Day of Atonement and Tabernacles -- will be fulfilled by Christ at His second coming.

Recognizing the role of the feasts as signposts we can conclude with confidence that the resurrection and rapture will occur on a Feast of Trumpets when "...*the Lord Himself will descend from heaven with **a shout**, with **the voice of an archangel**, and with **the trumpet of God**: And the dead in Christ will rise first [resurrection]. Then we who are alive and remain shall be caught up together with them in the clouds [rapture] to meet the Lord in the air*" (I Thessalonians 4:16-17).

The resurrection and rapture event is further amplified in 1 Corinthians 15:20-57, especially verses 51-52: "*Behold, I tell you a mystery; we will not all sleep, but we will all be changed, in a moment, in the twinkling of an eye, at **the last trumpet**; for the trumpet will sound, and the dead will be raised imperishable, and we will be changed.*"

Both of these passages echo Matthew 24:31: "*And He will send His angels **with a great sound of a trumpet**, and they will gather together His elect from the four winds, from one end of heaven to the other.*"

The Feast of Trumpets is identified in Leviticus 23 as *Zicharon Truah*, or *Yom Teruah*, meaning literally "a remembrance of blowing." This commemorates the anniversary of the creation of the world by God as described in Job 38:7 when "*all the sons of God shouted for joy.*" To this day, on the Feast of Trumpets Jews read the story of Abraham and Isaac in which God provided the ram as a sacrificial substitute for Isaac -- the theme of resurrection. That is why the trumpet blown on the Feast of Trumpets is a ram's horn (the *shofar*).

The resurrection and rapture on the Feast of Trumpets marks the end of the Great Tribulation (the trial) and beginning of the Wrath of God (the sentence on the guilty).

The "touchdown" of Christ to earth will occur ten days later on the Day of Atonement.

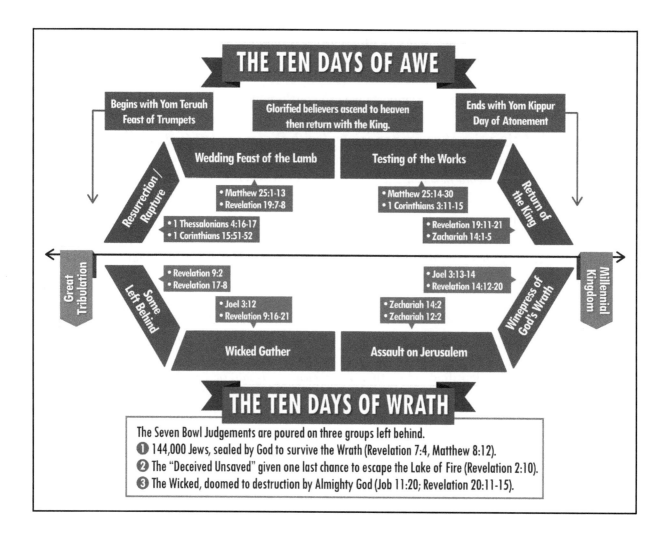

THE TEN DAYS OF AWE

"*Now in the seventh month, on the first day of the month, you shall also have a holy convocation; you shall do no laborious work. It will be to you a day for blowing trumpets....Then on the tenth day of this seventh month you shall have a holy convocation, and you shall humble yourselves; you shall not do any work*" (Numbers 29:1-7).

"*Do not fear what you are about to suffer. Look, the devil is about to throw some of you into prison to test you, and you will suffer tribulation for ten days. Be faithful even unto death, and I will give you the crown of life*" (Revelation 2:10).

In the Bible, a period of ten days is frequently a time of waiting and/or testing while God's decision about a matter hangs in the balance. A good example is Jeremiah 42:6-7: "*Whether it is pleasant or unpleasant, we will listen to the voice of the LORD our God to whom we are sending you, so that it may go well with us when we listen to the voice of the LORD our God.*" *Now at the end of ten days the word of the LORD came to Jeremiah.*"

Daniel's test of faithfulness in refusing to be defiled by King Nebuchadnezzar's "delicacies" was of ten days (Daniel 1:1-16).

And the waiting period of the disciples in the upper room, from the ascension of Christ to the outpouring of the Holy Spirit on Pentecost was ten days as well (Luke 24:49-51, Acts 1:3).

Thus, the ten day period beginning with the Feast of Trumpets and ending with the Day of Atonement is of special significance: it is the time in which God decides who among those "left behind" at the rapture will be redeemed or thrown into the lake of fire, and He puts on a grand show to contrast the fate of those who choose Yeshua Ha'Maschiach (Jesus the Christ) with those who reject Him.

These are the **Ten Days of Awe** for the redeemed (those who accepted Christ before the resurrection and rapture), and concurrently the **Ten Days of Wrath** for the wicked. During this time those who are called the Bride of Christ (having passed the tribulation test by "enduring to the end" per Matthew 24:13) are now in newly glorified bodies in the spiritual realm, where we will celebrate the Wedding Feast of the Lamb (Matthew 22:1-2, 25:1-13; Revelation 19:7-8) and have our works tested (1 Corinthians 3:11-15; Matthew 25:14-30) to determine our role in the Millennial Kingdom (Matthew 19:28-29).

Meanwhile, three groups of people who were "left behind" on earth at the rapture -- the 144,000 Jews sealed against death (Revelation 7:4-8), the "foolish virgins" and "lazy servants" of Matthew 25 (whom we call collectively the "deceived unsaved"), and the wicked, -- must endure the Wrath of God, including the seven bowl judgments, where there is much *"weeping and gnashing of teeth."* Our conclusion that this place is earth during the Ten Days of Wrath is explained in Chapter 3.

On the Day of Atonement, Christ will lead the Host of Heaven (including the Bride-become-Wife of God) in a dramatic rescue of Jerusalem and slaughter of His enemies as He returns to claim His throne (Revelation 19:11-21; Zechariah 14:1-5). This is followed by His Millennial Kingdom.

Can we know the day?

"But of that day and hour no one knows, not even the angels of heaven, nor the Son, but the Father alone" (Matthew 24:36).

What at first glance appears to be a warning against "date-setting" in Matthew 24:36 is actually a clue as to the date of the resurrection and rapture.

Importantly, the Feast of Trumpets was known by the Jews of antiquity as "the feast of which no man could know the day or hour"[2] because the official start of the feast required a ruling by the Jewish religious court, the Sanhedrin, upon the testimony of two witnesses assigned to watch the night sky for the first appearance of the new moon. There was enough ambiguity about the official start, therefore, that no one could predict in advance what date the feast would begin. In other words, the phrase "no man knows the day or hour" was a Jewish idiom meaning the Feast of Trumpets.

The requirement of "two witnesses" in this context has special significance relative to the two witnesses of Revelation 11:1-12. These are the witnesses against the Antichrist who are eventually struck dead by the "beast that comes up from the abyss" and lie dead in the streets of Jerusalem for three days. Then, in a scene directly parallel to the resurrection and rapture passage of 1 Thessalonians 4:16-17 (in which the dead rise first and then the living are caught up into the air with them) *"the breath of life from God entered the two witnesses, and they stood on their feet, and great fear fell upon those who saw them. And the witnesses heard a loud voice from heaven saying, 'Come up here.' And they went up to heaven in a cloud as their enemies watched them"* (Revelation 11:11-12). Thus, Revelation 11 would seem to strongly support our contention.

That believers can and should know the day is made clear in 1 Thessalonians 5:1-6

*"But of the **times and the seasons**, brethren, ye have no need that I write unto you. **For yourselves know perfectly that the day of the Lord so cometh as a thief in the night. For when they shall say, Peace and safety; then sudden destruction cometh upon them, as travail upon a woman with child; and they shall not escape. But ye, brethren, are not in darkness, that that day should overtake you as a thief.** Ye are all the children of light, and the children of the day: we are not of the night, nor of darkness. Therefore let us not sleep, as do others; but let us watch and be sober."*

The context-setting metaphor of the birth process alone makes clear that the timing of the blessed event can be calculated within a very small window of time long before it occurs. But more importantly, the phrase "times and seasons" is a direct reference to the seven feasts of the Lord in Leviticus 23:4: *"These are the appointed times of the LORD, holy convocations which you shall proclaim at the times [seasons] appointed for them."*

The phrase "…but My father only" in Matthew 24:36 is a separate Jewish idiom related to the timing of the arrival of the Bridegroom for the wedding feast since the father of the groom had exclusive authority over it. The resurrection and rapture marks the start of the wedding feast -- or perhaps more accurately the start of the final preparation for the wedding feast. The Bride of Christ, the church, in glorified bodies, ascends into the clouds where the Bridegroom has arrived for the ceremony.

In a further blow to the doctrine of "imminency" (the idea that the rapture could occur at any time without warning or the necessity of prerequisite events), Jesus analogized the rapture to the time of Noah's Flood in Matthew 24:37-41, saying the *wicked* would be caught by surprise. But obviously Noah's righteous family was *not* taken by surprise since they were following God's timetable in building the ark, whose necessary completion God awaited patiently (1 Peter 3:20).

THE SEVEN STAGES OF THE LAST DAYS

"And one of the elders said to me, 'Stop weeping; behold, the Lion that is from the tribe of Judah, the Root of David, has overcome so as to open the book and its seven seals' " (Revelation 5:5).

The 15-step chronology of Matthew 24-25 unfolds in six stages, ending with/culminating in the seventh stage: the Millennial Kingdom.

In Matthew 24-25, which includes the Olivet Discourse, the Parable of the Wise and Foolish Virgins, the Parable of the Talents, and the Separation of the Sheep and Goats, Jesus presents the teaching of the last days in a series of seven individual segments that align with the Seven Seals of Revelation. Again, the unrelated teaching in Matthew 26:1 begins with *"When Jesus had finished all these words..."* (referring back to the previous chapter) making clear that Matthew 24 and 25 are to be taken together.

1-4) The Beginning of Birth Pangs: Matthew 24:4-13

"For many will come in My name, saying, 'I am the Christ,' and will mislead many. You will be hearing of wars and rumors of wars. See that you are not frightened, for those things must take place, but that is not yet the end. For nation will rise against nation, and kingdom against kingdom, and in various places there will be famines and earthquakes. But all these things are merely the beginning of birth pangs" (Matthew 24:5-8).

"Then I saw when the Lamb broke one of the seven seals, and I heard one of the four living creatures saying as with a voice of thunder, 'Come.' I looked, and behold, a <u>white horse</u>, and he who sat on it had a bow; and a crown was given to him, and he went out conquering and to conquer. When He broke the second seal, I heard the second living creature saying, 'Come.' And another, a <u>red horse</u>, went out; and to him who sat on it, it was granted to take peace from the earth, and that men would slay one another; and a great sword was given to him. When He broke the third seal, I heard the third living creature saying, 'Come.' I looked, and behold, a <u>black horse</u>; and he who sat on it had a pair of scales in his hand. And I heard something like a voice in the center of the four living creatures saying, 'A quart of wheat for a denarius, and three quarts of barley for a denarius; and do not damage the oil and the wine.' When the Lamb broke the fourth seal, I heard the voice of the fourth living creature saying, 'Come.' I looked, and behold, an <u>ashen horse</u>; and he who sat on it had the name Death; and Hades was following with him. Authority was given to them over a fourth of the earth, to kill with sword and with famine and with pestilence and by the wild beasts of the earth" (Revelation 6:3-8).

In these four segments, which address the "Four Horsemen of the Apocalypse," Jesus compared the last-days events to the delivery of a woman in labor. The *"beginning of birth pangs"* is expressly analogized to the initial contractions that signal the start of labor. By doing so, He indicated the clear chronological sequence of the events. As any mother (or involved father) knows, once the actual contractions begin they do not stop until the entire process climaxes with the birth of the baby. That climax is represented in this lesson by the resurrection and rapture of the church, in which the believers are delivered from our bodies of flesh into new glorified forms, like a baby emerging from the womb.

It is a simple yet elegant presentation of the facts as only Jesus can tell them. And if we start with that premise, we will find that all other prophetic Scriptures can be comfortably harmonized with this chronology.

5) The Time of Testing: Matthew 24:9-28

The word tribulation comes from the word "tribulum," which is an ancient Roman threshing sledge, designed to separate chaff from wheat at the time of harvest (Job 41:30, Isaiah 41:15). Thus, the time of tribulation in the Bible is not a time of God's wrath but of His testing when believers (the wheat) are separated from their attachments to the things of this world (the chaff), prior to being taken up by Christ at His return.

In our timeline, the fifth stage of the end begins just before or upon the unveiling of the Antichrist and his "abomination of desolation" .

"Then [following the 'beginning of birth pangs'] they will deliver you to tribulation, and will kill you, and you will be hated by all nations because of My name. At that time many will fall away and will betray one another and hate one another. Many false prophets will arise and will mislead many. Because lawlessness is increased, most people's love will grow cold. But the one who endures to the end, he will be saved. This gospel of the kingdom shall be preached in the whole world as a testimony to all the nations, and then the end will come. Therefore when you see the Abomination of desolation which was spoken of through Daniel the prophet, standing in the holy place (let the reader understand), then those who are in Judea must flee to the mountains...For then there will be a great tribulation, such as has not occurred since the beginning of the world until now, nor ever will. Unless those days had been cut short, no life would have been saved; but for the sake of the elect those days will be cut short" (Matthew 24:9-22).

This corresponds to the fifth Seal of Revelation 6:9-11 (described from the perspective of the spiritual realm):

"When the Lamb broke the fifth seal, I saw underneath the altar the souls of those who had been slain because of the word of God, and because of the testimony which they had maintained; and they cried out with a loud voice, saying, 'How long, O Lord, holy and true, will You refrain from judging and avenging our blood on those who dwell on the earth?' And there was given to each of them a white robe; and they were told that they should rest for a little while longer, until the number of their fellow servants and their brethren who were to be killed even as they had been, would be completed also."

During this period of "great tribulation," defined by widespread apostasy and martyrdom, there will also occur an end-time revival which many believe will be a single global event designed both to harden the world against the church and to coalesce the remnant of believers in preparation for the final separation of the wheat and tares.

6) The Return of Christ

"But immediately after the tribulation of those days The <u>sun will be darkened, and the moon will not give its light, and the stars will fall from the sky</u>, and the powers of the heavens will be shaken. And then the sign of the Son of Man will appear in the sky, and then <u>all the tribes of the earth will mourn</u>, and they will see the Son of Man coming on the clouds of the sky with power and great glory. And He will send forth His angels with a great trumpet and they will gather together His elect from the four winds, from one end of the sky to the other" (Matthew 24:29-31).

This corresponds to the sixth seal of Revelation 6:12-17:

"I watched as he opened the sixth seal. There was a great earthquake. <u>The sun turned black like sackcloth made of goat hair, the whole moon turned blood red, and the stars in the sky fell to earth</u>, as figs drop from a fig tree when shaken by a strong wind. The heavens receded like a scroll being rolled up, and every mountain and island was removed from its place. Then <u>the kings of the earth, the princes, the generals, the rich, the mighty, and everyone else, both slave and free, hid in caves and among the rocks of the mountains</u>. They called to the mountains and the rocks, "Fall on us and hide us from the face of him who sits on the throne and from the wrath of the Lamb! For the great day of their wrath has come, and who can withstand it?"

In our analysis of Revelation, as plotted on our chart "Yeshua's Chronology of End-Time Events in Revelation 6-20" (below), the first five of the seven trumpet judgments occur during the period of the fifth seal, immediately preceding the return of Christ.

What John is describing as he reports his vision -- "Hail and fire," "a flaming mountain"… appears to be a series of meteors both large and small striking the earth.

Importantly, there was apparently no word for "asteroid" or "meteor" at the time the Bible was written, and thus "stars" should be interpreted as "asteroids" (i.e. "small stars"), or "meteors" (asteroids that have entered our atmosphere). This would explain the geologic upheavals, the darkening of the sky by massive volumes of dust and debris, and the attempts of people to hide in clefts and caves. Even the appearance (to people on the earth) of the sky being rolled up like a scroll would be explained if a large-enough meteor struck the earth so as to briefly slow its spin. The optical illusion created during that shudder would match the Bible's imagery. (Alternately, of course, God could accomplish these results supernaturally if He chose to.)

I believe the return of Christ will occur on a Feast of Trumpets and trigger the resurrection and rapture. During the Ten Days of Awe that begin with the Feast of Trumpets (*Yom Teruah*/Rosh Hashanah) and end with the Day of Atonement (Yom Kippur), the Bride of Christ/Messiah will celebrate the Wedding Feast of the Lamb and the testing of the works of the believers in the heavenly realm.

Meanwhile, those "left behind" on the earth (the wicked, the 144,000 Torah-faithful Hebrews sealed against death, and the "foolish virgins"/"lazy servants" who thought they were saved but weren't) will (for ten days, not seven years -- Revelation 2:10) experience the Wrath of God poured forth from the seven bowls during the Ten Days of Awe. These seven bowls of judgment are contained within the sixth trumpet.

7) The Millennial Kingdom

Again, we must remember here that the seven trumpets of Revelation are contained within the seventh seal like a "wheel within a wheel." Only the seventh trumpet describes that seventh stage of the end, the Millennial Kingdom.

Revelation 11:15 states "The *seventh angel sounded his trumpet, and there were loud voices in heaven, which said: 'The kingdom of the world has become the kingdom of our Lord and of his Messiah, and he will reign for ever and ever.'* "

The Matthew 25:31 corollary reads "*But when the Son of Man comes in His glory, and all the angels with Him, then He will sit on His glorious throne. All the nations will be gathered before Him; and He will separate them from one another, as the shepherd separates the sheep from the goats; and He will put the sheep on His right, and the goats on the left. Then the King will say to those on His right, 'Come, you who are blessed of My Father, inherit the kingdom prepared for you from the foundation of the world.'* "

Importantly, this is not describing Heaven, which is as yet a future destination for those who will spend eternity with Christ, whose reign will continue for all time. First, however, the earth must have its Sabbath, its seventh millennium that corresponds to the seventh "day" of creation. The earth will enjoy 1000 years of Christ's bodily reign on the planet earth, which has been regenerated to be similar to it's pre-sin, Edenic state. And we who have been "glorified" upon the advent of the rapture will rule and reign with Him during this time (2 Timothy 2).

As Jesus told the Apostles in Matthew 19:28: "*Truly I say to you, that you who have followed Me, **in the regeneration when the Son of Man will sit on His glorious throne, you also shall sit upon twelve thrones, judging the twelve tribes of Israel**.*"

The promise is repeated for all the faithful in Revelation 20:4-6:

"*Then I saw thrones, and they sat on them, and judgment was given to them. And I saw the souls of those who had been beheaded because of their testimony of Jesus and because of the word of God, and those who had not worshipped the beast or his image, and had not received the mark on their forehead and on their hand; and they came to life and reigned with Christ **for a thousand years**.*"

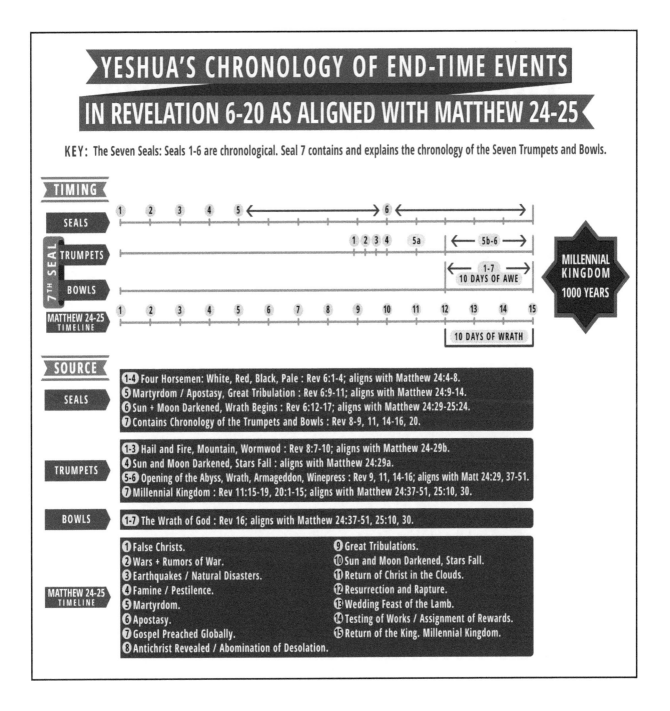

YESHUA'S CHRONOLOGY OF END-TIME EVENTS IN REVELATION 6-20

In the Book of Revelation, Jesus provided much more information about how the end-time events unfold, and how they relate to Old Testament prophecies. He first unsealed the events in a summary form, and we can see that the first six seals follow the exact pattern of the Gospel accounts. We have conjectured about what this might look like in a present-day context, but acknowledge that there are other equally plausible theories.

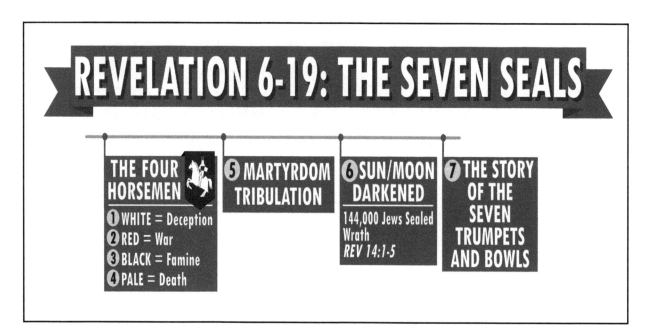

The Seven Seals

Seal #1. White Horse: The Antichrist spirit, bearing the symbol of the bow -- rainbow? -- begins accumulating power as well as conquering the world through guile and faked miracles.

Seal #2. Red Horse: Wars and rumors of wars trigger massive political upheavals which in turn trigger global economic collapse.

Seal #3 Black Horse: Global breakdown of social order results in widespread famine and starvation. Natural disasters compound the problems.

Seal #4. Pale Horse: Disease, pestilence, genocide, sectarian massacres, wild animals will kill many millions of people.

Seal #5. Martyrs Under the Altar: Description of the tribulation, including martyrdom, apostasy, the great end times revival (of the remnant of true believers who preach the Gospel to the entire world), the exposure of the Antichrist, and the "Great Tribulation" under his evil reign.

The martyrdom is exemplified by the beheading of Christians (which may be the work of Islamists who take advantage of the global chaos to rampage against all "infidels").

The fifth seal represents the time of great testing in which the sheep and goats are divided, and the final generation of believers prove their allegiance to Christ by "enduring" under suffering without renouncing Him, just as the Apostles and many first-century believers did (one of the most powerful proofs that the gospels were not of human invention or many would have recanted – suggesting that many in the last generation will similarly be moved to accept Christ by the example of the end time martyrs).

Seal #6   Return of Christ: The coming of the groom to rescue His bride is announced by the darkening of the sun and the moon. He appears in the clouds and sends His angels to gather His elect from the four corners of the world. The dead will be resurrected and rise first, and then we who are alive will join them in the air (per 1 Thessalonians 4:16-17 and 1 Corinthians 15:51-52).

Seal #7 Detailed overview: The seventh seal is not a subsequent event, but a broader and more detailed overview of what was summarized in the first six seals. Importantly, it contains the story of the seven trumpets, the first three of which occur during the time span of the fifth seal, the next three which occur during the sixth seal, and the seventh, final trumpet which announces the establishment of the Millennial Kingdom. In turn, the seven bowls of God's Wrath all occur during the time span of the fifth and sixth trumpets. In other words, like the "wheel within a wheel" revealed to Ezekiel, the seventh seal contains the seven trumpets, which in turn contain the seven bowls.

THE SEVEN TRUMPETS

1. Hail + Fire + Blood
2. Mountain of Fire
3. Wormwood
4. Sun/Moon Darkened
5. Satan/Locusts/Scorpions
6. Wrath (the Bowls)
7. The Millennial Kingdom (MK)

The Seven Trumpets

The seven trumpets begin during the fifth Seal, continue through the period of the sixth Seal, and end with the establishment of the Millennial Kingdom (the seventh seal). There is no clear indication of the precise starting point of the trumpets on the Matthew 24-25 timeline, but considering that they involve the most dramatic events of the Great Tribulation, they probably begin toward the end of it, on the cusp of the time of Wrath.

All of the first six trumpets may occur in a very short window of time – a period of weeks or even days, though the first three could span a period of months or even more than a year. The first three trumpets involve the pummeling of the earth by a series of meteorites of increasing size and import: hail and fire mixed with blood, a great mountain, and lastly the "star" Wormwood. Importantly, there is no separate word for meteor or asteroid in the Bible, but we can infer from the context that "Wormwood" is not a star like the sun, but merely a larger form of the same type of objects striking earth during the first two trumpets.

The fourth trumpet, the darkening of the sun and moon, clearly aligns with Matthew 24:29 and heralds the great pivotal moment of the return of Christ in the clouds. Once again, there is no clear indication of the time between the darkening of the sun and moon and the appearance of Christ. It could be almost immediate, or span a period of days, weeks or months, though it seems likely to be a shorter rather than longer span of time.

The biblical description of the fifth trumpet in Revelation 9:1-11 is the most challenging to our timeline. It involves the opening of the Abyss and the emergence of Satan to command the legions of the wicked. The passage neatly aligns with our timeline in numerous respects if we assume this trumpet describes the very last days of the Great Tribulation – but, this event can be no less than three and one-half days prior to the Resurrection and Rapture, since it must include the finalization of the ministry of the Two Witnesses of Revelation 11:7-12. This passage describes the ascension of the Two Witnesses after their three and a half days lying dead in Jerusalem following their murder by Satan. Their ascension seems to coincide with the Resurrection and Rapture on the Feast of Trumpets. In summary, Satan enters the world stage as King of Evil just before Christ, the King of Peace, departs with the righteous to celebrate the Wedding Feast of the Lamb in the heavenly realm, leaving the wicked to suffer the consequences of their rebellion during the Ten Days of Awe/Wrath on earth.

Additionally, Revelation 9:4 mentions the people sealed against death (the 144,000 Jews), left behind with the wicked to endure the Wrath, perfectly consistent with our timeline.

However, the fifth trumpet passage also introduces a very cryptic reference to scorpion-like locusts whose stings produce torturous pain that lasts *"for five months."* Since our timeline limits the Wrath to just ten days, this "five month" reference is problematic but not fatal. Since we know that many people survive the Wrath to repopulate the earth in the Millennial Kingdom, it is entirely plausible that the five months extends into the new millennium for those survivors afflicted with this agony.

Alternately, the "five months" could be a symbolic reference to the five days that fall between the Day of Atonement (Christ's "touchdown" on the earth on the last of the Ten Days of Awe/Wrath) and the Feast of Tabernacles (which is symbolic of the Millennial Kingdom, when God dwells with men) on the biblical calendar of Leviticus 23.

We have long considered that the actual or final fulfilment of the Feast of Tabernacles as a prophetic *moed* (appointed time) could be interpreted to be our entrance into Heaven at the end of the Millennial Kingdom, rather than at the beginning of the Millennial Kingdom. If so, the official start of the Millennial Kingdom wouldn't necessarily fall on the biblical calendar in the same way that Trumpets and Atonement do. In other words, Trumpets and Atonement will necessarily be fulfilled in the same year, just ten days apart, but Tabernacles might not technically be fulfilled for another thousand years. Even though Christ's reign in Jerusalem would seem to complete the prophetic calendar, it might serve as just a next-to-last iteration of the Tabernacles pattern, the last being heaven itself. If that were so, then we could consider the Millennial Kingdom to start the moment Christ sets foot on the Mount of Olives, and the "five months" to be a variation on the theme of the five days in the Tabernacles pattern.

In any case, it is reasonable to assume that there would be a natural transition from the old world to the new during the first weeks, months and years of the Millennial Kingdom, which would logically include the physical healing process of the survivors of the Wrath.

THE SEVEN BOWLS

1. Hail + Fire + Blood
2. Mountain of Fire
3. Wormwood
4. Sun/Moon Darkened
5. Satan/Locusts/Scorpions
6. Gathering for Armagedon
7. The Winepress of God's Wrath

The Seven Bowls

The sixth trumpet, described in Revelation 9:13-21, occurs during the Ten Days of Wrath when the seven bowls of wrath are poured out on the earth. The bowls are thus contained in the sixth trumpet, which marks the transition from the Tribulation (the trial) to the Wrath (the sentence on the guilty).

The seven bowls are described in Revelation 16:1-21:

"And I heard a great voice out of the temple saying to the seven angels, Go your ways, and pour out the vials of the wrath of God upon the earth. And **the first** *went, and poured out his vial upon the earth; and there fell a noisome and grievous sore upon the men which had the mark of the beast, and upon them which worshipped his image. And* **the second** *angel poured out his vial upon the sea; and it became as the blood of a dead man: and every living soul died in the sea. And* **the third** *angel poured out his vial upon the rivers and fountains of waters; and they became blood...And* **the fourth** *angel poured out his vial upon the sun; and power was given unto him to scorch men with fire...And* **the fifth** *angel poured out his vial upon the seat of the beast; and his kingdom was full of darkness; and they gnawed their tongues for pain, And blasphemed the God of heaven because of their pains and their sores, and repented not of their deeds....And* **the sixth** *angel poured out his vial upon the great river Euphrates; and the water thereof was dried up, that the way of the kings of the east might be prepared...And* **the seventh** *angel poured out his vial into the air; and there came a great voice out of the temple of heaven, from the throne, saying, It is done..."*

DECIPHERING THE REVELATION CHRONOLOGY

The Book of Revelation can be said in one sense to be the "graveyard" of prophecy gurus since its apparent complexity from a "Greek" perspective has produced innumerable false theories and interpretations. Its heavy emphasis on symbolism and lack of a clear and self-evident chronological sequence lays it open to imaginative, sometimes fanciful speculation. However, from the first-century Hebrew cultural perspective, the challenge of understanding Revelation is not nearly as daunting or problematic.

There are three keys to understanding Revelation. The first and master key is recognizing that Revelation should be recognized as an expanded and annotated version of the Olivet Discourse, which establishes a clear chronological timeline.

The second key is discerning the four types of passages in Revelation which reflect two alternate vantage points (either inside or outside of time) and two alternate locations of the events being observed (either on earth or in heaven). Thus, each of these four types of passages describe either:

1) the view of events on earth from the vantage point of earth,

2) the view of events on earth from the vantage point of heaven.

3) the view of events in heaven from the vantage point of earth, or

4) the view of events in heaven from the vantage point of heaven.

Most of the confusion in interpreting Revelation derives from the fact that the heavenly perspective is not time-bound and thus events observed or occurring there can't always be plotted on a linear time scale without reference to something else that is. In other words, the events of Revelation are not presented in strict chronological order but can be organized on a timeline by aligning the symbols and phrases in the passages describing observations or events in heaven with those observed or occurring on earth, always using the timeline of Matthew 24-25 as the template on which they all are plotted.

The third key to understanding Revelation is identifying the meaning of the symbols and phrases from their context in the Old Testament.

The two charts in this section lay out the Revelation chronology as it aligns with Matthew 24-25.

DECIPHERING THE REVELATION CHRONOLOGY

THREE KEY FACTS

1. Revelation is an expanded version of Yeshua's timeline in Matthew 24-25.

2. The story is told from four perspectives.

3. Passages from the heavenly perspective are not time bound and thus may be out of chronological sequence, but contains markers (symbols and phrases) that allow the events they describe to be plotted on the earthly timeline.

FOUR PERSPECTIVES

A. Earth seen from Earth.

B. Earth seen from Heaven.

C. Heaven seen from Earth.

D. Heaven seen from Heaven.

EVENTS OF REVELATION AS THEY APPEAR IN THE TEXT

① CHAPTER 1:1-9	② CHAPTER 1:10-19	③ CHAPTER 2-3	④ CHAPTER 4-5	⑤ CHAPTER 6-7:8
Introduction and Notice of John's Vision to the Seven Churches	The Lord's Instruction to John about Conveying His Message	Warnings: Some Will be "Left Behind" with One Last Chance	Jesus Presented with Sealed Scroll in the Throne Room of Heaven	Jesus Opens the Six Seals and Shields the 144K from Wrath

⑥ CHAPTER 7:9-8:4	⑦ CHAPTER 8:5-9:21	⑧ CHAPTER 10	⑨ CHAPTER 11:1-14	⑩ CHAPTER 11:15-19
Future Worship in Heaven of Those Now Suffering on Earth	Seventh Seal Shown to Contain Seven Trumpets. Six now Sound	John Receives and Seals Up Prophecy of Seven Thunders	The Two Witnesses During the Kingdom of the Antichrist	Seventh Trumpet Declares Start of the Millennial Kingdom

⑪ CHAPTER 12	⑫ CHAPTER 13	⑬ CHAPTER 7:9-8:4	⑭ CHAPTER 14:8-20	⑮ CHAPTER 15
Vision of Last Days as Displayed in Constellations of the Night Sky	The Beast: Cryptic Description of the Antichrist and his Kingdom	The Lamb and the 144,000 in the Throne Room of Heaven	Five Angels, Five Events: Gospel Preached through Winepress	Seven Angels Receive the Seven Bowls of Wrath

⑯ CHAPTER 16	⑰ CHAPTER 17	⑱ CHAPTER 18	⑲ CHAPTER 19:1-10	⑳ CHAPTER 19:11-16
The Pouring Out of the Bowls of Wrath on the Earth	ProÀle and History of Babylon the Great	Punishment of Babylon the Great Ending with Seventh Bowl	Exultation in Heaven Over Babylon's Destruction	The King of Kings Returns to Claim His Throne

㉑ CHAPTER 19:17-21	㉒ CHAPTER 20:1-10	㉓ CHAPTER 20:11-15	㉔ CHAPTER 21-22:5	㉕ CHAPTER 22:6-21
Defeat of the Wicked, the Beast and False Prophet	Beginning and End of the Millennial Kingdom	Great White Throne Judgement	The New Heaven and Earth in Eternity	Concluding Summary and Warnings

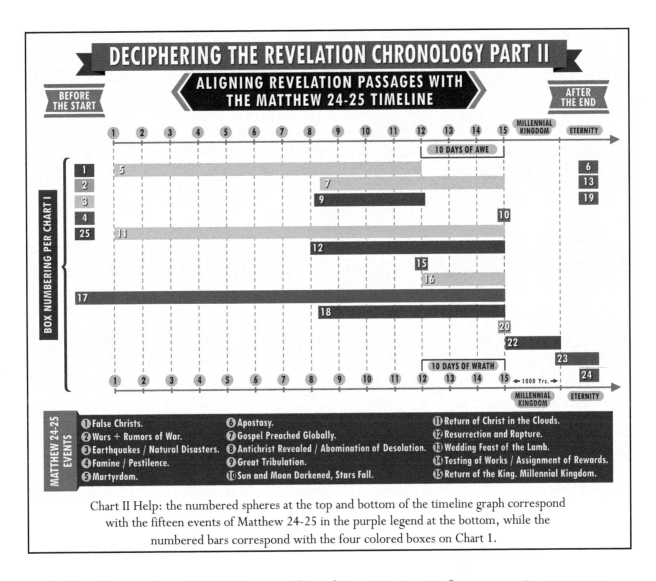

Chart II Help: the numbered spheres at the top and bottom of the timeline graph correspond with the fifteen events of Matthew 24-25 in the purple legend at the bottom, while the numbered bars correspond with the four colored boxes on Chart 1.

In the first chart we have divided the text of Revelation into twenty-five consecutive segments based upon the perspective of each passage. A few of these passages could conceivably be categorized differently or subdivided further, but since those changes would not substantively affect our conclusions regarding their place in the chronology we're satisfied with this arrangement. They are arranged in the order in which they appear in the text and color coded based on their perspective.

In the second chart we have arranged each segment to show its place on the Matthew 24-25 timeline. Importantly, the numbering of the colored boxes represents the twenty-five segments from Chart 1, while the numbering on the timeline (small grey circles) represents the fifteen events of Matthew 24-25. Keeping this in mind will prevent confusion in reading the charts.

For example, the first four colored boxes contain passages from Chapters 1-4 of Revelation, all of which occur before the Matthew 24-25 timeline begins. Colored box #5 (light green) begins the story of the four horses which align with the four events Jesus called "the beginning of birth pangs" (1-4 of the Matthew 24-25 timeline). Since these events have no clear end-point but could continue until the appearance of the Messiah, colored box #5 spans 1-12 of the Matthew 24-25 timeline. Colored box #6 (light blue) describes a vision of future worship in heaven by people whose time-bound activities are yet to play out on earth. Thus, that box is placed after the end of the Matthew 24-25 timeline.

Colored box #7 contains the story of the first six trumpets. The start of these occurs at some point following the event called the Abomination of desolation and encompasses all of the Great Tribulation and the Wrath, so it is placed on the chart accordingly. Colored box #17 contains the profile and history of "Babylon the Great," which begins long before the Matthew 24-25 timeline begins and ends with the return of the King. Colored box #23 contains the story of the Great White Throne Judgment told in Revelation 20:11-15. The events it describes begin toward the very end of – but still during – the Millennial Kingdom, just prior to the final judgment, and is placed thus on the chart.

Obviously, the topic is complex despite the assistance of these charts, but the entire book of Revelation can be deciphered relatively easily with these tools.

USING BIBLICAL SYMBOLISM TO ALIGN THE OLIVET DISCOURSE AND REVELATION

For simplicity's sake, we will limit this analysis primarily to the symbolism of a few segments of Revelation which describe events in heaven from the perspective of heaven (the dark blue squares on *Deciphering the Revelation Chronology*, Chart I), since these are the most difficult to plot chronologically.

In *Deciphering the Revelation Chronology*, Chart II, we show that the fifteen events of the Olivet Discourse in Matthew 24-25 begin with box #5 from Chart 1. Because Revelation is an expanded and augmented version of the Olivet Discourse it addresses additional matters that occur before and after the Olivet timeline.

It is like a modern book in which the Matthew 24-25 timeline is the main body, and additional materials are tacked on to the front and the back. The preliminary materials include a preamble (box#1), a general introduction (box #2), a special introductory note to a specific class of readers (box #3), and a foreword (box #4).

Box #4 contains the first example of events in heaven seen from heaven from Chart 1, and represents the final preliminary word before the Revelation version of the Matthew 24-25 chronology begins.

The key symbolism of the scroll in box #4 is a direct reference to Daniel's final prophecy in Daniel Chapter 12:1-13, of which we will quote the most relevant portion:

*"At that time Michael, the great prince who stands watch over your people, will rise up. There will be a time of distress such as never has occurred from the beginning of nations until then. But at that time your people—everyone whose name is found written in the book—will be delivered. And many who sleep in the dust of the earth will awake, some to everlasting life, but others to shame and everlasting contempt. Then the wise will shine like the brightness of the heavens, and those who lead many to righteousness, like the stars forever and ever. **But you, Daniel, shut up these words and seal the book until the time of the end.**"*

Of all the references to scrolls in the Bible, this is the only one that matches Revelation 4 and 5 (box #4). The passage concisely summarizes the entire end times chronology, with specific references to tribulation, resurrection/rapture, the Great White Throne Judgment, and eternity, in that order.

Box #5 then addresses the theme of tribulation with the very obvious "beginning of sorrows"/four horsemen alignment of Matthew and Revelation.

Box #6 (Revelation 7:9-84) is the next event in heaven as seen from heaven, describing the great ingathering of saints before the throne of God. The key symbols here include the "ingathering to God's presence" theme which is associated with the Feast of Tabernacles, itself a metaphor for the Millennial Kingdom. The Feast of Tabernacles is described in Leviticus 23:38-42, with an essential element being palm branches (23:40). It's "ingathering" theme is emphasized in Exodus 23:16b.

This helps us integrate Box #6 into the Matthew 24-25 timeline by association with the Hebrew religious calendar. The Feast of Tabernacles is the last of the seven feasts, beginning five days after Yom Kippur, the Day of Atonement, which is the day in which Christ touches down on the Mount of Olives to reclaim the earth and begin the Millennial Kingdom.

Box #6 is, in essence, a picture of the heavenly version of the Feast of Tabernacles, the perfect final ingathering in the spiritual realm, occurring in the text in the same order as in the Hebrew religious calendar on earth. Importantly, per Exodus 23:16, the Feast of Tabernacles pilgrimage encompasses all three of the fall feasts, beginning with the Feast of Trumpets, when the resurrection and rapture will occur for the Bride of Christ (and the 144,000 Jews are sealed against death to survive the Wrath), then the Day of Atonement, then five days later the Feast of Tabernacles itself, representing the start of the Millennial Kingdom. All three together represent the great ingathering.

Note that this sequence actually begins in Revelation 6:12 with the opening of the sixth seal. Revelation 6:12-8:2 (especially 6:12-17) clearly aligns with Matthew 24:29-32. Look at the sequence and order of symbols/themes common to both passages: darkness, falling stars, heavens shaken, figs, terror among men, four winds/corners of the earth, trumpets.

Studying the symbols used in the text allows us to recognize that the timeline of Revelation is not actually broken by the shift in perspective. What begins with events on earth from the perspective of heaven (in box #5) flows smoothly through the events of box #6 (events in heaven seen from the heavenly perspective): one continuous timeline.

The Season of the End. Matthew 24:32-35

"Now learn the parable from the fig tree: as soon as its branch has become tender and sprouts its leaves, you know that summer is near; so you too, when you see all these things, recognize that He is near, right at the door. Truly I say to you, this generation will not pass away until all these things take place." (32-34).

Jesus gave the parable of the fig tree as the clue which establishes the season in which the last days occur. This delineates the length of the season as the lifespan of the generation living at the time the metaphorical fig tree puts forth its leaves.

Throughout the Bible the fig tree is representative of the house of Judah which at the time of Christ was largely synonymous with the kingdom of Judea (while today it is defined by Yahweh worship through Judaism). In Jeremiah 24:1-10, the Lord compares two groups of Judeans (good and evil men, respectively) to good and bad figs. Then, Mark 11:12-13 and 20-21 records the cursing of the fig tree by Jesus in the short period between His triumphal entry into Jerusalem and the Olivet Discourse -- a context heavily emphasizing judgment against Judea.

I agree with the widespread view that this prophecy is being fulfilled today, that we are living in the last generation, and that all of the end times events leading to the start of the Millennial Kingdom will occur within the lifespan of those born in the generation of the fig tree.

There are disagreements as to the starting date of "this generation" involving the three most plausible options:

A. On or about Hanukkah of 1917, during World War 1, when British General Allenby marched into Jerusalem after liberating the Holy City from exactly 400 years of occupation by the Moslem Ottoman Turks and approximately 1800 years of exclusion of Jews from the land. Subsequently, British Foreign Secretary Arthur Balfour issued the famous Balfour Declaration inviting the Jewish people to repopulate "Palestine." The Balfour Declaration was in fact a letter from Balfour to Baron Walter Rothschild, de facto leader of world Jewry at that time.

Significantly, this was at the height of the popularity of the doctrine of "British Israelism," the belief (held by many, including Queen Elizabeth II) that the British monarchy was rooted in and a continuation of the royal lineage of the Judean kings and that the Anglo-Saxon people they ruled were the descendants of Ephraim, the dominant tribe of the House (and Kingdom) of Israel. We have not taken a firm position on these claims, the veracity of which is irrelevant to this study – what matters is that the British believed it at the time.

B. May 14, 1948, when the Jewish immigrants in the Holy Land declared the reestablishment of the State of Israel upon the expiration of the British Mandate.

C. June 6, 1967, when the Jews recaptured/liberated East Jerusalem, gaining full control over the entirety of the Holy City for the first time in nearly two millennia. Although the Jews had possession of West Jerusalem from 1948, East Jerusalem and the all-important Mount of Olives was in the possession of Jordan until 1967. The two territories were divided by a vacant strip through the center of Jerusalem called "No Man's Land."

Importantly in the study of prophecy, Jerusalem is the Center of the Universe in the priority and perspective of God and therefore is our point of reference for navigating our way, just as sailors plot their course by reference to the North Star. Thus, the liberation of Jerusalem is arguably a more significant spiritual event than the establishment of the State of Israel, and perhaps the most significant spiritual event of the 20th century.

Nevertheless, we think that May 14, 1948 is the most likely starting point, largely because it appears also to be the fulfillment of Isaiah 66:8: "*Who has heard such a thing? Who has seen such things? Can a land be born in one day? Can a nation be brought forth all at once? As soon as Zion travailed, she also brought forth her sons.*"

CHAPTER TWO:

THE SIGNIFICANCE OF THE SEVENS

"Remember the former things, those of long ago; I am God, and there is no other; I am God, and there is none like me. I make known the end from the beginning, from ancient times, what is still to come" (Isaiah 46:9-10).

God has arranged his time-keeping system in cycles of seven. Creation occurred according to this divine pattern of six 24-hour days of work and one of Sabbath rest. And the early Christians believed and taught that the totality of time allotted by God for physical creation to exist is seven thousand years: six thousand years of work and struggle by mankind followed by a thousand year Sabbath rest called the Millennial Kingdom. This in turn is followed by the destruction of all matter and our entrance into Heaven (2 Peter 3).

This is the same pattern of sevens found in the schedule of the biblical feasts in Leviticus 23, and the Jubilee calendar in Leviticus 25.

There are seven biblical feasts, which God instructs are His appointed times of fellowship with man: Passover, Unleavened Bread, First Fruits, Pentecost, Trumpets, Atonement, and Tabernacles. The Feast of Tabernacles or "Booths" is the "Sabbath" of the seven, representing God dwelling with man as He did during the Hebrew sojourn in the wilderness where they lived in tents (booths), following the Exodus from Egypt. In the prophetic sense, the feast of Tabernacles represents the future Millennial Kingdom when Christ will literally dwell on earth with men, ruling as King of Kings on the literal throne of David. Tabernacles is an eight-day festival, the eighth day representing the new beginning (prophetically, heaven).

The Jubilee calendar is a calendar of seven-year cycles, with each seventh year being the Sabbath year when the land must lie fallow (no planting of crops) and certain contracts between men must be considered fulfilled. Seven cycles of seven years round out the Jubilee and that final Sabbath year (the 49th year in the cycle) is called the High Sabbatical, ushering in the 50th, or Jubilee Year, the year of liberation: the land of the Hebrews must return to its original owners and captives are set free.

The importance of this pattern of sevens was burned into the minds of the Hebrews as they wandered in the desert, being fed daily by God's provision of manna. God provided manna for six days only and instructed men that they must gather a double portion on the sixth day because none would be provided on the seventh day, the Sabbath (Exodus 16:25). Importantly, the manna collected on the sixth day would last for two days, and not spoil in one day as it would at any other time. This teaching was so essential that a jar of manna was one of only three sacred items kept with the Ark of the Covenant, along with the stone tablets containing God's law, and Aaron's rod (Exodus 16:33, Hebrews 9:4).

The pattern of sevens (and of Jubilee) is also found in the way the feasts were kept. For example, the biblical feast of Pentecost falls on the 50th day after the feast of First Fruits (when Jesus rose from the dead, the first fruits of humanity (1 Corinthians 15:20), following seven weeks of watching and preparation called the "Counting of the Omer."

There are far too many examples of God's use of seven in Scripture to recount in this section, but we have cited enough of them for our purposes. Seven days, seven years, seven weeks, seven cycles of days, weeks and years, seven millennia, seven seals, trumpets and bowls, and on and on.

NOT EITHER/OR, BUT BOTH/AND

As we begin to recognize and contemplate the cyclical and organic nature of God's perfect system of timekeeping, the contrast between the human and the divine perspective on things becomes clearer. The unaided human perspective is flat, linear, two dimensional. But illuminated by the divine spark it perceives some of the depth and breadth of multiple dimensions. For example, it becomes possible to reconcile apparent contradictions in Scripture such as the doctrines of predestination and free will. The answer isn't that one must be true to the exclusion of the other, but that both can be true concurrently in different dimensions of reality: in this case from outside and inside of time (heaven and earth). Not "either this or that," but "both this and that."

Predestination is the perspective of timeless heaven, where the creation story has already finished but has not yet begun -- a paradox currently beyond our comprehension. Free will is the perspective of earth, where we human beings float in the river of time and perceive each successive moment and its very real choices as we pass from one to the next from the Alpha toward the Omega.

In like manner, any given passage of the Living Word of God may offer multiple perspectives of the truth it contains or teach multiple distinct and separate lessons based on the specific need or degree of spiritual maturity of the reader. A clue to this deeper reality is found in Isaiah 28:9-10:

"*Whom shall he teach knowledge? and whom shall he make to understand doctrine? them that are weaned from the milk, and drawn from the breasts. For precept must be upon precept,* **precept upon precept; line upon line, line upon line; here a little, and there a little.**"

The highest achievements of human reasoning and intellect from Pythagoras to Newton to Einstein are embodied in those first two steps: "*precept upon precept, line upon line.*" Deductive and inductive logic, the scientific method, mathematics, presuppositional theology, and every technological advance of humankind is made possible by our capacity to apply these rules of rationality written into our being by God.

But then he adds the third dimension of illumination: "*here a little, there a little.*" This passes beyond the realm of linear logic and the material world and draws from the eternal realm, a process in which Holy Spirit actively fulfils the promise of Christ that "*He will lead you into all truth*" (John 16:13). It is beyond our control but not random, available only to those who genuinely trust God to impart truth to us.

"Truth" is God's perspective of His creation. In His omniscience His perception is utterly infallible and He has three successively more illuminating ways of teaching us about it: three ways that match the three steps of the Isaiah passage above.

1) Through diligent observation of His creation for insights about Him whereby He reveals "precept upon precept." "*What may be known about God is plain to [everyone], because God has made it plain to them. For since the creation of the world God's invisible qualities—his eternal power and divine nature—have been clearly seen, being **understood from what has been made**, so that people are without excuse*" (Romans 1:19-20).

And "*when Gentiles, who do not have the law, do by nature things required by the law, they are a law for themselves, even though they do not have the law. They show that **the requirements of the law are written on their hearts***" (Romans 2:14-15). Since this is true of the highest intellectual abstractions of the moral law then, *a priori*, it is more obviously true of the more fundamental laws of material nature, many of which are self-evident to any rational thinker.

2) Through His Living Word, the Scripture, "line upon line." "*The testimony of the Lord is sure, making wise the simple*" (Psalms 19:7).

3) Through His Spirit, who dwells within us if we have accepted Christ and are sufficiently tuned in to Him to hear the still, small voice: "*here a little, there a little.*" God is like a divine tuning fork and His Holy Spirit is like the emanation of His vibration. The more we attune ourselves to His presence in us , the more we love Him and surrender to His will (Romans 8:28), the more we can perceive the truth in the supernatural "*here a little, there a little*" guidance of the Holy Spirit.

The more we appreciate that God's Word is living and active, not just dead words on a page, the easier it is to recognize that there is often more than one way to interpret a given passage. That perspective will be helpful as we reconsider some of the familiar dogma of modern end times theology.

DANIEL'S SEVENTY WEEKS AND THE PROBLEM OF THE 70TH WEEK

A common belief among mainstream Christians is that the Last Days Tribulation will last seven years and be preceded by the Rapture of the Church and the signing of some form of seven-year peace treaty. (The "weeks" of Daniel are years, not days.)

There are several problems with this doctrine, not the least of which is the sole proof text used to support the notion of a "seven-year tribulation" and a "peace treaty." That text is Daniel 9:24-27:

24Seventy weeks are determined upon thy people and upon thy holy city, to finish the transgression, and to make an end of sins, and to make reconciliation for iniquity, and to bring in everlasting righteousness, and to seal up the vision and prophecy, and to anoint the most Holy.

25Know therefore and understand, that from the going forth of the commandment to restore and to build Jerusalem unto the Messiah the Prince shall be seven weeks, and threescore and two weeks: the street shall be built again, and the wall, even in troublous times.

26And after threescore and two weeks shall Messiah be cut off, but not for himself: and the people of the prince that shall come shall destroy the city and the sanctuary; and the end thereof shall be with a flood, and unto the end of the war desolations are determined.

27And he shall confirm the covenant with many for one week: and in the midst of the week he shall cause the sacrifice and the oblation to cease, and for the overspreading of abominations he shall make it desolate, even until the consummation, and that determined shall be poured upon the desolate.

While this passage accurately prophesies the timing of the first coming of the Messiah and addresses the future second coming, the text does not state that there will be a seven-year tribulation or that it will begin with a peace treaty. Those conclusions are derived from the speculation of various prophecy teachers of the past, which are repeated as dogma by their current adherents. Granted, the seven-year peace treaty is a plausible theory, but it is not the only one.

It is equally plausible that the entire 70 weeks of Daniel was completed at the first coming of Christ, and the *pattern* of the 70th week will be repeated in the last days. I will address this alternative and the phenomenon of repeating biblical patterns below.

It is also plausible that it is Christ, not the Antichrist who "*confirms a covenant with many:*" the Covenant of God with Abraham, Isaac and Jacob.

As we read the passage carefully we see that v 25 says that 69 weeks lead up to the coming of the Messiah:

"unto Messiah the Prince there will be seven weeks and sixty-two weeks."

It seems apparent that countdown leads up to but does not include His first advent. It's like saying, "33 more shopping days until Christmas." Christmas is not included in the 33 days.

Verse 26 appears to supports this by saying:

"*AFTER threescore and two weeks shall Messiah be cut off.*"

In other words, the cutting off of the Messiah occurs IN the 70th week. It doesn't say "in the 69th week," it says "after." That precludes a 70th week being projected into the future even if just one day of it is adjacent to the 69ᵗʰ week.

The rest of verse 26 (26b) describes events that occur after the 69 weeks as well. We believe it is talking about the destruction of the Temple by Titus in 70AD. We think v26b is parenthetical, meaning it is stated as a side-comment. In other words, we should read it like this:

26a *"And after threescore and two weeks shall Messiah be cut off, but not for himself **26b** (and the people of the prince that shall come shall destroy the city and the sanctuary; and the end thereof shall be with a flood, and unto the end of the war desolations are determined.)"*

We view v27 as picking up from 26**a**:

"*And he [Messiah] shall confirm the covenant with many for one week: and in the midst of the week [He] shall cause the sacrifice and the oblation to cease...*"

This was precisely what Jesus came to do. He came to confirm the covenant made by Yahweh to Abraham, Isaac and Jacob, and in the midst of the week he was "cut off" by the Jewish and Roman authorities who crucified Him. In that "cutting off" He voluntarily became the Passover "lamb" whose sacrifice ended/fulfilled the purpose of that ritual. It's a perfect logical fit.

The rest of verse 27 reads (with our annotations in brackets):

"*and for [because of] the overspreading of abominations he [Messiah] shall make desolate, even until the consummation [of the end of the age], [when] that determined shall be poured upon the desolate. [i.e., those or him whose abominations have caused the desolation].*"

This is precisely the sentence that Jesus pronounced in Matt 23:38-39:

"*Behold, your house [House/Kingdom of Judah] is left unto you desolate. For I say unto you, Ye shall not see me henceforth, till ye shall say, Blessed is he that cometh in the name of the Lord.*"

Just before His arrest, Jesus pronounced this sentence on the Jews (which was partially fulfilled in 70AD with the destruction of Jerusalem and the Temple, and fully so in 135AD following the Simon bar Kokhba revolt which caused the Roman authorities to permanently banish all Jews from the land -- a ban/desolation that endured until the Balfour Declaration of the British Empire in 1917). HE is the one who makes desolate. This is the same desolation enacted by God to cleanse the land of Hebrew sin when He sent its inhabitants into exile in Babylon for 70 years.

GOD, NOT ANTICHRIST, IS THE ONE WHO "MAKES DESOLATE"

Abominations cause desolations, but God is the one who enacts the desolations.

Leviticus 26: <u>27</u> *"And if ye will not for all this hearken unto me, but walk contrary unto me...I will make your cities waste, and bring your sanctuaries unto desolation...<u>32</u>And I will bring the land into desolation: and your enemies which dwell therein shall be astonished at it. <u>33</u>And I will scatter you among the heathen, and will draw out a sword after you: and your land shall be desolate, and your cities waste. <u>34</u>Then shall the land enjoy her sabbaths, as long as it lieth desolate, and ye be in your enemies' land; even then shall the land rest, and enjoy her sabbaths. <u>35</u>As long as it lieth desolate it shall rest; because it did not rest in your sabbaths, when ye dwelt upon it."*

Isaiah 24:<u>1</u> *"Behold, the LORD maketh the earth empty, and maketh it waste, and turneth it upside down, and scattereth abroad the inhabitants thereof."*

Ezekiel 33:<u>28</u> *"For I [Yahweh] will lay the land most desolate, and the pomp of her strength shall cease; and the mountains of Israel shall be desolate, that none shall pass through."*

SEVEN YEARS OR THREE AND ONE HALF?

In the mainstream view, Daniel's 70th week is unfulfilled and projected some 2,000 years into the future, soon to begin in these last days. We acknowledge it is a plausible theory, and one that is NOT defeated by the gap of two millennia. There are other biblical examples of a time lapse in the fulfillment of prophecy, most importantly the gap implied by Jesus Himself in His reading of Isaiah 61:1-2 in the synagogue:

"1 The Spirit of the Lord GOD is upon me; because the LORD hath anointed me to preach good tidings unto the meek; he hath sent me to bind up the brokenhearted, to proclaim liberty to the captives, and the opening of the prison to them that are bound; 2a To proclaim the acceptable year of the LORD, 2b and the day of vengeance of our God..."

As recorded in Luke 4:16-21, Jesus read only through the verse 2a and closed the book because He was literally fulfilling the prophecy of Isaiah 6:1-2a, but not yet fulfilling 2b, *"the day of vengeance of our God,"* which would not occur until 2,000 years later at His second coming.

Importantly, this reading was an announcement of the Jubilee Year and (by some accounts) His first act of ministry (immediately following His testing by Satan in the wilderness). Look for the Antichrist, the counterfeit messiah, to possibly follow this pattern of declaring a Jubilee at the start of his reign.

Getting back to our question in this section, it does not necessarily follow, however, that the full seven years of the 70th "week" are waiting to be fulfilled. It may be that only the "half week" (3 ½ years) is unfulfilled. As we have conjectured above "*after threescore and two weeks shall Messiah be cut off, but not for himself…and in the midst of the [70th] week he shall cause the sacrifice and the oblation to cease.*" If this alternative view is correct, and the projecting of an unfulfilled portion of the prophecy into the future is also correct, the reign of the Antichrist could be just three and one half years, not seven years.

Interestingly, there is no mention of a seven-year reign of the Antichrist in Revelation, only three and one-half years (see Revelation 11:2, 12:6, 12:14, 13:5).

That having been said, we tend to believe that the Antichrist probably *will* reign a full seven years, and his reign may very well begin with a peace treaty. However, we don't expect it to comport with the details of Daniel 9:24-27 as closely as other prophecy teachers do, because we believe the Daniel 9 iteration of the Daniel pattern (all 70 weeks of it) was finished in sequence with no gap.

THE COMPLETION OF THE 70TH WEEK

After Jesus was "cut off" in the "middle of the week," the Apostles, whom Jesus trained to "do even greater works" than He, picked up the mantle of His authority and went out to continue the mission of Christ *to the Hebrews only*. For the remainder of that 70th week they made their best effort, but the Jews then hired Saul to stop the advance of the church. At the end of the "week" the first martyr of the church, Stephen, is killed by a mob as young Saul looks on, but not before Stephen delivers a final indictment of the Jews (Acts 7). He is essentially closing the door to the corporate House of Judah in fulfillment of the sentence of Jesus in Matthew 23.

Saul then becomes Paul, Apostle to the Gentiles, and at the close of the 70th week the primary mission of the church shifts as the Age of the Gentiles begins (Romans 11), and the sentence of Jesus unfolds upon the Jews, culminating in the near term with the destruction of Jerusalem and the Temple and eventually (135 AD) in their banishment from the Holy Land for more than 17 centuries.

In this way, Daniel's 70th week can be considered to have been completed, yet we believe it may soon be repeated prior to the return of Christ.

THE REPEATING PATTERN OF THE DESECRATION OF JERUSALEM

How can Daniel 9:27 be fulfilled and unfulfilled at the same time -- both things be true?

The flaw in the traditional view is that it attempts to compress three separate versions of the Daniel prophecy into one, rather than recognizing they are intended to describe three iterations of the same pattern, with three distinct Antichrist figures, three distinct "deliverer" figures, three distinct historical settings of the City of Jerusalem, and three distinct abominations that cause desolation.

Daniel 9:24-27

This is actually the second iteration of the desecration of Jerusalem pattern historically, though first in order in the text.

In this iteration, the Antichrist figure is the Roman general Titus, later to become Emperor Titus. The deliverer figure is Yeshua Hamashiach (Jesus Christ). And the setting is the City of Jerusalem in the last generation before the destruction of the Second Temple (which could arguably be called the Third Temple because it had been so dramatically enlarged by the wicked King Herod -- a descendant of Edomite converts to Judaism). The abomination that causes desolation (A of D) could be the rejection of the Messiah by the Jewish religious authorities despite His personal presence and appeal to them through signs and wonders and through reasoning from the Scriptures. If so, the desolation was decreed by Christ in Matthew 23: 37-38, and (in relation to the temple) was carried out by Titus in 70 AD. According to Philostratus, Titus refused to accept a wreath of victory for that campaign, saying he was merely the instrument of God's wrath on the Jews.[3]

Alternately, and perhaps more likely, the A of D could have been the erection of a statue of Roman emperor Caligula in the Temple in Jerusalem in AD 40.[4] Caligula was a definite Antichrist figure who, like Antiochus IV Epiphanes, claimed to be a god and hated the Jews for their monotheism.

Daniel 11:29-45

This iteration was the first in order of fulfillment, but second in order in the text. The Antichrist figure is Antiochus IV Epiphanes, King of the Seleucid Empire, headquartered in Babylon. The deliverer figure is Judah Maccabee (Judah the Hammer), founder of the Hasmonean Dynasty of Hebrew Kings (which ended a century later with a slaughter of the royal family by the Roman-backed usurper Herod the Great). The setting is the City of Jerusalem in 167 BC and the Second Temple.

Antiochus corrupted the priests with flattery and the Jewish youths with homosexuality, then defiled the temple with pigs' blood in an attempt to force the Jews to abandon their exclusive worship of Yahweh and embrace the polytheism of his empire in which he declared himself to be the "Epiphanes" ("The Manifest God.")

It is believed by scholars that the Abomination of desolation of Daniel 11:31 was a bust of Antiochus himself, placed on the altar of God. The brief period of desolation lasted until the temple was cleansed in a ritual which is today commemorated as Hannukah. (Regarding these events, the historical record of Daniel 11 is supplemented by the Apocryphal books of 1 & 2 Maccabees, which do not have the authority of Scripture but nonetheless offer a highly reliable account).

Daniel 12:1-4

The third iteration of the desecration of Jerusalem pattern is yet to come. The Antichrist figure will be the end-time Antichrist. The deliverer will again be Jesus Christ. The setting will be the City of Jerusalem during the reign of the Antichrist, and either a rebuilt Third Temple, or possibly just the altar (for which we see a precedent in Ezra 3:1-6). The Abomination of desolation is not clearly identified, but could very well be some artifact that depicts the Antichrist as God, set up on the altar.

Importantly, there are numerous elements of the prior two iterations of the pattern which may or may not be present in the end-time iteration. For example, much attention is given by prior prophecy teachers to the actions of the "King of the North" and "King of the South" in their predictions about the end times Antichrist. They may be correct, but it is also possible that those elements were unique to the first iteration, as indeed they precisely describe the people and events of Antiochus' time. Might they be repeated identically in the third iteration? Yes. Must they be? Not in our opinion.

Unique to the Daniel 12 iteration is the reference to "*a time of trouble, such as never was since there was a nation even to that same time*" (v. 1), a warning restated and expanded upon by Jesus in the Olivet Discourse: "*For then shall be great tribulation, such as was not since the beginning of the world to this time, no, nor ever shall be. And except those days should be shortened, there should no flesh be saved: but for the elect's sake those days shall be shortened*" (Matthew 24:21-22). That time is clearly still in the future.

THE REPEATING PATTERN OF PASSOVER

By way of reinforcing our hypothesis about God's use of repeating patterns with common elements but with varying contexts and manifestations, we offer a second more familiar example, that of the Passover story. Again, there are three iterations with several common elements in each: a father, a firstborn son, the sacrifice of a lamb, and an object on which the sacrifice was given effect.

Genesis 22:1-13. The first iteration of this biblical pattern was the near-sacrifice of Isaac by Abraham. Abraham was the father ready to sacrifice his firstborn son on the command of God. At the last moment God Himself provided a substitutionary sacrifice in the form of a sheep. The sheep, instead of Isaac, had his blood shed upon an altar. "*By faith Abraham, when he was tested, offered up Isaac on the altar. He who had received the promises was ready to offer his one and only son, even though God had said to him, 'Through Isaac your offspring will be reckoned.' Abraham reasoned that God could raise the dead, and in a sense, he did receive Isaac back from death*" (Hebrews 11:17-19).

Exodus 12:1-13. The second iteration of the Passover pattern is found in Exodus 12. All the firstborn males of the land were to be killed by God (as punishment for Pharaoh's slaughter of the firstborn of the Hebrews during the infancy of Moses.) "*Every firstborn son in Egypt will die, from the firstborn son of Pharaoh, who sits on the throne, to the firstborn son of the female slave, who is at her hand mill, and all the firstborn of the cattle as well*" (Exodus 11:5). Only those households displaying the blood of a sacrificial lamb on the lintels and doorposts of their homes were spared.

The father figure is Pharaoh, and his firstborn son is the first to suffer God's wrath. The sheep is a one-year-old male. The object on which the sacrificial blood is given effect is the door frame of the house.

The Gospels. The third iteration is found in each of the four gospels, in the story of the crucifixion of Christ, which occurred, literally, on Passover, immediately preceding the first day of the Feast of Unleavened Bread (Leviticus 23:4-6). "*Clean out the old leaven so that you may be a new lump, just as you are in fact unleavened. For Christ our Passover also has been sacrificed*" (1 Corinthians 5:7).

The Passover pattern was completed in the sacrifice of Jesus on the cross. God the Father gave His only son (John 3:16). The Father is God. The son is Christ. The lamb is Christ. The object on which His shed blood was given effect was the cross.

So we can see that God uses thematic patterns in the Bible to describe actual events of history, and that the iterations of these patterns, though they share common thematic elements, are each unique. This fact informs our view that Daniel's 70th Week was completed at the first coming of Christ, but will likely be repeated in a similar but unique manner at His second coming.

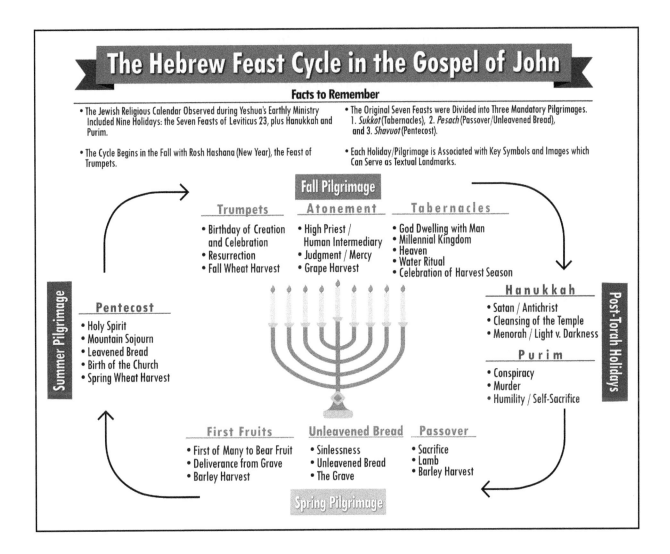

The Hebrew Feast Cycle in the Gospel of John

Facts to Remember

- The Jewish Religious Calendar Observed during Yeshua's Earthly Ministry Included Nine Holidays: the Seven Feasts of Leviticus 23, plus Hanukkah and Purim.

- The Cycle Begins in the Fall with Rosh Hashana (New Year), the Feast of Trumpets.

- The Original Seven Feasts were Divided into Three Mandatory Pilgrimages.
  1. *Sukkot* (Tabernacles), 2. *Pesach* (Passover/Unleavened Bread), and 3. *Shavuot* (Pentecost).

- Each Holiday/Pilgrimage is Associated with Key Symbols and Images which Can Serve as Textual Landmarks.

Fall Pilgrimage

Trumpets
- Birthday of Creation and Celebration
- Resurrection
- Fall Wheat Harvest

Atonement
- High Priest / Human Intermediary
- Judgment / Mercy
- Grape Harvest

Tabernacles
- God Dwelling with Man
- Millennial Kingdom
- Heaven
- Water Ritual
- Celebration of Harvest Season

Hanukkah
- Satan / Antichrist
- Cleansing of the Temple
- Menorah / Light v. Darkness

Purim
- Conspiracy
- Murder
- Humility / Self-Sacrifice

Pentecost
- Holy Spirit
- Mountain Sojourn
- Leavened Bread
- Birth of the Church
- Spring Wheat Harvest

Summer Pilgrimage

Post-Torah Holidays

First Fruits
- First of Many to Bear Fruit
- Deliverance from Grave
- Barley Harvest

Unleavened Bread
- Sinlessness
- Unleavened Bread
- The Grave

Passover
- Sacrifice
- Lamb
- Barley Harvest

Spring Pilgrimage

THE HEBREW FEAST CYCLE IN THE GOSPEL OF JOHN

The Gospel of John, written much later than the three synoptic (summary form) gospels, emphasizes the divinity of Jesus and addresses many topics and events not included in the others, while omitting some topics and events found in the earlier gospels. However, the most important difference in respect to our study is John's unique chronological narrative of the Lord's earthly ministry, directly tied to the cyclical Hebrew religious calendar.

Significantly, this calendar included not just the seven biblical feasts of Leviticus 23, but the later Hebrew holidays of Hanukkah and Purim as well, which were ritually observed in that generation. Hanukkah, also known as the Feast of Dedication and Feast of Lights was instituted by the Maccabees in 165 B.C.. Hanukkah plays a surprisingly important role in John's Gospel, its theme of Jesus as light to the world being prominently featured in the opening paragraphs of the first chapter, interwoven with Feast of Trumpets imagery as a part of the retelling of the Creation story. Hanukkah symbolism dominates a large section of John that spans three entire chapters (8-10), the second lengthiest treatment of any holiday in the book (the final Passover/Unleavened Bread/First Fruits pilgrimage – detailing the death, burial and resurrection of Christ – naturally being the longest and most thorough of all, spanning chapters 12-21).

Purim, also known as the Feast of Lots, celebrates the deliverance of the Jews from genocide by the sacrificial intervention of Queen Esther. (It is the least referenced of the holidays and even then only symbolically.)

The cyclical pattern of these nine feasts is found not just in the recounting of the Lord's schedule, but in the use of feast-related symbols, themes and images which are presented in the same chronological order as they occur in the calendar.

This is a good place to note that even today the Jews use two different forms of the Menorah which reflect the two alternative sets of holidays. The seven-branch Menorah represents the seven feasts of Leviticus 23. The nine-branch Menorah includes the same seven feasts plus the two later holidays, which both occur between Tabernacles and Passover.

To correctly track the holiday cycle in John it is necessary to know both the sequence of the holidays in the Hebrew calendar, and the themes and symbols associated with each holiday.

It is also helpful to know that the Hebrew civil calendar begins in the fall with Rosh Hashana (the Feast of Trumpets) rather than the spring -- much as the Hebrew day begins in the evening rather than the morning (Genesis 1:5).

To reiterate, the original seven holidays fall into three sets, each set representing a time of mandatory pilgrimage to Jerusalem:

- Pilgrimage 1) Trumpets through Tabernacles – collectively called the Feast of Tabernacles,

- Pilgrimage 2) Passover through First Fruits – collectively called the Feast of Unleavened Bread, officially, but referred to as Passover in John.

- Pilgrimage 3) Pentecost.

Hanukkah, which occurs a little over two months after Tabernacles, and Purim, which occurs about a month before Passover, were observed nationally at the time of Christ but were not biblically mandated.

Our charts in this section identifiy the nine holidays in sequence and key themes and symbols associated with them in the Bible and Jewish tradition.

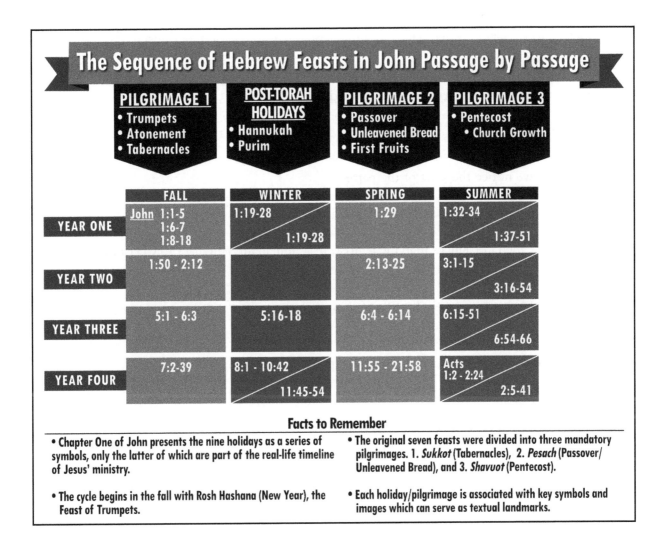

The Sequence of Hebrew Feasts in John Passage by Passage

PILGRIMAGE 1
• Trumpets
• Atonement
• Tabernacles

POST-TORAH HOLIDAYS
• Hannukah
• Purim

PILGRIMAGE 2
• Passover
• Unleavened Bread
• First Fruits

PILGRIMAGE 3
• Pentecost
• Church Growth

	FALL	WINTER	SPRING	SUMMER
YEAR ONE	John 1:1-5 1:6-7 1:8-18	1:19-28 1:19-28	1:29	1:32-34 1:37-51
YEAR TWO	1:50 - 2:12		2:13-25	3:1-15 3:16-54
YEAR THREE	5:1 - 6:3	5:16-18	6:4 - 6:14	6:15-51 6:54-66
YEAR FOUR	7:2-39	8:1 - 10:42 11:45-54	11:55 - 21:58	Acts 1:2 - 2:24 2:5-41

Facts to Remember

• Chapter One of John presents the nine holidays as a series of symbols, only the latter of which are part of the real-life timeline of Jesus' ministry.

• The cycle begins in the fall with Rosh Hashana (New Year), the Feast of Trumpets.

• The original seven feasts were divided into three mandatory pilgrimages. 1. *Sukkot* (Tabernacles), 2. *Pesach* (Passover/Unleavened Bread), and 3. *Shavuot* (Pentecost).

• Each holiday/pilgrimage is associated with key symbols and images which can serve as textual landmarks.

Feast of Trumpets: Birthday/Celebration of Creation, Resurrection, Fall Wheat Harvest.

Day of Atonement: High Priest/Human Intermediary, Judgment/Mercy, Grape Harvest.

Feast of Tabernacles: God Dwelling with Man, Millennial Kingdom, Heaven, Water Ritual, End of Harvest Season.

Hanukkah: Satan/Antichrist, Cleansing of the Temple, Menorah, Light vs Darkness.

Purim: Conspiracy, Murder, Humility/Self-Sacrifice.

Passover: Altar, Sacrifice, Lamb, Substitutionary Atonement, Barley Harvest.

Unleavened Bread: Sinlessness, Unleavened Bread, the Grave.

First Fruits: First of Many to Bear Fruit, Deliverance from Grave, Barley Harvest.

Pentecost: Holy Spirit, Water, Fire. Mountain Sojourn. Birth of the Church. Spring Wheat Harvest, Leavened Bread.

John 1: The Complete Hebrew Feast Calendar in Word Pictures

As we examine the text of the Gospel of John with these facts in mind, the association with the Hebrew feasts is unmistakable. Again, the civil calendar begins in the fall with the Feast of Trumpets, and immediately we notice the start of the pattern.

- John 1:1-5 describes the Creation, symbolically invoking the Feast of Trumpets.

- John 1:6-7 then introduces John the Baptist, first human intermediary to Christ in His earthly ministry, symbolically invoking the Day of Atonement.

- John 1:8-18 then proclaims that Christ is God made flesh to dwell among men, invoking the Feast of Tabernacles.

- John 1:19-28 emphasizes John's ministry of baptism, the cleansing of the body (the Temple) from sin, invoking Hanukkah.

- John 1:19-28 also emphasizes John's qualities of humility and self-sacrifice, which were Esther's defining qualities in the Purim story.

- John 1:29 declares of Jesus: "*Behold, the Lamb of God who takes away the sin of the world!*," invoking Passover.

There is no specific invocation of Unleavened Bread or First Fruits here, reflecting the cultural perspective of the three feasts of Passover as a single holiday pilgrimage but any of the key symbols of these feasts serve our purpose of tracking the religious cycle in the Gospel of John.

- John 1:32-34 describes the "*dove out of heaven*" descending upon Jesus, designating Him as "*the one who baptizes in the Holy Spirit*," invoking Pentecost.

Importantly, Pentecost (the last of the four biblical spring feasts fulfilled by Christ at His first coming) marks the beginning of the church age that will end on a Feast of Trumpets (the first of the biblical fall feasts which Christ will fulfill at His second coming). It makes perfect sense, therefore, that each invocation of the Pentecost holiday in the Gospel of John is followed by commentary on the church. In this first instance John 1:37-51 describes the gravitation to Jesus of John the Baptist's disciples, and His gathering of the apostles to Himself.

So we can see that this first chapter portrays one complete cycle of the Hebrew religious calendar in a single neat package through imagery and symbolism, but there is more.

A Brief Prophecy of the House of Israel

At the close of the first chapter, the prospective disciple Nathaniel has a brief exchange with Jesus: " *'Rabbi, You are the Son of God; You are the King of Israel. Jesus answered and said to him, 'Because I said to you that I saw you under the fig tree, do you believe? You will see greater things than these.' And He said to him, 'Truly, truly, I say to you, you will see the heavens opened and the angels of God ascending and descending on the Son of Man'* " (John 1:50-51).

Theologians have long grappled with the meaning of Christ's response about the opening of heaven and the ascending and descending of angels, their best guess being a figurative claim to divinity by Jesus by reference to Jacob's vision in Genesis 28:10-17. We agree that it is a statement of divinity by Jesus and does invoke Jacob's vision, but there's a deeper meaning to be found in the passage, which should be taken literally because it includes a specific express prophecy by the Lord.

Obviously, Nathaniel died in the first century without this prophecy having been fulfilled. But is there a time in the future when Nathaniel will see Christ and angels in the heavens? Of course there is, because Nathaniel will be resurrected at the second coming, along with everyone else who died in Christ.

We're not limited to mere deductive reasoning in reaching this conclusion. Consider the John 1:50-51 passage in the slightly wider context beginning with John 1:35 (Christ's gathering of the disciples) and continuing through the story of the wedding at Cana in John 2:1-11. From this wider context we recognize three significant things.

First, that the image of Jesus as the gateway to heaven (being attended by angels), followed by the image of a wedding feast is the same sequence seen in the Olivet Discourse, specifically Matthew 24:30-25:13. Note especially Matthew 24:30-31: *"At that time the sign of the Son of Man will appear in heaven....They will see the Son of Man coming on the clouds of heaven, with power and great glory. And He will send out His angels with a loud trumpet call, and they will gather His elect from the four winds, from one end of the heavens to the other."* Then note Matthew 25:10 *"[When] the bridegroom arrived. Those who were ready went in with him to the wedding banquet, and the door was shut."*

In other words, it is the imagery of the resurrection and rapture followed by the imagery of the Wedding Feast of the Lamb, that which we have addressed in our prior discussion and chart on the Ten Days of Awe.

Bolstering the linkage of these parallel passages and their end times implications is the mention of the "fig tree" in both passages: John 1:50 " *'Because I said to you that I saw you under the fig tree, do you believe?'* and Matthew 24:32-33 *"Now learn this lesson from the fig tree: As soon as its branches become tender and sprout leaves, you know that summer is near. So also, when you see all these things, you will know that He is near, right at the door.*"

As we have discussed previously, the fig tree is a metaphor/symbol for the House of Judah, which was symbolically cursed by Christ in Matthew 21:19, and literally verbally cursed by Christ as his last act in Matthew 23:3-39, before giving the Olivet Discourse. The effect of this sentence of judgment, which is described in Romans 11 as "*a partial hardening...until the fullness of the Gentiles has come in,*" will be lifted in the generation when the fig tree again puts forth its leaves per Matthew 24:32-34. We share the view that "*this generation*" began with the creation of the modern State of Israel.

Second, in the light of this symbolism and the "Two House" teachings in this book, these two events (the gathering of the disciples and the wedding at Cana) represent a pair of bookends between which is symbolically contained the entire history of the process of the redemption of the divorced house of Israel by Christ: from roughly 30 AD to (presumably) the near future.

Third, in using the imagery of resurrection and rapture to invoke the Feast of Trumpets, John completes Chapter 1 by emphasizing the turn of the cyclical calendar, because each new cycle starts with that holiday. But by invoking the Wedding Feast at the opening of Chapter 2 he identifies that *specific* Feast of Trumpets as the final occurrence of that holiday during the age of the Gentiles which the members of the Bride of Christ will celebrate in their human form, because the believers who transition to the Wedding Feast (to pass from betrothed "Bride of Christ" to "Wife of God") will be glorified in that process and assume their perfect spiritual state.

When the holiday cycle resumes in Chapter 2, it skips Hanukkah and Purim and begins with Passover.

It is helpful to remember here that the Hebrew calendar has two "beginning" holidays. The civil calendar begins with Rosh Hashana (the Feast of Trumpets), while the religious calendar begins with Passover. John 1 reflects the civil calendar. John 2 reflects the religious calendar.

John 2-11: The Hebrew Feasts in Jesus' Ministry

While John 1 portrayed the religious cycle primarily through symbolism, the remainder of the Gospel of John tracks the actual holiday calendar which dominated Hebrew life at the time of Christ. John supplements the narrative with symbolism wherever specific feasts are not mentioned by name. To be sure, there are events and teachings unrelated to the holidays interspersed through the book, especially in the latter chapters, but the holiday cycle and related symbolism follows an unmistakable thread through every chapter from beginning to end.

- **Passover**. John 2:13 states "*The Passover of the Jews was near, and Jesus went up to Jerusalem.*" Verses 13-25 describe His time there.

- **Pentecost**. John 3:1-15 tells the story of Jesus teaching Nicodemus about being born again through the Holy Spirit. The Holy Spirit is associated with Pentecost. Importantly, in verses 13-15, Jesus prophesies to Nicodemus about his impending ascension, which would occur just prior to Pentecost.

    - **Church Growth**. John 3:16-4:54 describes the growth of the church, which we have noted follows every iteration of the Pentecost holiday in John.

- **Tabernacles**. John 5:1 reads "*After these things there was a feast of the Jews, and Jesus went up to Jerusalem.*" This was the pilgrimage for the three feasts collectively called the Feast of Tabernacles. This chapter has special significance for those familiar with the 10 Days of Awe/Wrath, because it heavily emphasizes Christ's power of judgment and the choice of life or death for human beings based upon belief in Him and is heavily laced with resurrection symbolism. For example, note the key themes of resurrection and judgment in verses 25-29: "*Truly, truly, I say to you, an hour is coming and now is, when the dead will hear the voice of the Son of God, and those who hear will live. For just as the Father has life in Himself, even so He gave to the Son also to have life in Himself; and He gave Him authority to execute judgment, because He is the Son of Man. Do not marvel at this; for an hour is coming, in which all who are in the tombs will hear His voice, and will come forth; those who did the good deeds to a resurrection of life, those who committed the evil deeds to a resurrection of judgment.*"

This passage conflates the two resurrections (Revelation 20:5-6) at the beginning and the end of the Millennial Kingdom, which in turn evoke the Feast of Tabernacles.

The Tabernacles celebration in Jesus' time also included a daily water ritual called *Nissuch Ha-Mayim* in which the priests would draw water from the Pool of Siloam to be poured upon the altar the next morning, symbolizing the outpouring of the Holy Spirit at the time of the Messiah. John 5:1-6:3 opens with Jesus' healing miracle at the Pool of Siloam, and in the following year's Tabernacles pilgrimage Jesus proclaimed "*If anyone is thirsty, let him come to me and drink. Whoever believes in me, as the Scripture has said, streams of living water will flow from within him*" (John 7:37-38).

Hanukkah and Purim are not specifically addressed in this cycle in chronological order in the text of John, Chapter 5. However, if Chapter 5 can be viewed as "a summary of events that occurred between the Pentecost of John 3-4 and the Passover of John 6," and if we assume that the murderous intent of the Jewish authorities toward Jesus in John 5:16-18 is symbolic of Purim, its appearance in the text prior to the Trumpets symbolism (John 5:25-29) could reflect simple consistency in the narrative. What we mean is that Jesus' supposed "violation of the Sabbath" that led to the Jews *decision* to kill Him occurred before the Feast of Trumpets, while *acts* in furtherance of the conspiracy to murder Him occurred afterward, but both the decision and the acts were addressed in the same paragraph for narrative consistency.

The on and off inclusion of Hanukkah and Purim in the holiday cycle in John may simply reflect their lesser biblical status (notwithstanding Hanukkah's special treatment in chapters 8-10), or might serve to highlight the distinction between the seven-and nine-branch Menorahs, or both. In contrast, however, the three biblically-mandated pilgrimages honoring the seven biblical feasts of Leviticus 23 are presented in perfect sequential order from start to finish through John's Gospel.

- **Passover and Pentecost**. Chapter 6 of John spans the time period from just prior to Passover (6:4) to just prior to Trumpets (7:2). Interestingly, while John's narrative of Jesus' ministry centers on the feeding of the five thousand and seems to span just a few days time, the feast symbolism in the narrative covers all four holidays. Moreover, there is no indication in John that Jesus went to Jerusalem for either the Unleavened Bread or Pentecost pilgrimages during this particular holiday cycle.

  - **Passover**. John 6:4 states "*Now the Passover, the feast of the Jews, was near.*"

  - **First Fruits**. John 6:13 reports "*Here is a boy with five barley loaves and two small fish.*" Barley, as we have noted is symbolic of First Fruits, the third and final holiday of the Passover/Feast of Unleavened Bread pilgrimage.

  - **Pentecost**. John 6:15 states "*Then Jesus, realizing that they were about to come and make Him king by force, withdrew again <u>to a mountain by Himself</u>.* Remember that the original Pentecost featured Moses going up on Mt. Sinai to receive the Torah. Moses was the human witness provided to the people to testify about God's commands. In 6:32-33 after He (Jesus) had come down from the mountain, "*Jesus said to them, 'Truly, truly, I tell you, it was not Moses who gave you the bread from heaven, but it is My Father who gives you the true bread from heaven. For the bread of God is He who comes down from heaven and gives life to the world.*"

In John 6:35 Jesus expressly declares "*I am the bread of life; he who comes to Me will not hunger, and he who believes in Me will never thirst.*" Importantly, bread is symbolic both of the Passover (unleavened, it is called "*the bread of affliction*" in Deuteronomy 16:3) and Pentecost (leavened, per Leviticus 23:17 "*Bring two loaves of bread from your dwellings as a wave offering...baked with yeast, as the firstfruits to the Lord*"). The context of John 6:22-47 strongly suggests that Jesus was referring to Himself in His role as the Bread of Pentecost, in contrast to His role as the Bread of Passover.

- **Church Growth**. This chapter ends with a passage addressing church members (disciples) falling away because of a hard teaching (John 6:54-66). Again, every invocation of Pentecost in John is followed by information about the status of the church.

- **Tabernacles**. Chapter 7 of John takes place almost entirely in Jerusalem during the fall pilgrimage. As noted above, John 7:2 states "*Now the feast of the Jews, the Feast of Tabernacles, was near.*" Verses 37-38 state "*Now on the last day, the great day of the feast, Jesus stood and cried out, saying, "If anyone is thirsty, let him come to Me and drink. 'He who believes in Me, as the Scripture said, 'From his innermost being will flow rivers of living water.'*"

Remember that all three of the fall feasts, Trumpets, Atonement and Tabernacles, are celebrated in the pilgrimage called the Feast of Tabernacles. Trumpets and Atonement are celebrated over the first ten days, then five days later the eight-day feast of *Sukkot* (Tabernacles) begins. Traditionally, the eighth day of Tabernacles, "*the great day of the feast,*" was celebrated with a water ritual, illuminating the context of Jesus' teaching on living water/the Holy Spirit.

Importantly, this particular pilgrimage marked the beginning of Jesus' final year – or rather half-year -- of earthly ministry. The remainder of the Gospel of John shows the Lord's heavy ministry schedule in that it is loaded with teachings.

- **Hanukkah**. Chapters 8-10 of the Gospel of John are rich with Hanukkah imagery and symbolism. The story of Hanukkah is much bigger than the miracle of the holy lamp oil commemorated with the Menorah. As told in the Book of Daniel and the apocryphal books of 1 and 2 Maccabees, the first part of the Hanukkah story begins with the Satanic seduction and defilement of the Jewish people by the Antichrist figure Antiochus IV Epiphanes, who led Jerusalem and Judea into idolatry that culminated in the Abomination of Desolation. 1 and 2 Maccabees are essentially the fuller historical account of what is briefly summarized in Daniel 11:31-32 "*His forces will rise up and desecrate the temple fortress. They will abolish the daily sacrifice and set up the abomination of desolation. With flattery he will corrupt those who violate the covenant, but the people who know their God will firmly resist him.*"

The Hanukkah story continues with a second part, the narrative of the Maccabees family ("*the people who know their God*") who led a successful righteous revolt to overthrow Antiochus.

The cleansing of the temple after the Maccabees' victory is the third part of the much larger narrative and recounts and celebrates the miracle of the single day's worth of holy oil that lasted seven days.

John 8 opens with the story of the woman caught in adultery. While we accept that as a true story with major theological significance, we also recognize that adultery is the most common metaphor for idolatry in the Bible (see especially Hosea 1-3). As noted above, the Hanukkah story begins with the intentional defilement of the Jews by Antiochus through the introduction of idolatry.

When Jesus forgives this actual woman of her actual sin, His act is at the same time represents the forgiveness He offers the Jews for their past idolatry if they will accept Him as Savior.

This would not have been lost on the Jews of that day, for whom the Hanukkah story was a matter of relatively recent history (roughly as close in time to them as the US Civil War is to Americans). Indeed, the wounds of that painful experience had been freshly reopened by Herod the Great, the Edomite convert to Judaism who came to power by slaughtering (with the backing of the Romans) the entire royal family of the Hasmoneans, the descendants of the Maccabees. (This is the Herod, of course, who also tried to murder the toddler Jesus, and whose son Herod Antipas was the Tetrarch of Galilee who murdered John the Baptist.)

Be that as it may, the most direct connection between the adulterous woman account and the Hanukkah story, is John 8:6: *"Jesus bent down and began to write on the ground with His finger,"* an act unique in all the scripture. What Jesus wrote is one of the great mysteries of the Bible, but what was no mystery to the Jews of that day was the metaphor of "drawing a line in the sand" and its association with Antiochus IV Epiphanes. That metaphor originated in the famous historical account of Roman consul Gaius Popillius Laenas, who in 168 BC threatened Antiochus with war if he refused to immediately withdraw his forces from Egypt. Laenas drew a line in the sand around Antiochus, promising that a Roman declaration of war would be issued against him if he crossed the line without first capitulating. Antiochus famously backed down, shortly thereafter turning his attentions to Israel instead (in 167 BC) . The Jews of Jesus' day were undoubtedly intimately familiar with these facts.

Immediately following that account, Jesus declares in John 8:12, *"I am the light of the world. Whoever follows Me will never walk in the darkness, but will have the light of life."* Jewish legend holds that Herod's Temple boasted an eighty-foot tall Menorah, and it is suggested by Messianic Jewish leaders today that Jesus made his proclamation while standing beneath this Menorah. Whether or not that is true, we know with certainty that Hanukkah was also known as the Feast of Lights and the connection of His statement to the holiday theme would have been unmistakable to the hearers.

Hanukkah is also uniquely associated with Satan and the Antichrist because of the evil acts of Antiochus. In John 8:39-47 we find the clearest description of Satan by Jesus himself (e.g. verse 44: *"He was a murderer from the beginning, refusing to uphold the truth, because there is no truth in him. When he lies, he speaks his native language, because he is a liar and the father of lies."*

In John 9, Jesus again declares Himself to be the light of the world, and the entire chapter is devoted to the theme of blindness.

John 10:22 states specifically *"At that time the Feast of Dedication took place in Jerusalem,"* a closing bookend confirming the Hanukkah theme that began in John 8.

- **Purim**. In John 11:45-54 the Purim theme of conspiracy to murder is again seen in the plot to kill Jesus.

- **Passover**. John 11:55 then states "*Now the Jewish Passover was near, and many people went up from the country to Jerusalem to purify themselves before the Passover.*"

John 12-21: Jesus Fulfills the Spring Feasts Prophecy

We have learned that the spring feasts of Leviticus 23 were a prophecy of and preparation for the first coming of the Messiah: they foretold that He would die on Passover, be entombed as the Unleavened Bread for which the Spring Feasts are named, and rise from the dead on First Fruits. The entire Gospel of John points to this prophetic fulfilment from the beginning, when John the Baptist declares "*Behold the Lamb of God who takes away the sin of the world.*" All of the topical teachings throughout the book relate to His deity and most depict Him fulfilling various prophecies related to His authority and purpose, but fully half – the latter half – of John's Gospel is set during a short period of time centered on these three feasts when most of His teachings were given.

- **Passover**. As we noted, John 11:55 said Passover was near. Just three verses later, John 12:1 reads "*Six days before the Passover, Jesus came to Bethany, the hometown of Lazarus, whom He had raised from the dead.*"

Two days later, four days before Passover, was His triumphal entry into Jerusalem (John 12:12-16). This confirmed His role as the Passover Lamb per Exodus 12:1-13: "*...on the tenth day of this month each family must choose a lamb... The animal you select must be...with no defects...take special care of this chosen animal until the evening of the fourteenth day of this first month*" (four days).

John 13 begins with "*It was now just before the Passover Feast, and Jesus knew that His hour had come to leave this world and return to the Father.*" It is the third of three successive chapters to expressly invoke Passover. There can be no mistaking the heavy emphasis.

John 14-18 is packed with teaching and instruction by Jesus to the disciples. He knows his time is short, but they don't recognize the reality of what is about to happen.

In John 19:14 we find a fourth reference: "*It was the day of Preparation for the Passover, about the sixth hour.*" Very shortly thereafter, Jesus died on the cross. Importantly, the sixth hour was noon, the time when the Passover lambs were slaughtered in preparation for the Passover meal at twilight.

- **Unleavened Bread**. As recorded in Leviticus 23:5-8, "*The Passover to the LORD begins at twilight on the fourteenth day of the first month. On the fifteenth day of the same month begins the Feast* *of Unleavened Bread to the LORD. For seven days you must eat unleavened bread. On the first day you shall hold a sacred assembly; you are not to do any ordinary work. For seven days you are to present an offering made by fire to the LORD. On the seventh day there shall be a sacred assembly; you must not do any ordinary work.*" There are two high Sabbath days during Unleavened Bread, the first and last days. Passover is not a high Sabbath, nor is First Fruits.

Immediately after Jesus "*yielded up His spirit,*" in John 19:30, verse 31 tells that "*It was the day of Preparation (Passover), and the next day was a High Sabbath (Unleavened Bread).*"

And again in John 19:41-42: "*Now there was a garden in the place where Jesus was crucified, and in the garden a new tomb in which no one had yet been laid. And because it was the Jewish day of Preparation and the tomb was nearby, they laid Jesus there.*"

- **First Fruits**. John 20:1 states "*Early on the first day of the week, while it was still dark, Mary Magdalene went to the tomb and saw that the stone had been removed from the entrance.*"

The first day of the week was the day after the high Sabbath, meaning it was the Feast of First Fruits, per Leviticus 23:9-11 "*And the LORD said to Moses, 'Speak to the Israelites and say, 'When you enter the land I am giving you and reap its harvest, you are to bring to the priest the sheaf of the firstfruits of your harvest. And he shall wave the sheaf before the LORD so that it may be accepted on your behalf; the priest is to wave it on the day after the Sabbath.' *"

As Paul wrote in 1 Corinthians 15:20-23 "*Christ has indeed been raised from the dead, the firstfruits of those who have fallen asleep. For since death came through a man, the resurrection of the dead comes also through a man. For as in Adam all die, so in Christ all will be made alive. But each in his own turn: Christ the firstfruits; then at His coming, those who belong to Him.*"

Following His resurrection, "*He presented Himself to [His disciples] with many convincing proofs that He was alive. He appeared to them over a span of forty days and spoke about the kingdom of God.*" (Acts 1:3) and then "*Jesus…led them out as far as Bethany, He lifted up His hands and blessed them. While He was blessing them, He left them and was carried up into heaven*" (Luke 24:50-51).

Remember that Pentecost is a Greek word meaning "fiftieth day,' indicating that the period between Jesus' ascension and His return in the person of Holy Spirit was ten days. Thus His first coming ended with a foreshadowing of the still-future Ten Days of Awe/Wrath that frames His second coming: "*…each in his own turn: Christ the firstfruits; then at His coming, those who belong to Him*" (1 Corinthians 15:23).

The Gospel of John ends its holiday-anchored chronology with First Fruits, having closely linked the entire three and one-half year earthly ministry of the Lord to the framework and symbolism of the Hebrew religious calendar. The Book of Acts continues the chronology with a record of the first Christian Pentecost ten days after Jesus ascended, transitioning to the church history theme by featuring the official launch of the human-stewarded church age under the auspices of the Holy Spirit in Acts 2. The rest of Acts is devoted to the growth of the church.

	BEATITUDE	THEME	ISAIAH LINK	FEAST
1	Poor in spirit	Brokenness	61:1	Passover (the cross)
2	Those who mourn	Grief	61:2	Unleavened Bread (the grave)
3	Meek inherit earth	Earth	61:11	First Fruits (of the earth)
4	Hunger for righteousness	Being filled	61:7	Pentecost (Holy Spirit filled)
5	Merciful	Receiving mercy	61:3	Trumpets (saved from wrath)
6	Pure in heart	See God	61:6	Atonement (purity of high priest)
7	Peacemakers	Resembling God	61:9	Tabernacles (Dwell with God)
8	Persecution because of	Righteousness	61:10	Hanukkah (Antichrist of Dan 11)
9	Persecution by	Slander/false witness	61:8	Purim (Haman's conspiracy)

The Feast Cycle in the Beatitudes

Author's Note: During the final stage of creating this book, I had a troubling dream in which I faced serious personal tribulation and was directed specifically to Psalm 25 for answers. I didn't know why I was directed to Psalm 25, but when I read it, the part that jumped out at me was verse 8-13 *"Good and upright is the LORD; therefore He shows sinners the way. He guides the humble in what is right and teaches them His way....Who is the man who fears the LORD? He will instruct him in the path chosen for him. His soul will dwell in prosperity, and his descendants will inherit the land."*

I realized this was an Old Testament grounding of the third Beatitude (Matthew 5:5), offering God's definition of the "meekness" of those who inherit the earth: humble God-fearers.

This raised two questions, the first being "WHEN do the meek inherit the earth?" and reminded me that nearly all New Testament teachings have an Old Testament root that provides insight into meanings. "When" can only be the Millennial Kingdom since that is the only time in history or prophecy when the whole earth is literally in the possession of humble God-fearers, a topic we have addressed extensively in this book.

My second question was "WHERE is the Old Testament root of the Beatitudes?" And the Holy Spirit led me to Isaiah 61, all of it, but especially 61:1-2: "*The Spirit of the Lord GOD is upon me, Because the LORD anointed me to bring good news to the humble; He has sent me to bind up the brokenhearted, To proclaim release to captives, and freedom to prisoners; To proclaim the favorable year of the LORD And the day of vengeance of our God;*"

This reminded me that Jesus invoked this very passage in Luke 4:16-21, but stopped reading after reciting "*the favorable year of the Lord,*" before announcing that this Jubilee proclamation of liberation was His fulfilment of messianic prophecy. (As we have noted elsewhere, he stopped there because "*the day of vengeance of our God,*" refers to His second coming, not the first).

That invocation of Isaiah 61 was how He launched His ministry immediately after being tempted by Satan in the wilderness. Just a few weeks later He preached the most often-taught message in Scripture -- the Sermon on the Mount -- containing the nine "Beatitides" (meaning the nine "states of sublime bliss.")

As I reread Isaiah 61, I had an epiphany as my brain and spirit made the connection between Psalm 25, Isaiah 61 and the Beatitudes, for the first time noticing all of the specific thematic links with the Beatitudes (e.g. the "*poor in spirit*" theme of the first Beatitude aligning with Isaiah 61:1 and "*those who mourn*" in the second Beatitude with Isaiah 61:2) – suddenly realizing that these nine themes are the same themes of the nine Hebrew religious feasts that were in practice at the time of the Jesus' earthly ministry, as we have shown above. I have thus made a last-minute reorganization of the book to insert this short section where it is most relevant.

CHAPTER 3:

LETTERS TO THE "LEFT BEHIND"

The letters to the seven churches in Revelation 2-3 contain a message about the Ten Days of Awe/Wrath during which pseudo-Christians will have a chance to repent after the rapture if they endure till the tenth day (or their death). True believers are also exhorted not to deny Christ during the tribulation leading to the resurrection and rapture or they may lose their salvation, just as the Lord warned in Matthew 10:32-33. (While some readers may hold belief in "eternal security," meaning one cannot lose salvation under any circumstances, we have chosen to accept the plain meaning of the text at face value, while admitting that the doctrine of eternal security is plausible according to the internal logic of its arguments, but not definitive.)

The provision for repentance during a season of punishment (the outpouring of wrath over a period of time) is a central feature of the Mosaic Law in Leviticus 26:40-46, and was a feature of the Babylonian captivity of the Judeans centuries later: "But **if they will confess their iniquity** and that of their fathers in the unfaithfulness that they practiced against Me...**then I will remember My covenant** with Jacob and My covenant with Isaac and My covenant with Abraham, and I will remember the land. For the land will be abandoned by them, and it will enjoy its Sabbaths by lying desolate without them. **And they will pay the penalty for their iniquity**, because they rejected My ordinances and abhorred My statutes. **Yet in spite of this, when they are in the land of their enemies, I will not reject or despise them so as to destroy them**." This is the same general principle of Biblical law governing the "Left Behind" during the 10 Days of Awe/Wrath.

As explained in chapter two, the resurrection and rapture will occur on *Yom Teruah*, the Feast of Trumpets, when the members of the Bride of Christ will be glorified and enter into the spiritual realm for the Wedding Feast of the Lamb and the calculation of their reward (through the testing of their works by fire -- 1 Corinthians 3:11-15) before returning to the physical realm as a part of the host of heaven that accompanies the Messiah, when He will slay the wicked with "the sword of His mouth," and claim His rightful place as the King of Kings over all the earth (Revelation 19:11-16 and Zechariah 14). (*Yom Teruah* is the first, and *Yom Kippur* is the tenth of the Days of Awe, the final ten days of the tribulation.)

LETTERS TO THE "LEFT BEHIND" - REVELATION 2-3

FEAST OF TRUMPETS

Resurrection and Rapture for the Righteous

DAY OF ATONEMENT

Return of the King to Reclaim the Earth

WHITE THRONE JUDGMENT

Final Resurrection
Revelation 20:11-15

TRIBULATION TEN DAYS OF AWE 1000 YR MILLENNIAL KINGDOM HEAVEN

TRIBULATION TEN DAYS OF WRATH PRISON FOR SATAN AND THE WICKED LAKE OF FIRE

TRUE CHRISTIANS — Resurrected and raptured on Trumpets to join the Wedding Feast and return with the King on Atonement (Rev 19:11-21).

PSEUDO-CHRISTIANS — Left behind in "outer darkness" with ten days to repent and gain Heaven if they "endure to the end" (see below).

THESE INCLUDE:
the "Saved by Works" people of Matthew 7:21-23. "I never knew you" (v. 23).
the "Unprepared Wedding Guests" of Matthew 22:1-13. "Outer darkness" (v. 13).
the "Foolish Virgins" of Matthew 25:8-12. "I don't know you" (v.12).
the "Worthless Servants" of Matthew 25:14-30. "Outer darkness" (v. 30).

All or most will die during the 10 Days of Wrath but those who repent and endure to the end without renouncing Christ will have their names written in the book of life (Rev 2:10-11) and earn rewards retroactive to the Day of Atonement (Rev 19:11-21) which they can claim in heaven after the final resurrection and the White Throne Judgment (Rev 20:12).

LETTER 1: EPHESUS — Ephesus and Laodicea are bookends to the other letters with a common theme: If you repent before the rapture you will not face the wrath. Ephesus message: all 7 letters are for all believers (Rev 2: 7). Ephesus reward: Tree of Life (Rev 22:14).

LETTER 2: SMYRNA

Smyrna message: if you do not repent, you will face the wrath for 10 days and will probably die.

However, if you repent during the 10 days and do not renounce Christ you will not face the second death, which is the lake of fire (Rev 20:14).

Smyrna reward: The crown of life (Rev 19:12).

LETTER 3: PERGAMUM

Pergamum message: Those who fail to repent during the 10 days will be numbered with the wicked and slain by Christ the returning King with "the sword of His mouth" (Rev 19:15).

Pergamum rewards: hidden manna (Rev 11:19). White stone with new name (Rev 19:12). (Per Roman custom, contest winners got this prize.)

LETTER 4: THYATIRA

Thyatira message: those who do not repent of adultery with Jezebel will face the wrath in which they will be judged by their deeds.

Those not aligned with Jezebel have no other duty but to endure through the Tribulation.

Thyatira reward: reign with Christ and wield "iron scepter" during Millennial Kingdom (Rev 19:15).

LETTER 5: SARDIS

Sardis message: many believe they are saved but aren't and will be left behind to face the wrath.

Those who repent during the wrath will not have their names blotted out of the book of life.

Sardis reward: wear white garments in eternity (Rev 7:9) (but not "walk with Him" during Millennial Kingdom (Rev 19:14)).

LETTER 6: PHILADELPHIA

Philadelphia message: those who have been faithful to Christ and do not deny His name will not face the wrath.

Those left behind who repent and endure during the wrath will be accepted into heaven.

Philadelphia Reward: bear the name of God and the new Jerusalem (Rev 21:1-21).

LETTER 7: LAODICEA — If you repent before the rapture you will not face the wrath. Laodicea message: buy gold refined by fire (Rev 3: 18 & 1 Peter 1:7), white garments (Rev 3:18 & Rev 3:4) and eye salve, items associated with the righteous at the time of the rapture. Reward: to sit with Jesus on a throne (Rev 3:21 & Matt 19:28), a reference to the Millennial Kingdom.

Meanwhile, three groups of people will be left behind to face the wrath of God that will be poured out on the earth in the form of the bowl judgments (Revelation 16). These groups are:

1. The wicked (the willful God-haters).
2. The 144 thousand Torah-faithful Hebrews (sealed against death -- Revelation 7:2-8).
3. The deceived unsaved followers of false religions and pseudo-Christians -- all of whom hold false beliefs that caused them to trust in something other than the blood of Christ for their salvation, and who (for various reasons) do not take the mark of the Beast during the tribulation.

This section will address the psuedo-Christians, whom I believe are the intended recipients of the teaching in the letters to the seven churches. ["Pseudo-Christians" is a sub-category of the deceived unsaved, just as "foolish virgins" is a sub-category of "pseudo-Christians."]

First, let's identify who these pseudo-Christians are. Importantly, they are not "the wicked" who are defined by depravity and extreme rebellion against God, people who (during the wrath) *blasphemed the God of heaven because of their pains and their sores; and they did not repent of their deeds*" (Revelation 16:11). Obviously, neither are they the Torah-faithful 144,000 Hebrews or members of false religions (e.g. Buddhism) though the tenets of false religions are often a factor in the confusion of pseudo-Christians.

The pseudo-Christians believe themselves to be Christians but through false thinking accept false notions about salvation. These would include members of various cults such as Jehovah's Witnesses and Mormons who, because of false doctrines, worship a false version of Christ. Similarly, those whose embrace of "gay theology" causes them to believe in a "nicer-than-Jesus" version of Christ -- one who condones what God has condemned as abomination -- may also be pseudo-Christians (though I believe that there are repentant homosexual strugglers who genuinely believe in the true Christ and receive His mercy). Many Roman Catholics and others who put their faith in their own works rather than the atonement of Christ are also pseudo-Christians.

I want to be clear that I believe there are genuinely saved people (true believers in Christ per Romans 10:9-10) in every Christian and quasi-Christian denomination and bible-based cult, irrespective of whatever false doctrines these individuals may also hold. Likewise, I also believe there are unsaved pseudo-Christians in every authentically bible-believing denomination. Salvation is by faith alone in Christ alone.

The Bible addresses pseudo-Christians in several passages. The first and most striking is Matthew 7:21-23:

"*Not every one that saith unto me, Lord, Lord, shall enter into the kingdom of heaven; but he that doeth the will of my Father which is in heaven. Many will say to me in that day, Lord, Lord, have we not prophesied in thy name? and in thy name have cast out devils? and in thy name done many wonderful works? And then will I profess unto them,* **I never knew you: depart from me, ye that work iniquity.**' "*

These people apparently believed they were saved by works but had no relationship with Christ.

Another example is the Parable of the Ten Virgins in Matthew 25:8-12:

"*Then shall the kingdom of heaven be likened unto ten virgins, which took their lamps, and went forth to meet the bridegroom. And five of them were wise, and five were foolish…And the foolish said unto the wise, Give us of your oil; for our lamps are gone out. But the wise answered, saying, Not so; lest there be not enough for us and you: but go ye rather to them that sell, and buy for yourselves. And while they went to buy, the bridegroom came; and they that were ready went in with him to the marriage: and the door was shut. Afterward came also the other virgins, saying, Lord, Lord, open to us.* **But he answered and said, Verily I say unto you, I know you not.**"*

Also in Matthew 25:14-30: is the familiar Parable of the Talents, in which the recipient of the single talent proved to be an unfaithful steward who made no effort to serve his master, and heard the fateful rebuke, "**cast ye the unprofitable servant into outer darkness: there shall be weeping and gnashing of teeth**" (v. 30).

Similarly, the Parable of the Wedding Banquet in Matthew 22:1-13 highlights a wedding guest who is disqualified because he is not wearing wedding clothes (he is not properly prepared to enter the banquet) and meets a bad end:

"*But when the king came in to see the guests, he noticed a man there who was not wearing wedding clothes. He asked, 'How did you get in here without wedding clothes, friend?' The man was speechless.* **Then the king told the attendants, 'Tie him hand and foot, and throw him outside, into the darkness, where there will be weeping and gnashing of teeth**' " (v.11-13).

This "darkness" is the same place to which Jews (i.e. the 144,000) are sent who have not yet accepted Christ at the time of the resurrection and rapture:

"I say to you that many will come from east and west, and recline at the table with Abraham, Isaac and Jacob in the kingdom of heaven; **but the sons of the kingdom will be cast out into the outer darkness; in that place there will be weeping and gnashing of teeth**" (Matthew 8:12).

THE KINGDOM OF HEAVEN AND THE OUTER DARKNESS

To properly understand these parables we must first recognize that the "kingdom of heaven" is not the heaven of eternity, but the Millennial Kingdom. The following is an excerpt from "Jesus' Teaching on the Kingdom & Land Inheritance," by Pastor Tim Warner of Answers in Revelation:

> "Jesus' teaching is often misunderstood by modern Christians because it is usually divorced from the Old Testament prophecies. Jesus frequently spoke of the 'Kingdom of heaven' in His parables. Many assume that this refers to a kingdom IN heaven. From such statements Christians often suppose that He meant believers would fly away to heaven to live in this 'Kingdom.' This thinking is the result of imposing false presuppositions onto Jesus. When His words are understood from a Jewish perspective, compared with other statements He made, and in light of a host of Old Testament prophecies, it is quite evident that the "Kingdom of heaven" is not a kingdom IN heaven, but the Kingdom FROM heaven.

> "The phrase 'Kingdom of heaven' was used by Matthew only. It always refers to Christ's future reign from Jerusalem, when the dominion of heaven will be imposed on the earth. The places where Matthew records Jesus referring to the "Kingdom of heaven" all have "Kingdom of God" in the parallel passages in Mark and Luke. Thus, the terms are synonymous. The "Kingdom" is the one prophesied by Daniel. "'*And in the days of these kings the God of heaven will set up a kingdom which shall never be destroyed; and the kingdom shall not be left to other people; it shall break in pieces and consume all these kingdoms, and it shall stand forever.*'

> "Thus, the full title is really 'the Kingdom of the God of Heaven,' which the Gospel writers shortened to 'Kingdom of God' and 'Kingdom of heaven.' And this is the Kingdom 'under heaven' that Daniel said would be given to the 'Son of Man' and all of the 'saints.' www.answersinrevelation.org/Jesus.pdf.

Again, the Kingdom of Heaven is the Millennial Kingdom, not eternal spiritual heaven, a fact with enormously significant implications for our theology, which every reader of this study should take time to ponder (consider, for example 1 Corinthians 6:9-11).

Likewise, the "outer darkness" is (we believe) not eternal spiritual hell, but an earthly "hell" during the 10 Days of Awe/Wrath, where the deceived unsaved are "left behind" with a final chance to repent and have their names written in the Lamb's book of life.

The Bible identifies two different places where there is "*weeping and gnashing of teeth.*" One of them is a place of fire, which may represent either a place of torment for the wicked dead prior to the Great White Throne Judgment (Luke 16:23-24), or the lake of fire (Revelation 20:11-15), or both.

"*As therefore the tares are gathered and burned in the fire; so shall it be in the end of this world. The Son of man shall send forth his angels, and they shall gather out of his kingdom all things that offend, and them which do iniquity; And shall cast them into a furnace of fire: there shall be wailing and gnashing of teeth*" (Matthew 13:40-42).

The other place of "*weeping and gnashing of teeth*" is called "outer darkness," and I believe it will be earth during the bowl judgments of the Ten Days of Awe, for indeed there will be such great suffering that "*they gnawed their tongues because of pain, and they blasphemed the God of heaven because of their pains and their sores*" (Revelation 16:10-11). Importantly, the "outer darkness" is the place outside the "Wedding Feast of the Lamb" which we have shown takes place in the spiritual realm while the bowl judgments are poured out on earth.

SALVATION WILL STILL BE POSSIBLE DURING THE 10 DAYS OF AWE

In Hebrew teaching, the Ten Days of Awe is the time when God decides whether one's name will be written in the book of Life or the book of Death. How fitting that teaching is in light of this study and our assumption that those left behind will have a second chance to accept Christ and spend eternity with Him. They do miss out on being a part of the Bride of Christ, and have to die as humans (most likely during the wrath) and wait till the end of the Millennial Kingdom to be resurrected and receive their spiritual bodies.

"*Then I saw a great white throne and Him who sat upon it, from whose presence earth and heaven fled away, and no place was found for them. And I saw the dead, the great and the small, standing before the throne, and books were opened; and another book was opened, which is the book of life; and the dead were judged from the things which were written in the books, according to their deeds. And the sea gave up the dead which were in it,* **and death and Hades gave up the dead which were in <u>them</u>**; *and they were judged, every one of them according to their deeds. Then death and Hades were thrown into the lake of fire. This is the second death, the lake of fire. And* **if** *anyone's name was not found written in the book of life, he was thrown into the lake of fire*" (Revelation 20:11-15).

There are two separate holding pens for those who die after the resurrection and rapture. The deceived unsaved get a second chance to have their names written in the Lamb's book of life. However, it's not going to be easy! That is the message of the letters to the seven churches.

THE LETTERS TO THE LEFT BEHIND

This section is not intended to be a comprehensive study of Revelation 2-3, nor to contradict any other teaching on it. As we have stated, we believe the Bible offers multiple layers of meaning and supports multiple interpretations. This analysis will only address the aspects of the seven letters that speak to the consequences to pseudo-Christians of not repenting of false beliefs and their consequent actions.

The theme and purpose of the Ten Days of Awe is the final chance for repentance as God decides whose name will be written in the Lamb's book of life and who will be written in the book of death. The final decision is not made until the Day of Atonement, when all of those who have not accepted Christ as Savior will be killed.

The letters taken together contain a dual message: favor for those who repent and remain faithful unto death, but increasing levels of punishment for those who fail to repent. *"God is not willing that any should perish, but that all should come to repentance* (2 Peter 3:9). The letters to the seven churches (and the Ten Days of Awe foretold in them) are His last effort to persuade men to turn from their sin.

EPHESUS -- FIRST WARNING: REPENT TO BE SPARED THE WRATH

Both Ephesus (the first letter) and Laodicea (the seventh and final one) advise the readers in general terms that if they repent they will be spared the wrath. In this way they are bookends that point to and emphasize the messages between them.

But the letter to Ephesus makes it clear that the messages of all seven letters are relevant to all individual believers and should be taken together as one teaching:

*"**Whoever has ears, let them hear what the Spirit says <u>to the churches</u>**. To the one who is victorious, I will give the right to eat from the tree of life, which is in the paradise of God"* (Revelation 2:7).

All are exhorted to heed the warnings of Revelation 2-3, and those who do (both the members of the Bride of Christ and those who accept Christ during the wrath) will be with Him in eternity. This exhortation is repeated throughout the seven letters.

The Tree of Life is not found in the Millennial Kingdom but in heaven (Revelation 22:2) after the physical world has been destroyed (Revelation 21:1). In other words, the letters address all of those who will come to salvation, whether or not they are "left behind" during the Ten Days of Awe.

Likewise, all must "overcome" to receive their reward, a reminder that there is great pressure to deny Christ during the suffering of the tribulation as well as during the wrath.

SMYRNA -- 'LEFT BEHIND," YES. BUT FOR HOW LONG?

The letter to Smyrna is the first letter to warn of a specific consequence for not repenting before the time of wrath.

"*Fear none of those things which thou shalt suffer: behold,* **the devil shall cast** <u>**some**</u> **of you into prison, that ye may be tried; and ye shall have tribulation** <u>**ten days**</u>**: be thou faithful unto death, and I will give thee a crown of life...** *He that overcometh shall not be hurt of the* <u>*second death*</u>" (Rev. 2:10-11).

Remember that all those who are not in Christ have not been ransomed by His blood and are thus owned by Satan (John 3:18). They will not be resurrected or raptured as a member of the Bride of Christ, but will be left behind, in the hands of the evil one.

They will suffer wrath, not for seven years, but for ten days! These are the Ten Days of Awe/Wrath.

Importantly, those among the "left behind" who receive Christ and remain faithful to Him *until death* will win the crown of life that saves them from the second death at the end of the Millennium. In other words, their names will be written in the Lamb's book of life but many or most will probably not survive the time of wrath.

PERGAMUM -- ABANDON FALSE DOCTRINES OR DIE WITH THE WICKED

The letter to Pergamum warns that those left behind to face the wrath who then fail to repent during those ten days will be killed with the wicked upon the return of Christ on the Day of Atonement.

"*But I have a few things against thee, because thou hast there them that hold the doctrine of Balaam, who taught Balac to cast a stumblingblock before the children of Israel, to eat things sacrificed unto idols, and to commit fornication. So hast thou also them that hold the doctrine of the Nicolaitans, which thing I hate.* **16 Repent; or else I will come unto** <u>**thee**</u> **quickly, and will fight against** <u>**them**</u> **with the sword of my mouth.**...*To him that overcometh will I give to eat of the hidden manna, and will give him a white stone, and in the stone a new name written, which no man knoweth saving he that receiveth it*" (Revelation 2:14-17).

Note the clear reference to Revelation 19: 11-16, which describes the return of Christ in power on the Day of Atonement, especially the reference in verse 15 of the "sword of His mouth." This is unmistakably classifying the unrepentant pseudo-Christians with the wicked whom Christ slays upon his return with the host of heaven.

"*And I saw heaven opened, and behold a white horse; and he that sat upon him was called Faithful and True, and in righteousness he doth judge and make war. His eyes were as a flame of fire, and on his head were* <u>*many crowns*</u>*; and he had a* <u>*name written, that no man knew, but he himself*</u>*. And he was clothed with a vesture dipped* *in blood: and his name is called The Word of God. And the armies which were in heaven followed him upon white horses, clothed in <u>fine linen, white and clean</u>. **15And out of his mouth goeth a sharp sword**, that with it <u>he should smite the nations: and he shall rule them with a rod of iron:</u> and he treadeth the winepress of the fierceness and wrath of Almighty God. And he hath on his vesture and on his thigh a name written, KING OF KINGS, AND LORD OF LORDS."*

Note also the references to some of the rewards of the repentant in this same Revelation passage: a crown of life (Smyrna), a secret name (Pergamum), "my new name" (Philadelphia), clean white linens (Laodicea), authority over the nations (Thyatira). These all align the teaching of Revelation 2-3 with the Ten Days of Awe.

The Pergamum letter emphasizes two false doctrines that may help to identify why the pseudo-Christians are left behind. First, the reference to Balaam invokes the demonic idolatry of the Canaanites, involving sexual perversion and child sacrifice and in the present-day context would seem to encompass believers and churches compromised by worldly attitudes on sexual morality and abortion. Second, the reference to the Nicolaitans relates to human-created doctrines taught as equivalent or superior to Scripture (the "the leaven of the Pharisees"), especially by ecclesiastical authorities who, by virtue of their titles, hold themselves out as superior to the laity, and in the modern context would seem to encompass both pseudo-Christian cults and some aspects of denominationalism in mainstream Christianity.

There is another spiritual bombshell in Revelation 2:17, *"To the one who is victorious, I will give some of the hidden manna."* Does this suggest that God will supernaturally sustain some of those who repent during the wrath, allowing them to survive it? Or is this the hidden manna of the Ark of the Covenant in Revelation 11:19 (the perfect spiritual Ark on which the earthly Ark was designed), suggesting that the subjects of verse 17 are killed during the wrath? Intriguing questions, but I think the former is correct. Some will survive the wrath and be a part of the "mixed multitude" of Jerusalem who are rescued by Christ on the Day of Atonement (Zechariah 14). (Very significantly, the "mixed multitude of Hebrews and Gentiles" theme originates in Exodus 12:38). Shortly thereafter we find this mixed multitude of sealed-Jews and post-rapture saved Gentiles, dwelling safely together in the Millennial Kingdom:

"For the LORD will have mercy on Jacob, and will yet choose Israel, and set them in their own land: and the strangers shall be joined with them, and they shall cleave to the house of Jacob" Isaiah 14:1.

THYATIRA -- SECOND WARNING ABOUT CAANANITE IDOLATRY AND PERVERSION

Those who do not repent of their adultery with Jezebel will face the wrath.

*"I have a few things against thee, because thou sufferest that woman Jezebel, which calleth herself a prophetess, to teach and to seduce my servants to commit fornication, and to eat things sacrificed unto idols. And I gave her space to repent of her fornication; and she repented not. **Behold, I will cast her into a bed, and them that commit adultery with her into great tribulation, except they repent of their deeds.** And I will kill her children with death; and all the churches shall know that I am he which searcheth the reins and hearts: and I will give unto every one of you according to your works.*

*"**But unto you I say, and unto the rest in Thyatira, as many as have not this doctrine, and which have not known the depths of Satan, as they speak; I will put upon you none other burden. But that which ye have already hold fast till I come.** And he that overcometh, and keepeth my works unto the end, to him will I give power over the nations: And he shall rule them with a rod of iron; as the vessels of a potter shall they be broken to shivers: even as I received of my Father. And I will give him the morning star"* (Revelation 2:19-28).

Two groups of church members are contrasted here: those unfaithful who suffer the wrath v. those faithful who will reign with Christ in the Millennial Kingdom. Note that the unfaithful Jezebel's "*children*" are "*killed with death*" – an otherwise very peculiar turn of phrase that makes perfect sense in the context of the "*second death*" in the lake of fire. Indeed, the warning could even be rephrased "her children will be killed, along with death itself, in the lake of fire."

Jezebel here appears to be synonymous with the great prostitute of Revelation 17 which suggests that one purpose of the letter to Thyatira may be to confirm that the Ten Days of Awe is the time in which the bowl judgments will be poured out on the earth:

"One of the seven angels who had the seven bowls came and said to me, 'Come, I will show you the punishment of the great prostitute, who sits by many waters. With her the kings of the earth committed adultery, and the inhabitants of the earth were intoxicated with the wine of her adulteries...'" Revelation 17:2-3.

Let us also remember, however, that the historical Jezebel was the wife of Ahab, who *"as though it had been a trivial thing for him to walk in the sins of Jeroboam the son of Nedab, ... [dared to defy God even more egregiously, and] married Jezebel the daughter of Ethbaal king of the Sidonians, and went to serve Baal and worshiped him. So he erected an altar for Baal in the house of Baal which he built in Samaria. Ahab also made the Asherah. Thus Ahab did more to provoke the LORD God of Israel than all the kings of Israel who were before him"* (1 Kings 16:30-33). What made Jezebel such a symbol of evil was her association with Canaanite idolatry involving sexual perversion and child sacrifice.

SARDIS -- DON'T BE UNPREPARED LIKE THE FOOLISH VIRGINS

*"I have not found thy works perfect before God. Remember therefore how thou hast received and heard, and hold fast, and repent. If therefore thou shalt not watch, I will come on thee as a thief, and thou shalt not know what hour I will come upon thee. **Thou hast a few names even in Sardis which have not defiled their garments; and they shall walk with me in white: for they are worthy.***

"He that overcometh, the same shall be clothed in white raiment; and I will not blot out his name out of the book of life, but I will confess his name before my Father, and before his angels" (Revelation 3:1-5).

Only a few are already credited as righteous. The others will be among those caught by surprise at the return of Christ and will face the wrath, but if they repent and remain faithful their names will be found written in the Lamb's book of life at the Great White Throne Judgment, when Christ will confess their names before the Father.

This letter is a warning for believers to be prepared for the return of Christ, urging diligence in discerning the times and seasons.

*"But of the <u>times and the seasons</u>, brethren, ye have no need that I write unto you. **For yourselves know perfectly that the day of the Lord so cometh as a thief in the night. For when <u>they</u> shall say, Peace and safety; then sudden destruction cometh upon <u>them</u>, as travail upon a woman with child; and <u>they</u> shall not escape. <u>But ye, brethren, are not in darkness, that that day should overtake you as a thief.</u>** Ye are all the children of light, and the children of the day: we are not of the night, nor of darkness. Therefore let us not sleep, as do others; but let us watch and be sober"* (1 Thessalonians 5:1-6).

"Times and seasons" refers to the feasts or *moedim* of the Lord in Leviticus 23, provided to the Hebrews as signposts and rehearsals for the first and second coming of Christ. *"These are the feasts of the LORD, even holy convocations, which ye shall proclaim in their seasons"* (Leviticus 23:4). The Hebrew words for both "feasts" and "seasons" in Leviticus 23:4 are variations of the word "*moed*," or "appointed times." The Greek word *kairos* ("seasons" in 1 Thessalonians 5:1) is used in the Septuagint to translate *moed*.

Thus, the Sardis letter is also a warning to Christians to pay attention to the Hebrew roots of Scripture so as not to avoid being taken by surprise by the return of the Lord.

PHILADEPHIA -- SALVATION REQUIRES ENDURANCE

This church is unified in righteousness, but believers are warned not to waver in their commitment to Christ. They will lose their reward (*"thy crown"*) if they deny His name before the end of the tribulation.

*"<u>I know thy works: behold, I have set before thee an open door, and no man can shut it: for thou hast a little strength, and hast kept my word, and hast not denied my name. Behold, I come quickly:</u> **hold that fast which thou hast, that no man take thy crown.** Him that overcometh will I make a pillar in the temple of my God, and he shall go no more out: and I will write upon him the name of my God, and the name of the city of my God, which is new Jerusalem, which cometh down out of heaven from my God: and I will write upon him my new name"* (Revelation 3:8-12).

"If you deny me before men, I will deny you before my Father in Heaven," Jesus warned the disciples in Matthew 10:32-33, a teaching found throughout the New Testament (e.g., John 15:1-6; 1 Corinthians 15:1-2).

LAODICEA -- FINAL WARNING: REPENT TO BE SPARED THE WRATH

The Letter to Laodicea, like the Letter to Ephesus, contains a general warning to repent or face the wrath, and reminds us that testing through tribulation is a part of God's plan.

"<u>So then because thou art lukewarm, and neither cold nor hot, I will spue thee out of my mouth....</u> **<u>As many as I love, I rebuke and chasten: be zealous therefore, and repent</u>**. *Behold, I stand at the door, and knock: if any man hear my voice, and open the door, I will come in to him, and will sup with him, and he with me. To him that overcometh will I grant to sit with me in my throne, even as I also overcame, and am set down with my Father in his throne"* (Revelation 3:15-21).

POSTSCRIPT

The letters to the seven churches were written to all believers in every generation from the time John the Apostle first published them, and contain a wealth of knowledge and revelation supporting a wide variety of teachings and interpretations. This section has touched on just a fraction of the truth available in these two short chapters of Revelation that is highly relevant to these last days. The message is a warning to the last generation that the final years leading to the reign of Christ will be defined by increasing persecution, but that all who repent and thereafter cling firmly to Christ will spend eternity with Him in heaven, even those whose error causes them to miss the wedding feast and end up in the outer darkness of the Ten Days of Awe/Wrath.

CHAPTER FOUR:

THE WINEPRESS OF GOD'S WRATH

"And another angel came out of the temple, crying with a loud voice to him that sat on the cloud, Thrust in thy sickle, and reap: for the time is come for thee to reap; for the harvest of the earth is ripe" (Revelation 14:15).

"Put ye in the sickle, for the harvest is ripe: come, get you down; for the press is full, the fats overflow; for their wickedness is great" (Joel 3:13).

The winepress of God's wrath is a metaphor for the punishment of the wicked on the Day of Atonement. It is the final event of the six thousand years of man: a sort-of final house-cleaning before the start of the Millennial Kingdom. It occurs on the last of the Ten Days of Awe.

THE HARVEST OF THE GRAPES

The seven feasts of the Lord of Leviticus 23 are associated with agricultural harvests in Israel. The spring feasts of Passover, Unleavened Bread and First Fruits were related to the barley harvest. Christ rose from the dead literally on the Feast of First Fruits: *"But now is Christ risen from the dead, and become the firstfruits of them that slept"* (1 Corinthians 15:20). Pentecost was associated with the spring wheat harvest, and celebrated by the baking of two loaves of leavened bread representing both Jews and the Gentiles (Judah and Israel) together as the followers of Christ in the newly formed church.

The fall feasts of *Yom Teruah* (Trumpets) and *Yom Kippur* (Atonement) are associated with the fall wheat harvest and grape harvest respectively.

The harvest of the wheat represents the resurrection and rapture of the Bride of Christ on the Feast of Trumpets. Believers in Christ are the "wheat" (Matthew 13:24-30).

The harvest of the grapes represents the crushing of the wicked beneath the feet of Christ as will be described below.

Before we focus in on the grape harvest, let us consider its importance in combination with the wheat harvest, which we believe is specially emphasized by Jesus in "The Lord's Supper."

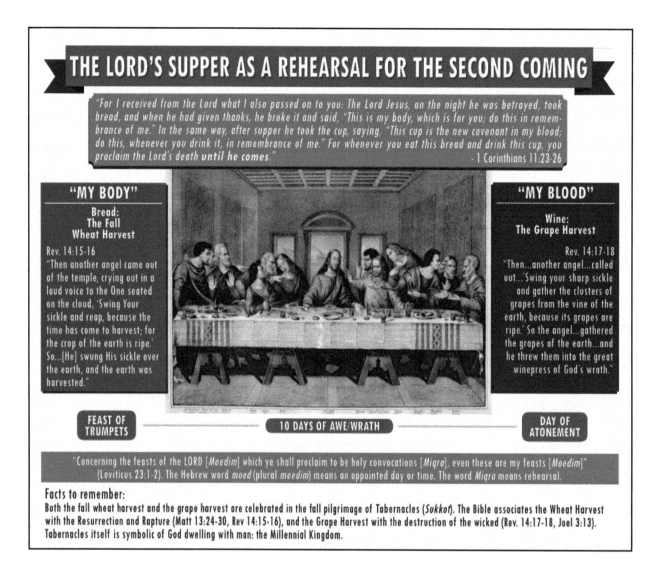

THE LORD'S SUPPER AS A REHEARSAL FOR THE SECOND COMING

"For I received from the Lord what I also passed on to you: The Lord Jesus, on the night he was betrayed, took bread, and when he had given thanks, he broke it and said, "This is my body, which is for you; do this in remembrance of me." In the same way, after supper he took the cup, saying, "This cup is the new covenant in my blood; do this, whenever you drink it, in remembrance of me." For whenever you eat this bread and drink this cup, you proclaim the Lord's death until he comes." — 1 Corinthians 11:23-26

"MY BODY"

**Bread:
The Fall
Wheat Harvest**

Rev. 14:15-16
"Then another angel came out of the temple, crying out in a loud voice to the One seated on the cloud, 'Swing Your sickle and reap, because the time has come to harvest; for the crop of the earth is ripe.' So...[He] swung His sickle over the earth, and the earth was harvested."

"MY BLOOD"

**Wine:
The Grape Harvest**

Rev. 14:17-18
"Then...another angel...called out...'Swing your sharp sickle and gather the clusters of grapes from the vine of the earth, because its grapes are ripe.' So the angel...gathered the grapes of the earth...and he threw them into the great winepress of God's wrath."

| FEAST OF TRUMPETS | 10 DAYS OF AWE/WRATH | DAY OF ATONEMENT |

"Concerning the feasts of the LORD [*Moedim*] which ye shall proclaim to be holy convocations [*Miqra*], even these are my feasts [*Moedim*]" (Leviticus 23:1-2). The Hebrew word *moed* (plural *moedim*) means an appointed day or time. The word *Miqra* means rehearsal.

Facts to remember:
Both the fall wheat harvest and the grape harvest are celebrated in the fall pilgrimage of Tabernacles (*Sukkot*). The Bible associates the Wheat Harvest with the Resurrection and Rapture (Matt 13:24-30, Rev 14:15-16), and the Grape Harvest with the destruction of the wicked (Rev. 14:17-18, Joel 3:13). Tabernacles itself is symbolic of God dwelling with man: the Millennial Kingdom.

THE LORD'S SUPPER AS A *MOED* FOR THE RAPTURE AND WRATH

"And the LORD spake unto Moses, saying, Speak unto the children of Israel, and say unto them, Concerning the feasts of the LORD [moedim] which ye shall proclaim to be holy convocations [miqra], even these are my feasts [moedim]" (Leviticus 23:1-2).

To reiterate, the Hebrew word *moed* (plural *moedim*) means an appointed day or time. The word *miqra* means rehearsal. Thus, the Feasts of the Lord are appointed times designed to be prophetic rehearsals for the first and second coming of Christ. The rituals associated with these holidays identify the clues to their fulfillment. For example, the Feast of Unleavened Bread is celebrated with the *matzah* wafer of unleavened bread, pierced and striped, just as sinless Christ was pierced and striped for our transgressions (Isaiah 53:5). The Hebrew ritual of burying and then resurrecting the "middle *matzah*" in the Passover celebration is a rehearsal for the death and resurrection of Christ (though it is not recognized as such by most Jews).

Jesus established only one ritual for His followers during His earthly ministry: what we call The Lord's Supper, or Communion (Luke 22:14-20). We contend that this ritual is also a *moed* and a *miqra*.

If we consider the bread to represent the wheat harvest (resurrection and rapture) on *Yom Teruah* and the wine to represent the grape harvest (punishment of the wicked) on *Yom Kippur*, we can recognize the Lord's Supper as an "appointed time" that serves as a rehearsal for His second coming.

THE RETURN OF CHRIST "TO JUDGE AND MAKE WAR"

Before we discuss the winepress, let's first set the stage of the context of Christ's return, looking backward from the Day of Atonement and reviewing some of what we've learned.

On *Yom Teruah* (Feast of Trumpets) Christ had appeared in the clouds to call up the Bride of Christ from the earth:

"Then will appear the sign of the Son of Man in heaven. And then all the peoples of the earth will mourn when they see the Son of Man coming on the clouds of heaven, with power and great glory. And he will send his angels with a loud trumpet call, and they will gather his elect from the four winds, from one end of the heavens to the other" (Matthew 24:30-31).

With the righteous then removed, the Ten Days of Awe/Wrath begin, with its series of increasing punishments represented in the bowl judgments of Revelation 16: *"Then I heard a loud voice from the temple saying to the seven angels, 'Go, pour out the seven bowls of God's wrath on the earth' "* (v.1). But the wicked would not repent (v.11) but instead gathered to make war against God's holy city, Jerusalem, as John writes in verses 12-16:

*"The sixth angel poured out his bowl on the great river Euphrates, and its water was dried up to prepare the way for the kings from the East. I saw three impure spirits that looked like frogs; they came out of the mouth of the dragon, out of the mouth of the beast and out of the mouth of the false prophet. They are demonic spirits that perform signs, and **they go out to the kings of the whole world, to gather them for the battle on the great day of God Almighty...Then they gathered the kings together to the place that in Hebrew is called Armageddon.**"*

This is the army of 200 million men (like a plague of locusts on the land), described in Revelation 9:13-21, for, as we have noted above, the bowl judgments are contained within the sixth trumpet, like a wheel within a wheel.

From the Valley of Armageddon, the mighty army of the wicked, cursing and blaspheming God, march on Jerusalem. This is described in Zechariah 14:1-5:

*"A day of the Lord is coming, Jerusalem, when …**I will gather all the nations to Jerusalem to fight against it;** the city will be captured, the houses ransacked, and the women raped. Half of the city will go into exile, but the rest of the people will not be taken from the city. **Then the Lord will go out and fight against those nations, as he fights on a day of battle**. On that day his feet will stand on the Mount of Olives, east of Jerusalem, and the Mount of Olives will be split in two from east to west, forming a great valley, with half of the mountain moving north and half moving south. You will flee by my mountain valley, for it will extend to Azel. You will flee as you fled from the earthquake in the days of Uzziah king of Judah. Then **the Lord my God will come, and all the holy ones with him.**"*

And in Joel 2:1-2

*"Blow the trumpet in Zion; sound the alarm on my holy hill. Let all who live in the land tremble, for the day of the Lord is coming. It is close at hand— a day of darkness and gloom, a day of clouds and blackness. **Like dawn spreading across the mountains a large and mighty army comes, such as never was in ancient times nor ever will be in ages to come**."*

God's response to this army of the wicked is the winepress, the harvest of the grapes, but first He rescues the faithful remnant of His people from Jerusalem, just as He rescued His people from Egypt.

THE EXODUS PATTERN IN THE WINEPRESS STORY

In Egypt, God brought ten plagues against the Egyptians that represented an escalating series of judgments upon them, in a close parallel to the bowl judgments of the Ten Days of Awe. Several of the symbols of the Exodus judgment are repeated during those ten days: blood (Exodus 7:20, Revelation 16:3-6), frogs (Exodus 8:6, Revelation 16:13-14), sores (Exodus 9:10, Revelation 16:2), ans darkness (Exodus 10:21, Revelation 16:10-11).

But even more interesting is the parallel of the exodus flight itself. Just as the Hebrews (and others who had chosen to flee with them -- Exodus 12:37-38) were pursued by the wicked Egyptians as they fled eastward, so does a "mixed multitude" (the 144,000 sealed-Jews and an unknown number of post-rapture saved Gentiles) then flee the City of Jerusalem eastward upon the return of Christ:

"On that day his feet will stand on the Mount of Olives, east of Jerusalem, and the Mount of Olives will be split in two from east to west, forming a great valley, with half of the mountain moving north and half moving south. You will flee by my mountain valley" (Zechariah 14:4-5).

The Lord Jesus, returning with the host of heaven, will split the Mount of Olives just as God parted the Red Sea in Exodus 14:21-28.

And just as God collapsed the Red Sea upon the pursuing Egyptians, killing every one of them, so will the Lord Yeshua Hamashiach kill the wicked who pursue His people who flee through the Valley of the Mount of Olives:

"Then the Lord will go out and fight against those nations, as he fights on a day of battle... the Lord my God will come, and all the holy ones with him" (Zechariah 14:3).

This crushing of the wicked by the Lord is the winepress of God's Wrath. Watch it unfold in the following passages:

Revelation 19:11-21:

*"And I saw heaven opened, and behold a white horse; and he that sat upon him was called Faithful and True, and **in righteousness he doth judge and make war**. His eyes were as a flame of fire, and on his head were many crowns; and he had a name written, that no man knew, but he himself. **And he was clothed with a vesture <u>dipped in blood</u>**: and his name is called The Word of God. And the armies which were in heaven followed him upon white horses, clothed in fine linen, white and clean. And out of his mouth goeth a sharp sword, that with it he should smite the nations: and he shall rule them with a rod of iron: **<u>and he treadeth the winepress of the fierceness and wrath of Almighty God</u>**. ... And I saw the beast, and the kings of the earth, and their armies, gathered together to make war against him that sat on the horse, and against his army... And the remnant were slain with the sword of him that sat upon the horse, which sword proceeded out of his mouth."*

This same scene is described with even more detail in Revelation 14:15-20:

*"And another angel came out of the temple, crying with a loud voice to him that sat on the cloud, **Thrust in thy sickle, and reap: for the time is come for thee to reap; for the harvest of the earth is ripe. And he that sat on the cloud thrust in his sickle on the earth; and the earth was reaped.** And another angel came out of the temple which is in heaven, he also having a sharp sickle. And another angel came out from the altar, which had power over fire; and cried with a loud cry to him that had the sharp sickle, saying, **Thrust in thy sharp sickle, and gather the clusters of the vine of the earth; for her grapes are fully ripe. And the angel thrust in his sickle into the earth, and gathered the vine of the earth, and cast it into the great winepress of the wrath of God. <u>And the winepress was trodden without the city, and blood came out of the winepress, even unto the horse bridles, by the space of a thousand and six hundred furlongs</u>**."*

Thus, does the Lord of Hosts create a Red Sea of the blood of the very army of the wicked who expected in the depths of their insanity to defeat God by destroying His holy city and His chosen people.

Chapter Five:

The Salvation of "the Jews"

In Matthew 23:37-39, near the end of His earthly ministry, Jesus passed a sentence of judgment upon the House of Judah. Standing on the Mount of Olives, looking across the narrow Kidron Valley at the holy city spread out before Him, he lamented:

"Jerusalem, Jerusalem, who kills the prophets and stones those who are sent to her! How often I wanted to gather your children together, the way a hen gathers her chicks under her wings, and you were unwilling. **'Behold, your house is being left to you desolate! For I say to you, from now on you will not see Me until you say, 'Blessed is He who comes in the name of the Lord'** ".

Three and a half years later the implementation of that sentence would be initiated and the long 2000-year "age of the Gentiles" would begin upon the final indictment of the Jews by Stephen, the first martyr of the church (Acts 7). And the man who orchestrated Stephen's murder, Saul of Tarshish, would very soon become Paul (Acts 9), the apostle to the Gentiles (Romans 11:13).

That age of the gentiles is nearing its end today, as we await the return of Christ to His city when the Jews will finally recognize their Messiah and *"weep for Him as for an only son"* (Zechariah 12:10), and *"all Israel will be saved."* (Romans 11:26).[5]

"And I will pour upon the house of David, and upon the inhabitants of Jerusalem, the spirit of grace and of supplications: and they shall look upon me whom they have pierced, and they shall mourn for him, as one mourneth for his only son, and shall be in bitterness for him, as one that is in bitterness for his firstborn. (Zechariah 12:10, cited in John 19:37).

"And the Redeemer shall come to Zion, and unto them that turn from transgression in Jacob, saith the LORD" (Isaiah 59:20, cited in Romans 11:26).

On the Day of Atonement, the last of the Ten Days of Awe, "all Israel" (those who repent of their unbelief in Christ) will receive their salvation when the Messiah arrives to rescue Jerusalem from the army of the wicked which have overrun it (Zechariah 14).

"And it will come about that whoever calls on the name of the LORD will be delivered; For on Mount Zion and in Jerusalem there will be those who escape, As the LORD has said, Even among the survivors whom the LORD calls" (Joel 2:32).

These are represented by the 144,000 Hebrews, 12,000 from each of the 12 tribes of Jacob: faithful Torah-believing men who were sealed against death by God in order to preserve them through the time of wrath.

"And I saw another angel ascending from the east, having the seal of the living God: and he cried with a loud voice to the four angels, to whom it was given to hurt the earth and the sea, Saying, Hurt not the earth, neither the sea, nor the trees, till we have sealed the servants of our God in their foreheads. And I heard the number of them which were sealed: and there were sealed an hundred and forty and four thousand of all the tribes of the children of Israel" (Revelation 7:2-4).

The "seal of the living God" is His name, written upon their foreheads:

"And I looked, and, lo, a Lamb stood on the mount Sion, and with him an hundred forty and four thousand, having his Father's name written in their foreheads. And I heard a voice from heaven, as the voice of many waters, and as the voice of a great thunder: and I heard the voice of harpers harping with their harps: And they sung as it were a new song before the throne, and before the four beasts, and the elders: and no man could learn that song but the hundred and forty and four thousand, which were redeemed from the earth" (Revelation 14:1-3).

These two passages, offering snapshots of the Hebrew elect before and after their rescue by the Messiah, evoke a pattern seen in the Passover and subsequent exodus from Egypt, and (to a lesser extent) in the rescue of Lot from Sodom, but most especially in Ezekiel's vision in Ezekiel 8-9, which contains a description of the sealing of the righteous Jews before the execution of God's wrath:

*"And the LORD said unto him, Go through the midst of the city, through the midst of Jerusalem, and **set a mark upon the foreheads of the men that sigh and that cry for all the abominations that be done in the midst thereof.** <u>And to the others he said in mine hearing, Go ye after him through the city, and smite</u>: let not your eye spare, neither have ye pity: Slay utterly old and young, both maids, and little children, and women: but come not near any man upon whom is the mark; and <u>begin at my sanctuary</u>"* (Ezekiel 9:4-6).

Interestingly, what defines the righteousness of these men is not their actions, but the grief in their hearts over the apostasy that surrounds them. This was also true of covetous, incestuous Lot who nevertheless is described as "righteous" in 2 Peter 2:9.

*"He rescued **righteous** Lot, oppressed by the sensual conduct of unprincipled men (for by what he saw and heard that righteous man, while living among them, felt his righteous soul tormented day after day by their lawless*

deeds), then the Lord knows how to rescue the godly from temptation, and to keep the unrighteous under punishment for the day of judgment."

Importantly (relative to God's command that judgment on the wicked begin at His sanctuary), Mount Zion is traditionally identified as being the site of the Temple Mount (not the hill immediately to the south of the Old City that is so designated today). This location is referenced by Revelation 14:1, Isaiah 59:20 and Ezekiel 9:6 all of which are cited above. In other words, "God's sanctuary" is Mount Zion and Mount Zion is traditionally considered to be the site of the Temple Mount.

JEWS, ISRAELITES AND HEBREWS: WHO'S WHO?

*"Behold, I am going to make Jerusalem a cup that causes reeling to all the peoples around; and when the siege is against Jerusalem, it will also be against **Judah**…But I will watch over the **house of Judah**, while I strike every horse of the peoples with blindness. "**Then the clans of Judah will say in their hearts, 'A strong support for us are the inhabitants of Jerusalem through the LORD of hosts, their God' "*** (Zechariah 12:2-5).

Zechariah Chapter 12 describes the end-time siege of Jerusalem before its rescue by Christ and identifies "the clans of Judah" as the leaders of the city's defense. This is a reference to the tribe of Judah (into which Jesus was born). But Judah is also a reference to the house of Judah, which includes the tribes of Judah and Benjamin (and, *de-facto*, Levi).

The "Jews" are, technically, the members of the house of Judah (two tribes) and are first designated by that nickname in the Bible when the House of Judah was at war with the House of Israel (the other ten tribes, led by Ephraim).

"Then Rezin king of Syria and Pekah son of Remaliah king of Israel came up to Jerusalem to war: and they besieged Ahaz, but could not overcome him. At that time Rezin king of Syria recovered Elath to Syria, and drave the Jews from Elath" (2 Kings 16:5-6).

Properly differentiating the house of Judah from the house of Israel is absolutely essential to understanding both biblical history and prophecy. This can be difficult, because the word "Israel" is sometimes used to designate all 12 tribes such as "all Israel" in Romans 11:26, and sometimes the house/kingdom of Israel. When the Bible uses the name "Jacob" to designate the Hebrews it means all the tribes. Similarly, the designation house of David (as in Zechariah 12:10 above) means all 12 tribes, because David's kingdom was united, before the division caused by his son Solomon's great sin.

Whenever the Bible addresses the house (or kingdom) of Israel or the house (or kingdom) of Judah by name, it is done purposefully and precisely to distinguish it from the other. But there is potential for additional confusion in that sometimes each house/kingdom is designated by its capital: i.e. Jerusalem (for Judah) or Samaria (for Israel). And sometimes the house/kingdom is designated by its leading tribe: Judah or Ephraim. Thus it is often necessary to search the context to know which entity is being addressed, but that is an important exercise.

In the next section we will study this little-recognized aspect of biblical teaching in greater depth and explore the relationships of the two houses to God, to each other and to the world in light of both history and prophecy.

WHO ARE THE JEWS TODAY?

Modern mainstream Christianity and most Bible versions identify all Hebrews as "Jews," but that is not entirely accurate. They are correct only in the sense that most self-identified Hebrews are modernly aligned with the house of Judah and its system of Torah and/or Talmud-based synagogue worship, and can thus properly be labeled as Jews. But many Hebrews are secular, and others align with Christianity (which we will show in the next section that these latter make up the house of Israel).

There is an additional factor to consider within Judaism related to the Talmud (the collected commentaries on the Old Testament by Jewish sages) and the degree to which individual Jews and religious factions adhere to those human writings and opinions more attentively than to God's Torah itself. This tendency was the cause of Christ's numerous rebukes of the Scribes and Pharisees, and has many parallels in Christian denominations which elevate human traditions and extra-biblical church rules to the status of doctrine, sometimes even in contradiction to the Scripture. True Judaism and true Christianity are defined by God's Word, not the writings or teachings of human beings or institutions, no matter how esteemed.

Dangerous Ground

I want to pause for a moment here and acknowledge that we have now begun to tread some theologically dangerous ground, in the sense that some of the facts and perspectives we will next explore are shared in part by various cults and racist groups. Further, even within authentic Christianity there are deeply entrenched and polarized ideological camps which (at the extremes) either believe the Jews can do no wrong, or alternately that the Jews are behind all of the ills of the world. The truth lies somewhere in the middle.

We will need to take out our scalpels and be prepared to carve the truth away from falsehood very precisely so as not to be misunderstood.

Jews Who Are Not Jews

"I know the blasphemy of them which say they are Jews, and are not, but are the synagogue of Satan" (Revelation 2:9).

Clearly, the Bible warns that some who call themselves Jews are not. This is not to say that non-Hebrews cannot become Jews through conversions, as noted in Easton's Bible Dictionary (under proselyte):

> "The law of Moses made specific regulations regarding the admission into the Jewish church of such as were not born Israelites (Exodus 20:10 ; 23:12 ; Exodus 12:19 Exodus 12:48 ; Deuteronomy 5:14 ; Deuteronomy 16:11 Deuteronomy 16:14 , etc.). The Kenites, the Gibeonites, the Cherethites, and the Pelethites were thus admitted to the privileges of Israelites...[I]n New Testament times, we read of [Jewish] proselytes in the synagogues (Acts 10:2 Acts 10:7 ; Acts 13:42; Acts 13:43; Acts 13:50, 17:4 ; 18:7; Luke 7:5). The 'religious proselytes' here spoken of were proselytes of righteousness, as distinguished from proselytes of the gate....the 'proselytes of the gate' (half proselytes) were not required to be circumcised nor to comply with the Mosaic ceremonial law. They were bound only to conform to the so-called seven precepts of Noah, viz., to abstain from idolatry, blasphemy, bloodshed, uncleanness, the eating of blood, theft, and to yield obedience to the authorities...abstain from work on the Sabbath, and to refrain from the use of leavened bread during the time of the Passover. The 'proselytes of righteousness', religious or devout proselytes (Acts 13:43), were bound to all the doctrines and precepts of the Jewish economy, and were members of the synagogue in full communion"[6]

[Note that even in this dictionary entry the word "Jewish" is incorrectly used to identify all Hebrews and Hebrew culture, even regarding events that predate the existence of the house of Judah or nation of Judea. This misunderstanding is unfortunately nearly universal in modern Christendom.]

Importantly, some people were (temporarily or permanently) forbidden, due to race or circumstances of birth, from full conversion.

"No one who is emasculated or has his male organ cut off shall enter the assembly of the LORD. No one of illegitimate birth [a "mamzer"] shall enter the assembly of the LORD; none of his descendants, even to the tenth generation, shall enter the assembly of the LORD. No Ammonite or Moabite shall enter the assembly of the LORD; none of their descendants, even to the tenth generation, shall ever enter the assembly of the LORD...You shall not detest an Edomite, for he is your brother; you shall not detest an Egyptian, because you were an alien in his land. The sons of the third generation who are born to them may enter the assembly of the LORD" (Deuteronomy 23:1-8).

The term "assembly of the Lord" means the population of legally acceptable marriage partners. Thus the grandchildren of half-proselyte Edomites (descendants of Esau) and Egyptians could become full proselytes and marry full-blooded Hebrews. However, a *mamzer*, meaning a person of illegitimate birth could never become a full proselyte, thus every Ammonite and Moabite was permanently excluded because these two nations were established through the incestuous, and therefore illegitimate, union of Lot and his two daughters, respectively. However, scholars have noted that this apparently rule did not apply to females, and thus Ruth, a Moabite is found in the genealogy of Jesus.

Marriage was also forbidden with any descendants of Canaan, the grandson of Noah whose family line established the demon-worshiping religions of the post-flood world:

"When the LORD thy God shall bring thee into the land whither thou goest to possess it, and hath cast out many nations before thee, the Hittites, and the Girgashites, and the Amorites, and the Canaanites, and the Perizzites, and the Hivites, and the Jebusites, seven nations greater and mightier than thou ; And when the LORD thy God shall deliver them before thee; thou shalt smite them, and utterly destroy them; thou shalt make no covenant with them, nor shew mercy unto them: Neither shalt thou make marriages with them; thy daughter thou shalt not give unto his son, nor his daughter shalt thou take unto thy son. **For they will turn away thy son from following me, that they may serve other gods**: so will the anger of the LORD be kindled against you, and destroy thee suddenly* (Deuteronomy 7:1-4). [*These seven tribes are all ethnically Canaanite though they are identified here by different tribal affiliations.]

Importantly, this prohibition seems to be related more to Canaanite idolatry and its destructive social and spiritual consequences than to bloodline. There isn't enough detail in the scriptural context of the incidents mentioning Hebrew/Canaanite intermarriage in Genesis 24:3; 26:34; 27:46; 28:8 to assert this conclusion definitively. But these were all prior to the giving of the Torah through Moses when the rules regarding both intermarriage and idolatry were more clearly codified. However, in mentions of the marriage ban or its violation *after* the giving of the Torah, the justification for the ban is expressly linked to Canaanite idolatry, defined by human sacrifice and sexual perversion (see Leviticus 18, especially v. 24-28).

Interestingly, this Canaanite demon-worship was also adopted by the Moabites and Ammonites per Numbers 25:1-3 and 1 Kings 11:5-7 and is referenced indirectly in Deuteronomy 23:4 (i.e. Balaam's curse) as the reason for the prohibition on marriage with them (since it was Balaam who advised King Balak to send in Moabite women to sexually and spiritually corrupt the Hebrew men -- 2 Peter 2:15).

Thus, in Ezra's purification of the assembly of marriageable Hebrews after the Babylonian exile (in Ezra 9:1-2), the reason given for Ezra's policy -- applying even to Egyptian and Edomite proselytes who were *exempted* under Torah law from a permanent ban on marriage with Hebrews (per Deuteronomy 23:7-8) -- was demon worship. So it was *not ethnicity but culturally-based idolatrous conduct* that condemned these "foreign wives."

"*Now when these things were done, the princes came to me, saying, The people of Israel, and the priests, and the Levites, have not separated themselves from the people of the lands,* **doing according to their abominations**, *even of the Canaanites, the Hittites, the Perizzites, the Jebusites [all Canaanites by bloodline], the Ammonites, the Moabites ["mamzers"], the Egyptians, and the* ~~Amorites~~" (Ezra 9:1-2). *[We agree with scholars who conclude that, due to scribal error, "Amorites" should be "Edomites" in this verse.]*

Again, it was demon worship by the Egyptians and Edomites that disqualified them from inclusion in the pool of marriageable partners, even though they would otherwise have qualified.

BY THEIR FRUIT

We must now consider who are those "*who say they are Jews but are really of the synagogue of Satan.*" In light of the above, this designation must be based on conduct, not bloodline, since so many authentic "Jews," including Jesus, have a mixed racial heritage (among His ancestors, Ruth was a Moabite, Rahab was a Canaanite).

Now at the time of Christ's earthly ministry until just before John's publication of Revelation, the nation of Judea was ruled by the Herodian Dynasty, under Roman auspices. The Herods were Edomites whose ancestors (along with the entire population of Edom) had been forced to convert to Judaism about a hundred years earlier. The Herodians, established as the ruling family of Judea by the Romans beginning with Herod the Great, were uniformly wicked. Herod began his reign with the slaughter of the Hasmonean (Hebrew) royalty, descendants of the legendary Maccabee family of the tribe of Judah, which had thwarted the antichrist prototype Antiochus IV Epiphanes in 164 BC (Daniel 11). (The Maccabees presided over the rededication of the temple, an event celebrated annually today as Hanukkah). Herod also attempted to kill the infant Christ by slaughtering all the children in and around Bethlehem.

Surely Herod and many of his administration, his family, and successors would deserve the label of "false-Jew."

During this entire Herodian period the designation "Jew" was far less indicative of Hebrew origins since it described all of the residents of the then pluralistic nation of Judea, integrated culturally and demographically into the Roman Empire. And even the house of Judah, such as it was, was heavily influenced, if not controlled, by non-Hebrews (the Herodians).

ARE MODERN "JEWS" EVEN JEWS? (YES!)

Confusion about the above matters have bolstered the claims of various cults and racist groups (both Black and White) whose members insist that they themselves are the "true Jews" while asserting that those identifying themselves as Jews modernly (such as the "Zionists") are imposters. These racist contenders for the Jewish title (and other adversaries) also cite the influence of Turkish Kazar conversions in the history of the Ashkenazic Judaism of Europe as evidence that today's Jews are not really Jews.

However, missing from the debate over these facts is the identity, history and role of the house of Judah, which has always been strongly tied to the Torah and self-measured by faithfulness to its teachings. By that standard, it is clear to see that a core of authentic Judaism survived the Herodians, the Romans, the Turks, the Catholics, the Protestants, the Nazis, etc., and exists today in distinct communities around the world, including Israel. And, as in Christianity, persecution has served as a purifying "refiner's fire" for the faithful, and a powerful motivation for the unfaithful to abandon Judaism.

Whereas the identification "Jew" might have been confused in the pluralistic Roman-controlled Judea of the early church period (the label in those days including both Judaic religious and Judean national identity -- reminiscent of today's blurry distinction between religious and ethnic Jews), frequent and often long-lasting persecution and hardship in the Hebrew diaspora largely ensured that only those willing to suffer for their faith would openly claim the label.

Who would claim to be a Jew who wasn't over most of the past two millennia? I suggest that very few would do so, and in my estimation that is one of the greatest proofs that the house of Judah is composed primarily of authentic Jews today, including both Hebrews of all the tribes of Jacob, as well as non-Hebrew converts and their descendants -- all defined not by their bloodline, but by the measure of their Torah faithfulness.

As Paul wrote in his Letter to the Romans:

"For he is not a Jew who is one outwardly, nor is circumcision that which is outward in the flesh. But he is a Jew who is one inwardly; and circumcision is that which is of the heart, by the Spirit, not by the letter; and his praise is not from men, but from God....For we maintain that a man is justified by faith apart from works of the Law. Or is God the God of Jews only? Is He not the God of Gentiles also? Yes, of Gentiles also, since indeed God who will justify the circumcised by faith and the uncircumcised through faith is one" (Romans 2:28-29; 3:28-30).

SECTION TWO

THE TWO HOUSE PROPHECY

THE DIVISION AND REUNIFICATION OF THE HOUSE OF JACOB AS THE BACKDROP TO THE STORY OF CHRISTIANITY

INTRODUCTION TO SECTION TWO

In the early days of my prophecy studies, I read *The United States and Great Britain in Prophecy* (1954) by Herbert W. Armstrong of the Worldwide Church of God, a now-defunct organization considered by most Christian authorities to have been a cult. However, I found most of the book to be quite interesting and biblically sound, though some portions were in my view not scriptural. Shortly afterward I learned that the portions of the book I found so intriguing had actually been plagiarized nearly word-for-word by Armstrong from a much earlier book, *Judah's Scepter and Joseph's Birthright*, written by J.H. Allen in 1902. I quickly obtained a copy of Allen's book and have since read it three separate times. It is by far the most fascinating and illuminating book I have ever read and I highly recommend it.

I later learned that Allen, a founder of the Holiness Movement in the 19th century, had, without attribution, borrowed heavily from an earlier work on the same theme: H.L. Chamberlain's 1887 book *Judah and Israel, Or, The Kingdom of the God of Heaven (Dan. 2-14) as it is Now: And the Kingdom of the Son of David (Dan. 7-13,14) as it Will be*, which in turn drew upon an 1840 book of lectures written and published by historian John Wilson under the title *Our Israelitish Origins*, which was inspired by Sharon Turner's 1799 work *History of the Anglo-Saxons*, and based upon Wilson's own research into the ancient writings of Ptolemy, Diodorus, Herodotus, and Josephus. So, this is a topic with deep and scholarly roots, though I think Allen's version is by far the most readable.

Judah's Scepter and Joseph's Birthright develops and interweaves two separate and distinct doctrines: 1) the Two House teaching and 2) British Israelism. I can confirm from long and diligent study that the first of these, regarding the two houses is 100% Biblically sound, as I will show in this section.

The latter doctrine, known alternately as British Israelism or Anglo-Israelism is beyond the scope of our current study. I can attest that the doctrine is not entirely sound as presented by Allen, relying in part on highly questionable extra-biblical sources, although the portions of the teaching grounded in the Bible are quite plausible and very intriguing, and whatever errors may exist do not detract from the readability of Allen's enjoyable and engaging style.

Unfortunately, while Allen's book is decidedly *not* Anti-Semitic (nor is the authentic Two House teaching itself), twisted, non-biblical versions of the Two House teaching were so thoroughly exploited and misused by various cults and Anti-Semitic groups in the 20th century that the subject began to be shunned by mainstream Christianity around a century ago and eventually forgotten. The average American Christian today has never even heard of the Two House teaching.

In my view, what the Bible teaches about the two houses is not only extremely illuminating, it is essential to understanding both Bible history and end times prophecy.

This beautiful illustration from the Sephardic Jewish Cervera Bible, published 1299 AD in Spain, depicts the vision of Zechariah in Chapter 4 of his prophecy: *Then the angel who was speaking with me returned and woke me, as a man is awakened from his sleep. "What do you see?" he asked. "I see a solid gold lampstand," I replied, "with a bowl at the top and seven lamps on it, with seven spouts to the lamps. There are also two olive trees beside it, one on the right side of the bowl and the other on its left." "What are these, my lord?" I asked the angel who was speaking with me....So he said, "These are the two anointed ones who are standing beside the Lord of all the earth."* The meaning is further clarified in Jeremiah 11:16-17 *"The LORD called thy name, A green olive tree, fair, and of goodly fruit: with the noise of a great tumult he hath kindled fire upon it, and the branches of it are broken. For the LORD of hosts, that planted thee, hath pronounced evil against thee, for the evil of the house of Israel and of the house of Judah."* In other words, the olive tree symbolizes the house of Jacob, represented by the house of Judah and the house of Israel, giving special insight into many prophetic passages, including particularly Romans 11.

CHAPTER SIX:

JUDAH'S SCEPTER
AND JOSEPH'S BIRTHRIGHT

God's 7-Point Covenant with the Hebrews

When God chose Abraham to be the progenitor of His chosen people He made seven promises to him.

"When Abram was ninety-nine years old, the Lord appeared to him and said, 'I am God Almighty; walk before me faithfully and be blameless. Then I will make my covenant between me and you and will greatly increase your numbers.' Abram fell face down, and God said to him, 'As for me, this is my covenant with you:

[1] You will be the father of many nations. No longer will you be called Abram; your name will be Abraham, for I have made you a father of many nations. I will make you very fruitful; **I will make nations of you, and**

[2] **Kings will come from you**.

[3] **I will establish my covenant as an everlasting covenant** *between me and you and your descendants after you for the generations to come, to be your God and the God of your descendants after you.*

[4] **The whole land of Canaan, where you now reside as a foreigner, I will give as an everlasting possession to you and your descendants after you; and I will be their God'"** (Genesis 17:1-8).

Later, when Abraham's faith was tested by God in the command to sacrifice his son, Isaac upon an altar, God added a codicil to His covenant that included four new terms:

"'By Myself I have sworn, declares the Lord, because you have done this thing and have not withheld your son, your only son, indeed I will greatly bless you, and

[5] *I will greatly multiply your seed as the stars of the heavens and as the sand which is on the seashore; and*

[6] *your seed shall possess the gate of their enemies.*

[7] *In your seed all the nations of the earth shall be blessed, because you have obeyed My voice'* " (Genesis 22:16-18).

With this codicil, God established that the Messiah would come through the line of Isaac (#7). This has been termed the **"scepter promise,"** because it covenants that the King of Kings would come through Isaac. (Unlike the other covenantal terms, the word "seed" in term #7 is singular, as attested by Paul in Galatians 3:16).

It also established that the **"birthright promise,"** already previously covenanted, would be expanded in term #5 to guarantee vast numbers of descendants.

Significantly, term #5 of the "birthright promise" was given a second expression in the prophecy of Rebecca's brothers, when she left their family to become Isaac's wife: "*May you, our sister, become thousands of ten thousands, and may your descendants possess the gate of those who hate them*" (Genesis 24:60).

Importantly for our study, the story of Abraham and Isaac represents the first iteration of the Passover pattern in Scripture. It introduces the theme of resurrection from the dead, as it necessarily assumes that Abraham believed God would raise Isaac from the dead following the sacrifice (since Isaac was the son of promise through whom God had covenanted to bring many kings and nations). Isaac was also metaphorically "raised from the dead" by the substitutionary offering of the young ram: "*Abraham reasoned that God could raise the dead, and in a sense, he did receive Isaac back from death*" (Hebrews 11:19).

Genesis 22 is the passage of Scripture read by Jews even to this day on the Feast of Trumpets, accompanied by the blowing of the shofar, the ram's horn. These are powerful symbolic supports for our conclusion that the Resurrection and Rapture of the church will occur on a Feast of Trumpets.

After Abraham's death, God confirmed His promises to Isaac:

"*The Lord appeared to him and said, 'Do not go down to Egypt; stay in the land of which I shall tell you. Sojourn in this land and I will be with you and bless you, for to you and to your descendants I will give all these lands, and I will establish the oath which I swore to your father Abraham. I will multiply your descendants as the stars of heaven, and will give your descendants all these lands; and by your descendants all the nations of the earth shall be blessed'* " (Genesis 26:2-4).

Isaac was the first son born of God's promise and first generation with the ostensible right of choice of which of his sons to bless as his heir to that promise (though God had preordained that choice).

His choice of Jacob over Esau (though it was by the conspiracy of Rebecca and Jacob) also introduced a new pattern in the unfolding of God's plan: the passing over of the firstborn son in the assignment of the birthright promises, in exception to the law of seniority by the firstborn in the right of inheritance.

That law, called primogeniture, is featured prominently in the Two House prophecy, both in the observance and in the exception, especially the right of the firstborn to a *double portion* of the inheritance (Deuteronomy 21:17).

In any case, Isaac passed the blessing of God's promises to Jacob, saying in Genesis 28:3-4, "*May God Almighty bless you and make you fruitful and multiply you, that you may become a company of peoples. May He also give you the blessing of Abraham, to you and to your descendants with you, that you may possess the land of your sojournings, which God gave to Abraham.*"

God then ratified Isaac's prayer in Genesis 28:13-14:

"'*I am the Lord, the God of your father Abraham and the God of Isaac; the land on which you lie, I will give it to you and to your descendants. Your descendants will also be like the dust of the earth, and you will spread out to the west and to the east and to the north and to the south; and in you and in your descendants shall all the families of the earth be blessed.*'"

Thus, God not only extended to Jacob all of the promises He had made to Abraham and Isaac, He also proclaimed a blessing to "all the families of the earth" through the very existence of Jacob and his descendants, who would be thoroughly dispersed throughout the world. By His own mouth, God declared His chosen people, the Hebrews, to be a blessing to all humanity.

THE DIVISION OF THE PROMISES TO TWO SEPARATE HOUSES

This diffusion throughout the world of Hebrew "seed," and the effect of the promises God had attached to it, was accomplished by the establishment of twelve tribes through four distinct genetic lines. These are the twelve tribes of Israel, through Leah, her handmaiden Zilpah, Rachel, and her handmaiden Bilhah. Four women, four bloodlines that would eventually be scattered to the four directions per Genesis 28:14.

The laws and customs of his father-in-law Laban required Jacob to accept Leah as his first wife, but her younger sister Rachel was Jacob's chosen and favored wife. **The two Hebrew houses were founded in these two marriages, and God divided the promises between them.**

The house of Judah was rooted in the marriage with Leah, and it held the scepter promise which was fulfilled when the Messiah, Jesus Christ, the King of Kings was born in the lineage of Judah.

The house of Israel arose from the marriage with Rachel, and it held the birthright promise through Joseph, the firstborn son of Jacob's favored bride.

We will now explore the fascinating biblical history of the origin and significance of the division between the houses. First, let us remember the law of primogeniture and look at the seniority of Jacob's male heirs, and how the promises of God were allocated. This is the order of birth of Jacob's sons:

1. Rueben by Leah
2 Simeon by Leah
3. Levi by Leah
4. **Judah by Leah**
5. Dan by Jacob's concubine Bilhah, handmaid of Rachel
6. Naphtali by Bilhah
7. Gad by Jacob's concubine Zilpah, handmaid of Leah
8. Asher by Zilpah
9. Issachar by Leah
10. Zebulun by Leah
11. **Joseph by Rachel**
12. Benjamin by Rachel

Reuben was the firstborn by Leah, but was disqualified from receiving the firstborn blessing (1 Chronicles 5:1) because he slept with his father's concubine Bilhah (Genesis 35:22).

"*Now the sons of Reuben the firstborn of Israel (for he was the firstborn, but because he defiled his father's bed, his birthright was given to the sons of Joseph the son of Israel; so that he is not enrolled in the genealogy according to the birthright. Though Judah prevailed over his brothers, and from him came the leader, yet the birthright belonged to Joseph)*" (1 Chronicles 5:1-2). Note that the blessing went to the firstborn of the other wife, Rachel, not to any of the later-born sons of the first wife, Leah.

Simeon and Levi were the second and third sons by Leah, but they were disqualified from leadership of her house (Genesis 49:5-7) because of their excessive and treacherous revenge against the men of Shechem in retaliation for the rape of their sister Dinah (Genesis 34).

Thus Judah, while not given the firstborn birthright (which instead went to Joseph, firstborn of Rachel), became the political leader of the twelve tribes and received the scepter promise. As prophesied by Jacob before he died:

"*The scepter shall not depart from Judah, Nor the ruler's staff from between his feet, Until Shiloh [Christ] comes, And to him shall be the obedience of the peoples*" (Genesis 49:10).

So at this point, the promises that had been held as a single package by Abraham, Isaac and Jacob, are now divided in two, one portion held by each of the houses of Jacob's two wives, represented by Judah and Joseph respectively.

But remember that the birthright promise carries the special blessing of a double portion of the inheritance. Thus, Joseph's position among his brothers received special honor in that his two sons, Ephraim and Manasseh were elevated to equal status with their uncles. Instead of the tribe of Joseph, there was now the tribe of Ephraim and the tribe of Manasseh. Joseph's double portion encompassed two nations of the twelve instead of one, which was one sixth of the territory of the promised land.

[The reason that this did not add up to thirteen tribes and thirteen shares of land was that the Levites were not considered a tribe but were set apart as the priests of God -- He was their "portion" and their territory was limited to the six Cities of Refuge, per Joshua 20:1-9: *"Kedesh in Galilee in the hill country of Naphtali, Shechem in the hill country of Ephraim, and Kiriath Arba (that is, Hebron) in the hill country of Judah. East of the Jordan (on the other side from Jericho) they designated Bezer in the wilderness on the plateau in the tribe of Reuben, Ramoth in Gilead in the tribe of Gad, and Golan in Bashan in the tribe of Manasseh."*]

Here, again, the younger son of Joseph, Ephraim, benefitted from an exception to the rule of primogeniture. Ephraim received the firstborn blessing at the hand of his grandfather Jacob/Israel superceding his older brother Manasseh.

*"Joseph took them both, Ephraim with his right hand toward Israel's left, and Manasseh with his left hand toward Israel's right, and brought them close to him. But Israel stretched out his right hand and laid it on the head of Ephraim, who was the younger, and his left hand on Manasseh's head, crossing his hands, although Manasseh was the firstborn....When Joseph saw that his father laid his right hand on Ephraim's head, it displeased him; and he grasped his father's hand to remove it from Ephraim's head to Manasseh's head. Joseph said to his father, 'Not so, my father, for this one is the firstborn. Place your right hand on his head.' But his father refused and said, 'I know, my son, I know; he also will become a people and he also will be great. However, his younger brother shall be greater than he, and **his descendants shall become a multitude of nations'** "* (Genesis 48:13-19).

"For I am a father to Israel [says the Lord God] And Ephraim is My firstborn" (Jeremiah 31:9).

So, at the time of Jacob's death, when "all Israel" was living in Egypt, in the Land of Goshen, centuries before the entrance into the promised land, and long before the kingdom of David would be divided into the nations of Judah and Israel, the two houses were already well established. They were represented by Judah and Joseph (via Ephraim), holding the scepter promise and the birthright promise respectively.

Now that we are aware of the special roles and relationship of Judah and Ephraim in Bible history and prophecy, numerous Bible stories take on a new meaning and significance.

Consider for example the incident at Kadesh Barnea, where twelve Hebrew spies were sent into the promised land to scout out the prospects for its conquest in fulfillment of God's promise to Abraham, Isaac and Jacob. It is not generally remembered that the only two spies who (trusting God) advocated for immediate invasion represented the tribes of Ephraim (Joshua, Numbers 13:8, 16) and Judah (Caleb, Numbers 13:6).

However, for the purposes of our study, we will now jump ahead to the post-Davidic establishment of the nations of Judah and Israel on the foundations of these two Hebrew houses.

THE TWO HOUSES UNDER KING DAVID

After the conquest of Canaan, and a long period of God's provision to the Hebrew tribes through a series of Judges, the people demanded the formation of a Hebrew monarchy. Subsequently, via the prophet Samuel (who unsuccessfully warned the people against it on God's behalf), Saul was anointed King over all twelve tribes.

In due season, Saul (who became a type of Antichrist) was rejected by God in favor of David, the shepherd. David became a type of Christ and the "apple of God's eye" because He served God with his whole heart and because he unified the two houses under one righteous authority. Yes, Saul had briefly united the houses early in his reign, but then, per Samuel 15:3-10, he led them into rebellion against God. In contrast, note how central the two house perspective was in the plans of God for David:

"...*the LORD has sworn to David...to transfer the kingdom from the house of Saul and* **to establish the throne of David over Israel and over Judah,** *from Dan even to Beersheba*" (2 Samuel 3:9-10). (This was many years before the houses of Israel and Judah were formed into two kingdoms!)

Importantly, David's role as a model of Christ is not primarily related to the first coming of Christ, but to the second.

In His second coming Christ will not come as a baby, or a suffering servant, but as the King of Kings to first "*judge and make war*" and then "*rule the nations with a rod of iron*" (Revelation 19:11-16) much as David had done (1 Chronicles 28:3).

And perhaps the most significant thing that Christ will do at His second coming, a fact almost entirely missed in the church today, is to unify the two houses! Consider God's emphasis in His message to Mary via the angel Gabriel:

"*And behold, you will conceive in your womb and bear a son, and you shall name Him Jesus. He will be great and will be called the Son of the Most High; and* **the Lord God will give Him the throne of His father**

David; and He will reign over the house of Jacob forever, and His kingdom will have no end" (Luke 1:31-33).

Why the term "house of Jacob?" Because the house of Jacob encompasses all twelve tribes, while the house of Israel does not.

We will consider one more item regarding the soon second coming of Christ before we turn back to the past and chronicle the division of David's kingdom into two. That item is the prophecy of Ezekiel 37. Very often this chapter, which begins with the prophecy of the dry bones, is wrongly interpreted (due to lack of understanding about the two houses) to describe the return of the Jews to the land of Israel. This is despite God's very clear explanation of the prophecy in verse 11: "*Son of man, these bones are the whole <u>house of Israel</u>.*"

One might question whether the emphasis on the "whole" house of Israel is intended to incorporate all twelve tribes, but that notion is definitively quashed in verses 16-24, in the second of the three chronologically sequential and interrelated proverbs:

"*[S]on of man, take for yourself one stick and write on it, 'For Judah and for the sons of Israel, his companions'; then take another stick and write on it, 'For Joseph, the stick of Ephraim and all the <u>house of Israel</u>, his companions.' Then join them for yourself one to another into one stick, that they may become one in your hand. When the sons of your people speak to you saying, 'Will you not declare to us what you mean by these?' say to them,* **'Thus says the Lord GOD, "Behold, I will take the stick of Joseph, which is in the hand of Ephraim, and the tribes of Israel, his companions; and I will put them with it, with the stick of Judah, and make them one stick, and they will be one in My hand.** *The sticks on which you write will be in your hand before their eyes. Say to them, 'Thus says the Lord GOD,* **"Behold, I will take the sons of Israel from among the nations where they have gone, and I will gather them from every side and bring them into their own land; and I will make them one nation in the land, on the mountains of Israel; and one king will be king for all of them; and they will no longer be two nations and no longer be divided into two kingdoms.** *They will no longer defile themselves with their idols, or with their detestable things, or with any of their transgressions; but I will deliver them from all their dwelling places in which they have sinned, and will cleanse them. And they will be My people, and I will be their God.* **My servant David will be king over them, and they will all have one shepherd; and they will walk in My ordinances and keep My statutes and observe them.'*** "

We will return to this chapter later for a closer examination but for now simply note that the prophecy is clearly related to two distinct kingdoms founded on the two houses (Ephraim and Judah), and that, at a yet-future date, these two kingdoms will be reunited by Christ, who will rule them from the throne of David.

CHAPTER SEVEN:

THE TWO HOUSES
BECOME TWO KINGDOMS

After he completed the building of the Temple, David's son Solomon received a conditional promise from God that if he remained righteous before Him, his father's kingdom would belong to him and his descendants in perpetuity -- the same promise God made to David (2 Samuel 7:12-16):

"As for you, if you walk before me faithfully with integrity of heart and uprightness, as David your father did, and do all I command and observe my decrees and laws, I will establish your royal throne over Israel forever, as I promised David your father when I said, 'You shall never fail to have a successor on the throne of Israel. But if you or your descendants turn away from me and do not observe the commands and decrees I have given you and go off to serve other gods and worship them, then I will cut off Israel from the land I have given them and will reject this temple I have consecrated for my Name' " (1 Kings 9:4-7).

Sunday school lessons about Solomon tend to emphasize the great wisdom he displayed in his youth, but when he grew old, his wisdom waned and he broke faith with God, becoming one of the most idolatrous men generally and the single most prolific polygamist in all of Scripture:

"King Solomon, however, loved many foreign women besides Pharaoh's daughter—<u>Moabites, Ammonites, Edomites, Sidonians and Hittites</u> [Mamzers and Canaanites]. They were from nations about which the Lord had told the Israelites, **'You must not intermarry with them, because they will surely turn your hearts after their gods.'** *Nevertheless, Solomon held fast to them in love. He had seven hundred wives of royal birth and three hundred concubines, and his wives led him astray.* **As Solomon grew old, his wives turned his heart after other gods**, *and his heart was not fully devoted to the Lord his God, as the heart of David his father had been.* **He followed Ashtoreth the goddess of the Sidonians, and Molek the detestable god of the Ammonites.** *So Solomon did evil in the eyes of the Lord; he did not follow the Lord completely, as David his father had done"* (1 Kings 11:1-6).

Consider just how deep was Solomon's betrayal of God:

"On a hill east of Jerusalem, Solomon built a high place for Chemosh the detestable god of Moab, and for Molek the detestable god of the Ammonites. He did the same for all his foreign wives, who burned incense and offered sacrifices to their gods" (1 Kings 11:7-8).

What was the hill east of Jerusalem? And how were Chemosh and Molech worshipped?

That hill is known to us today as the Mount of Olives, and these demons were worshiped with sexual perversion and human sacrifices -- child sacrifices to be exact (Leviticus 18:21). In other words, it was King Solomon himself who led the Hebrews into the demon worship on the very hillside where Jesus would be betrayed by Judas, that would first split David's kingdom in two and then lead eventually to the banishment from the promised land of each of those kingdoms in turn.[7]

Here, then, was the cause of the division of David's kingdom and the origin of the two kingdoms:

"*The Lord became angry with Solomon because his heart had turned away from the Lord, the God of Israel, who had appeared to him twice. Although he had forbidden Solomon to follow other gods, Solomon did not keep the Lord's command. So the Lord said to Solomon,* **'Since this is your attitude and you have not kept my covenant and my decrees, which I commanded you, I will most certainly tear the kingdom away from you and give it to one of your subordinates. Nevertheless, for the sake of David your father, I will not do it during your lifetime. I will tear it out of the hand of your son. Yet I will not tear the whole kingdom from him, but will give him one tribe for the sake of David my servant and for the sake of Jerusalem, which I have chosen'** " (1 Kings 11: 9-13).

TAKE CAREFUL NOTICE OF THIS TRUTH. From the instant of this division, until the second coming of Christ and the establishment of the Millennial Kingdom, the priority of God was and is the eventual restoration of the two houses. Every historical and prophetic event of the Bible, every teaching, every parable, every word and action of Jesus Christ relates in some way to this central focus of God. Indeed, the very purpose of Christianity -- "to seek and to save *that which was lost*" -- is inextricably linked to this plan, as we will see. But let us continue to chronicle the historical events as they unfolded.

REHOBOAM AND JEROBOAM

Despite Solomon's phenomenal wealth, beyond that of all the other kings of the earth (described in 1 Kings 10: 14-29), he was not satisfied. In the latter days of his reign he enslaved the Hebrew population with an enormous tax burden and a system of forced labor for building public works. When Solomon died, his son Rehoboam succeeded him in a ceremony at Shechem in the territory of Ephraim. (Significantly, Shechem is the site where the Bible first identifies Abraham by the term "Hebrew" -- Genesis 14:13 -- and where he built the first Hebrew altar to God -- Genesis 13:4.)

"*Rehoboam went to Shechem, for all Israel had gone there to make him king. When Jeroboam son of Nedab heard this (he was still in Egypt, where he had fled from King Solomon), he returned from Egypt. So they sent for Jeroboam, and he and the whole assembly of Israel went to Rehoboam and said to him: 'Your father put a heavy yoke on us, but now lighten the harsh labor and the heavy yoke he put on us, and we will serve you'... The king answered the people harshly. Rejecting the advice given him by the elders, he followed the advice of the young men and said, 'My father made your yoke heavy; I will make it even heavier. My father scourged you with whips; I will scourge you with scorpions' "* (1 Kings 12:1-4; 13-14).

Jeroboam the Ephraimite had been a high-level servant of Solomon, who had appointed him head over the labor forces of the house of Joseph (Ephraim and Manasseh). After the prophet Ahijah of Shiloh prophesied that Jeroboam would become king over the northern ten tribes, Solomon tried to kill him, so he fled to Egypt (1 Kings 10:26-40). Upon his return, and Rehoboam's refusal to enact reforms, the people rebelled against Rehoboam and made Jeroboam king over them: by that act establishing the Kingdom of Israel.

"King Rehoboam sent out Adoram, who was in charge of forced labor, but all Israel stoned him to death...and made [Jeroboam] king over all Israel. Only the tribe of Judah remained loyal to the house of David. [Then] Rehoboam ... mustered all Judah and the tribe of Benjamin—a hundred and eighty thousand able young men—to go to war against Israel and to regain the kingdom for Rehoboam son of Solomon. But this word of God came to Shemaiah the man of God ...Do not go up to fight against your brothers, the Israelites. Go home, every one of you, for this is my doing.' So they obeyed the word of the Lord and went home again, as the Lord had ordered" (1 Kings 12:18-24).

Thus the former unity of the twelve tribes of Israel was shattered and the House of Jacob was divided in two: the house and kingdom of Judah and the house and kingdom of Israel.

WAYWARD ISRAEL

"Jeroboam thought to himself, 'The kingdom will now likely revert to the house of David. If these people go up to offer sacrifices at the temple of the Lord in Jerusalem, they will again give their allegiance to their lord, Rehoboam king of Judah. They will kill me and return to King Rehoboam. After seeking advice, the king made two golden calves. He said to the people, 'It is too much for you to go up to Jerusalem. Here are your gods, Israel, who brought you up out of Egypt.' One he set up in Bethel, and the other in Dan....Jeroboam built shrines on high places and appointed priests from all sorts of people, even though they were not Levites. He instituted a festival on the fifteenth day of the eighth month, like the festival held in Judah, and offered sacrifices on the altar. This he did in Bethel, sacrificing to the calves he had made. And at Bethel he also installed priests at the high places he had made" (1 Kings 12:26-32).

The kingdom of Israel got off to a bad start and never recovered. King Jeroboam was afraid that his subjects would defect to Judah because the temple of God was located in its capital, Jerusalem, and their religious duty was to make pilgrimage there three times per year (for the feasts of Passover, Pentecost, and Tabernacles). So Jeroboam the Ephraimite, fresh from exile in Egypt, and likely mindful of his Egyptian heritage (the wife of Joseph, mother of Ephraim and Manasseh, was a daughter of the Egyptian priest of On -- Genesis 46:20), created his own religion: a hybrid version of "Judaism" centered on the golden calf rather than the temple-based worship of God.

Jeroboam further departed from Judaism by ignoring God's exclusive assignment of priestly duties to the tribe of Levi and making priests of the non-Levites. It would seem almost a foregone conclusion that the Levites would gravitate back to Judah, since their very identity was enmeshed in the rituals and upkeep of the temple and since they could no longer be priests in any Torah-prescribed capacity.

"For the Levites left their pasture lands and their property and came to Judah and Jerusalem, for Jeroboam and his sons had excluded them from serving as priests to the LORD. He set up priests of his own for the high places, for the satyrs and for the calves which he had made. [As Jeroboam had feared] Those from all the tribes of Israel who set their hearts on seeking the LORD God of Israel followed them to Jerusalem, to sacrifice to the LORD God of their fathers" (2 Chronicles 11:14-16).

So as a practical matter, Jeroboam would have needed to recruit clergy from outside the legitimate priesthood. And we must remember that Levi was not actually one of the "ten tribes of Israel" anyway, since their special relationship with God substituted for a land inheritance -- they were assigned the six cities of refuge instead of a twelfth portion of the promised land (Joshua 18:7). (Why then were there not just eleven tribes if Levi wasn't counted among them? Because Joseph, recipient of the firstborn blessing from his father Jacob, received a double portion per Deuteronomy 21:17, meaning that Joseph's inheritance was a full share of land for each of his two sons, who were listed as equal partners with their uncles as the tribes of Ephraim and Manasseh.)

God was angry with the Kingdom of Israel for its pagan idolatry, but His mercy endured from generation to generation until the rise of King Ahab.

"Ahab the son of Omri did evil in the sight of the LORD more than all who were before him. It came about, as though it had been a trivial thing for him to walk in the sins of Jeroboam the son of Nedab, that he married Jezebel the daughter of Ethbaal king of the Sidonians, and went to serve Baal and worshipped him. So he erected an altar for Baal in the house of Baal which he built in Samaria. Ahab also made the Asherah. Thus **Ahab did more to provoke the LORD God of Israel than all the kings of Israel who were before him**" (1 Kings 16:30-33).

Ahab's sin represented the "straw that broke the camel's back," as it were, and the prophet Micaiah declared the outcome of it, saying to Ahab *"I saw all Israel scattered upon the hills, like sheep without a shepherd"* (1 Kings 22:17). The immediate context of this comment related to the result of Ahab's imminent battle with the Syrians, but the phrase "sheep without a shepherd" carries a much deeper meaning, and prophetically describes the future identity of the Israelites of the Northern Kingdom as "lost sheep."

Importantly, the "lost sheep" metaphor in the Bible is primarily used as a symbol of the house of Israel (though it is sometimes used for all the sons of Israel). Its first use in Scripture is by the soon-to-die Moses, praying for a worthy successor to lead the twelve tribes *"so that the congregation of the LORD will not be like sheep which have no shepherd"* (Numbers 27:17). That man was to be Joshua the

Ephraimite. Note that the Hebrews were not "lost sheep" at this time under the good shepherding of Joshua.

We are most familiar with the New Testament references to Jesus as the Good Shepherd of John 10, and Luke 15 who seeks after the lost sheep, and especially the parallel passages in Mark 6:34 and Matthew 9:36 : *"Jesus…had compassion on them [the huge crowds of Galileans who began following him] because they were like sheep without a shepherd."* This was the same spiritual and geographical frame of reference in which he first sent out the twelve disciples, saying, *"Do not go in the way of the Gentiles, and do not enter any city of the Samaritans; but rather go to the lost sheep of the house of Israel"* (Matthew 10:5-6, parallel to Mark 6:7).

Galilee is at this time, of course, a Roman-controlled province in the northern-most territory of what had once been the Northern Kingdom (of Israel), populated with descendants of Hebrew exiles who had drifted back to the land over the centuries (though the majority had been scattered throughout the nations).

In these passages, Jesus is directly fulfilling the prophecy of Ezekiel 34, as spoken by God to Ezekiel:

*"…They were scattered for lack of a shepherd, and they became food for every beast of the field and were scattered. My flock wandered through all the mountains and on every high hill; My flock was scattered over all the surface of the earth, and there was no one to search or seek for them…***Behold, I Myself [Jesus] will search for My sheep and seek them out.** *As a shepherd cares for his herd in the day when he is among his scattered sheep, so I will care for My sheep and will deliver them from all the places to which they were scattered on a cloudy and gloomy day…I will seek the lost, bring back the scattered, bind up the broken and strengthen the sick; but the fat and the strong I will destroy. I will feed them with judgment….***Then they will know that I, the LORD their God, am with them, and that they, <u>the house of Israel</u>, are My people***… As for you, My sheep, the sheep of My pasture, you are men, and I am your God"* (Ezekiel 34:5-6; 11-12; 16; 30-310).

Ezekiel 34 (primarily the portion not quoted above) relates in part to the coming Millennial Kingdom, and is in part a rebuke to faithless spiritual leaders (shepherds) who exercise authority over the exiles during Ezekiel's ministry to them (he lives among them per Ezekiel 1:1) over a century after the fall of the Northern Kingdom. As noted above, while "sheep" sometimes is used for all the Hebrews, in the Old Testament it is most often used in association with the house of Israel, and this is true of the prophecy of Jesus as Shepherd in Ezekiel 34.

Again, Ezekiel prophesied from exile among the ten Tribes of Israel during the conquest of Judah by Babylon, and throughout the Book of Ezekiel he clearly delineates his comments and prophesies about Israel from those about Judah. Ezekiel 23 and 37 are two of the best examples. Ezekiel 34, a message to the house of Israel (v30) falls in the middle of a set of rebukes and warnings to Gentile nations, because that's where Israel was at the time, both physically and spiritually.

In contrast to the shepherdless house of Israel (whose "shepherds" had always been illegitimate in God's eyes), the house of Judah was never separated from its legitimate spiritual shepherds, the Levites, whom He had placed over them. Even to this day, the Levites maintain the role they were assigned, one that was expressly endorsed by Jesus in Matthew 23:2 (though He did not endorse the heretical Pharisees and Sadducees who had usurped the Levitical "seat of Moses" for themselves). Neither was the House of Judah ever divorced by God, despite her great sin. Judah's status remains in a sort-of spiritual suspended animation "*until the fullness of the Gentiles has come in*" (Romans 11).

ISRAEL BUT NOT JUDAH DIVORCED BY GOD

Although the sentence would not be carried out immediately, God finally lost patience with Israel due to Ahab's escalation of evil behavior and issued a writ of divorce, banishing the kingdom of Israel -- all ten tribes -- from His presence, which is how they became the "lost ten tribes of Israel."

*"Then the LORD said to me in the days of Josiah the king, 'Have you seen what faithless Israel did? She went up on every high hill and under every green tree, and she was a harlot there. I thought, After she has done all these things she will return to Me'; but she did not return, and her treacherous sister Judah saw it. **And I saw that for all the adulteries of faithless Israel, I had sent her away and given her a writ of divorce**, yet her treacherous sister Judah did not fear; but she went and was a harlot also. Because of the lightness of her harlotry, she polluted the land and committed adultery with stones and trees. Yet in spite of all this her treacherous sister Judah did not return to Me with all her heart, but rather in deception, declares the LORD*" (Jeremiah 3:6-10).

Notice that Judah *did* return (quite imperfectly) but Israel never did (until after the divorce). Thus God used the Assyrians to carry out His sentence of desolation and in 722BC the entire territory of Israel was emptied of Israelites.

Importantly, God promised to eventually bring Israel back to the land. We will now explore how He has been working to fulfill that promise over the centuries.

THE TWO HOUSES AS "WIVES" AND "SONS" OF GOD

God's relationship with Judah and Israel is always described in familial terms in the Old Testament, with the two houses addressed alternately as wives or sons of God, depending on the aspects of the relationship being emphasized in the passage. Importantly, the New Testament also addresses Christians alternately as sons of God and the Bride of Christ.

Ezekiel Chapter 23 is entirely devoted to the portrayal of Judah and Israel as wives of God:

"The word of the LORD came again unto me, saying, Son of man, there were two women, the daughters of one mother: And they committed whoredoms in Egypt; they committed whoredoms in their youth: there were their breasts pressed, and there they bruised the teats of their virginity. **And**

the names of them were Aholah the elder, and Aholibah her sister: and they were mine, and they bare sons and daughters. Thus were their names; Samaria [Israel] is Aholah, and Jerusalem [Judah] is Aholibah. And <u>Aholah played the harlot when she was mine; and she doted on her lovers, on the Assyrians</u> her neighbours....<u>And when her sister Aholibah saw this, she was more corrupt in her inordinate love than she</u>, and in her whoredoms more than her sister in her whoredoms....<u>And the Babylonians came to her into the bed of love</u>, and they defiled her with their whoredom, and she was polluted with them' " (Ezekiel 23:1-17).

The remainder of Ezekiel 23 continues with a heavy emphasis on the adulterous behavior of Aholah and Aholibah (Israel and Judah respectively). We must remember how closely idolatry and sexual immorality and perversion are linked in the perspective of God, e.g. Leviticus 18.

We are also reminded that the roots of the two houses are in Leah and Rachel respectively (Ruth 4:11).

In the Book of Hosea (written in the generation preceding the Assyrian conquest of Israel) the two houses are also portrayed as wives, in part to emphasize the sexual metaphor for the idolatrous conduct that separates them from God. But even more importantly, the story of Hosea highlights the Hebrew marriage laws and customs as a framework for interpreting the prophecies related to the two houses. These interpretations would include the way in which the significance of marriage is expanded in Jeremiah 3 and in Ephesians 5, for example:

"If a man put away his wife, and she go from him, and become another man's, shall he return unto her again? shall not that land be greatly polluted? (Jeremiah 3:1).

"Husbands, love your wives, even as Christ also loved the church [the House of Israel], and gave himself for it [God Himself dying on the cross to free the her from the law against remarriage]; That he might sanctify and cleanse it with the washing of water by the word, That he might present it to himself a glorious church [the "Bride of Christ"], not having spot, or wrinkle, or any such thing; but that it should be holy and without blemish....For this cause shall a man leave his father and mother, and shall be joined unto his wife, and they two shall be one flesh. This is a great mystery: but I speak concerning Christ and the church" (Ephesians 5:25-32).

The prophecy of Hosea relates almost entirely to Israel, though Judah's conduct and God's response to it is shown contrasted to Israel.

The prophecy is set as an allegorical skit in which Hosea represents God, Gomer represents Israel, and their grandchildren -- Jezreel (boy), Loruhamah (girl) and Loammi (boy) -- represent prophetic events and seasons in the life of the Israelites.

"And the LORD said to Hosea, 'Go, take unto thee a wife of whoredoms and children of whoredoms: for the land hath committed great whoredom, departing from the LORD. So he went and took Gomer the daughter of Diblaim;

which conceived, and bare him a son. And the LORD said unto him, **Call his name Jezreel; for yet a little while, and I will avenge the blood of Jezreel upon the house of Jehu, and <u>will cause to cease the kingdom of the house of Israel</u>. And it shall come to pass at that day, that I will break the bow of Israel in the valley of Jezreel.'** *"*

"And she conceived again, and bare a daughter. And God said unto him, **'Call her name Loruhamah: for I will no more have mercy upon the house of Israel; but I will utterly take them away.** <u>*But I will have mercy upon the house of Judah,*</u> *and will save them by the LORD their God, and will not save them by bow, nor by sword, nor by battle, by horses, nor by horsemen.'* *"*

"Now when she had weaned Loruhamah, she conceived, and bare a son. Then said God, **Call his name Loammi: for ye are not my people, and I will not be your God.'**

'Yet the number of the children of Israel shall be as the sand of the sea, which cannot be measured nor numbered; and it shall come to pass, that in the place where it was said unto them, Ye are not my people, there it shall be said unto them, Ye are the sons of the living God.'

<u>*'Then shall the children of Judah and the children of Israel be gathered together, and appoint themselves one head, and they shall come up out of the land*</u>*: for great shall be the day of Jezreel'* *"* (Hosea 1:2-11).

This opening chapter of the Book of Hosea is a simple summary of the future history of Israel, with both immediate and long-term iterations. The immediate future involved King Jehu's reward and punishment related to the slaughter of the 70 sons of King Ahab. Though God had assigned him this task, Jehu's heart was both tainted by self-interest and faithless regarding the continuing worship of the golden calves. His reward was to head a four-generation royal dynasty, but his punishment was to bear responsibility for failure to redeem Israel in the aftermath of Ahab's far greater (Baal-worshipping) defilement of the land (2 Kings 10). In this iteration Jezreel represents the Assyrian conquest of Israel.

The long-term iteration of Hosea's prophecy has far greater significance to our study. The Valley of Jezreel is also known as the Plain of Megiddo or the Valley of Armageddon (Revelation 16:16), the last days battlefield on which Christ will conquer His enemies. Jezreel is placed in the Hosea summary like a pair of bookends with the first iteration of the Jezreel theme representing the Assyrian conquest and second iteration representing the restoration of Israel to the land in the Millennial Kingdom.

In between these bookends, the Israelites are first rejected and banished from the Holy Land:

"Call her name Loruhamah: for I will no more have mercy upon the house of Israel; but I will utterly take them away."

And then, while they are scattered and multiplied throughout the pagan world, the rejection is reaffirmed:

"*Call his name Loammi: for ye are not my people, and I will not be your God. Yet the number of the children of Israel shall be as the sand of the sea, which cannot be measured nor numbered...*"

However, while sojourning in the pagan world, they will be redeemed:

"*and it shall come to pass, that in the place where it was said unto them, Ye are not my people [after Lorumahah, during Loammi], there it shall be said unto them, Ye are the <u>sons of the living God</u>.*" [Note that this verse is quoted by Paul in Romans 9, the entire chapter of which is devoted to showing that Israelite identity under the new covenant is defined by faith in Christ, not by bloodline. He makes that point even more clearly and succinctly in Galatians 3:26: "*For you are all <u>sons of God</u> through faith in Christ Jesus*"].

Finally, Israel will be reunited with Judah under Christ in the Holy Land following the Battle of Armageddon:

"*Then shall the children of Judah and the children of Israel be gathered together, and appoint themselves one head, and they shall come up out of the land: for great shall be the day of Jezreel .*"

DIVORCED ISRAEL IN THE WILDERNESS

The second and third chapters of Hosea address divorced Israel's experience among the pagans.

She will be lost in the wilderness, and abandon the pseudo-Judaic rituals invented by Jeroboam:

"*Say to your brothers, 'Ammi,' and to your sisters, 'Ruhamah.' 'Contend with your mother, contend, For she is not my wife, and I am not her husband...behold, I will hedge up her way with thorns, And I will build a wall against her so that she cannot find her paths...I will also put an end to all her gaiety, Her feasts, her new moons, her sabbaths And all her festal assemblies*" (Hosea 2:1-11).

But God will seek her out in the wilderness and give her a path to redemption:

"*Therefore, behold, I will allure her, Bring her into the wilderness, and speak kindly to her. Then I will give her vineyards from there, And* **the valley of Achor as a door of hope**. *And she will sing there as in the days of her youth, As in the day when she came up from the land of Egypt*" (Hosea 2:14-15). [Just as the Valley of Achor -- just north of Jericho -- was the doorway to the promised land for the Hebrews under Joshua, so Christ is the doorway of hope for lost Israel.]

That path of redemption is betrothal to God. Israel will be the Bride of Christ:

"It will come about in that day," declares the LORD, That you will call Me Ishi [my husband] And will no longer call Me Baali [my master]. For I will remove the names of the Baals from her mouth, So that they will be mentioned by their names no more...I will betroth you to Me forever; Yes, **I will betroth you to Me** *in righteousness and in justice, In lovingkindness and in compassion, And I will betroth you to Me in faithfulness.* **Then you will know the LORD**" (Hosea 2:16-20).

In the end, God will restore Israel to the land:

"I will sow her for Myself in the land. I will also have compassion on her who had not obtained compassion, And I will say to those who were not My people, 'You are My people!' And they will say, 'You are my God!' " (Hosea 2:23). (Again, see Romans 9:25-26 for the direct association of this prophecy with Christianity.)

ISRAEL IN THE AGE OF THE GENTILES

Hosea chapter 3 addresses the time of Israel's betrothal to God. Importantly, she is the same "woman" (Israel), but enters into an entirely new relationship with God as a Bride and not a Wife.

"Then the LORD said to me, 'Go again, love a woman who is loved by her husband, yet an adulteress, even as the LORD loves the sons of Israel, though they turn to other gods....You shall not play the harlot, **nor shall you have a man; so I will also be toward you**' *" Hosea 3:1-3). [Note the dual identity of Israel, both wife and betrothed woman, with emphasis on premarital celibacy to clearly establish the distinction from a marriage.]*

The long length of the betrothal is emphasized as well as the complete disassociation of Israel from both Judaism and "household idols."

"For the sons of Israel will remain for <u>*many days*</u> *without king or prince, without sacrifice or sacred pillar and without ephod or household idols' "* (Hosea 3:4).

And finally, to remove any doubt as to the long-term prophetic nature of the passage it ends as follows:

*"**Afterward** [after the "many days"] the sons of Israel will return and seek the LORD their God and David their king; and they will come trembling to the LORD and to His goodness* **in the last days**' *"* (Hosea 3:5).

To summarize, Hosea 1-3 describe Israel as one of two Wives of God (along with Judah), who is divorced by Him for adultery (while Judah is not). Israel is sent as a divorced woman into the wilderness to live among the pagans, but while there is allured by God into a new relationship as a betrothed bride. After a very long engagement, she is brought back into the land in the last days.

This is the story of Christianity!

Hosea 4-13 address the sins of Israel that caused the divorce, ending with a reiteration of the promise of future restoration in chapter 14.

Before we explore how God orchestrates the betrothal and remarriage of Israel to Himself -- and how that illuminates the story of salvation -- let's jump ahead to the New Testament for confirmation of the Two House thesis in the teachings of Jesus.

THE TWO HOUSE TEACHING OF JESUS IN THREE PARABLES

In Luke Chapter 15, Jesus tells three parables relating to His mission to restore Israel. The Parable of the Lost Sheep, the Parable of the Lost Coin, and the Parable of the Prodigal Son. Each of these addresses a separate aspect of the thesis. As we proceed, we must keep in mind that the Bible, approached as one unified document, usually provides the clues for determining the meaning of the symbols that it employs, and where it doesn't, the best place to look is the historic cultural context of the story being told.

THE PARABLE OF THE LOST SHEEP

This parable emphasizes that the first focus of Christ's mission is Israel, not Judah or non-Hebrews. "Lost sheep" is a biblical metaphor associated almost exclusively with the house of Israel (e.g 1 Kings 22:17), and indeed Jesus made clear that His mission was limited (at first) to that house:

"*But He answered and said, 'I was sent only to the <u>lost sheep of the house of Israel</u>'*" (Matthew 15:24), and, when sending out the 12 Disciples on their first evangelistic crusade, told them "*Do not go in the way of the Gentiles, and do not enter any city of the Samaritans; but rather go to the <u>lost sheep of the house of Israel</u>*" (Matthew 10:5-6).

Notice further, that when Jesus later addresses the house of Judah, He uses an entirely different metaphor: a mother hen and chicks, not a shepherd and sheep (Matthew 23:37).

Now let's look at the "lost sheep" symbolism in Luke 15:

"*What man among you, if he has a hundred sheep and has lost one of them, does not leave the ninety-nine in the open pasture and go after **the one which is lost** until he finds it? When he has found it, he lays it on his shoulders, rejoicing. And when he comes home, he calls together his friends and his neighbors, saying to them, 'Rejoice with me, for I have found my sheep which was lost!' I tell you that in the same way, there will be more joy in heaven over one sinner who repents than over ninety-nine righteous persons who need no repentance*" (Luke 15:4-7).

And compare this to the "lost sheep" prophecy of Ezekiel, who lived on the Euphrates in formerly

Assyrian territory (now Babylonian at the time of the prophecy), among the exiles of the house of Israel (Ezekiel 1:1).

" 'For this is what the Sovereign Lord says: **I myself will search for my sheep and look after them.** *As a shepherd looks after his scattered flock when he is with them, so will I look after my sheep. I will rescue them from all the places where they were scattered on a day of clouds and darkness.* **I will bring them out from the nations and gather them from the countries, and I will bring them into their own land.** *I will pasture them on the mountains of Israel, in the ravines and in all the settlements in the land...I myself will tend my sheep and have them lie down...**I will search for the lost and bring back the strays...**"* (Ezekiel 34:11-16).

Compare it also to the "lost sheep" prophecy of Jeremiah: *"**Then I Myself will gather the remnant of My flock out of all the countries where I have driven them** and bring them back to their pasture...they will not be afraid any longer, nor be terrified, **nor will any be missing,** declares the LORD...Therefore **behold, the days are coming...when they will no longer say, 'As the LORD lives, who brought up the sons of Israel from the land of Egypt', but 'As the LORD lives, who brought up and led back <u>the descendants of the household of Israel</u> from the north land and from all the countries where I had driven them' "** (Jeremiah 23:3-8).

THE PARABLE OF THE LOST COIN

"Or what woman, if she has ten silver coins and loses one coin, does not light a lamp and sweep the house and search carefully until she finds it? When she has found it, she calls together her friends and neighbors, saying, 'Rejoice with me, for I have found the coin which I had lost!' In the same way, I tell you, there is joy in the presence of the angels of God over one sinner who repents" (Luke 15:8-10).

This parable is a bit more cryptic, because there is not as clear a biblical source for the symbolism of the coin. However, Bible scholars believe that the ten silver coins refer to a bridal necklace or headband worn by betrothed women in those days,[8] which would imply a far more ennobling motive for the woman in this story than materialism. Instead of a woman merely looking for lost property, she is a bride desperate to present herself whole and pure to her husband, "...*as a glorious church, without stain or wrinkle or any such blemish, but holy and blameless"* (Ephesians 5:27). The woman in this case is the Bride of Christ, Israel.

This bridal jewelry hypothesis is supported by Jeremiah 2:31-32: *"O generation, heed the word of the LORD. Have I been a wilderness to **Israel**, Or a land of thick darkness? Why do My people say, 'We are free to roam; We will no longer come to You'? **Can a virgin forget her ornaments, Or a bride her attire?** Yet My people have forgotten Me Days without number."*

It seems significant, as well, that the woman has ten coins, in that the house of Israel has ten tribes.

The Parable of the Prodigal Son

This is the most direct Two House parable of the three. The parable is found in Luke 15:11-32:

Jesus said, *"**A man had two sons. The younger of them said to his father, 'Father, give me the share of the estate that falls to me.' So he divided his wealth between them. And not many days later, the younger son gathered everything together and went on a journey into a distant country, and there he squandered his estate with loose living.** Now when he had spent everything, a severe famine occurred in that country, and he began to be impoverished. So he went and hired himself out to one of the citizens of that country, and he sent him into his fields to feed swine. And he would have gladly filled his stomach with the pods that the swine were eating, and no one was giving anything to him. But **when he came to his senses, he said,** 'How many of my father's hired men have more than enough bread, but I am dying here with hunger! **I will get up and go to my father, and will say to him, "Father, I have sinned against heaven, and in your sight. I am no longer worthy to be called your son**; make me as one of your hired men.' So he got up and came to his father. But while he was still a long way off, his father saw him and felt compassion for him, and ran and embraced him and kissed him. And the son said to him, 'Father, I have sinned against heaven and in your sight; I am no longer worthy to be called your son.' **But the father said to his slaves, 'Quickly bring out the best robe and put it on him, and put a ring on his hand and sandals on his feet; and bring the fattened calf, kill it, and let us eat and celebrate; for this son of mine was dead and has come to life again**; he was lost and has been found.' And they began to celebrate.*

*"Now **his older son** was in the field, and when he came and approached the house, he heard music and dancing. And he summoned one of the servants and began inquiring what these things could be. And he said to him, 'Your brother has come, and your father has killed the fattened calf because he has received him back safe and sound.' But he became angry and was not willing to go in; and his father came out and began pleading with him. But he answered and **said to his father, 'Look! For so many years I have been serving you and I have never neglected a command of yours; and yet you have never given me a young goat, so that I might celebrate with my friends; but when this son of yours came, who has devoured your wealth with prostitutes, you killed the fattened calf for him.' And he said to him, 'Son, you have always been with me, and all that is mine is yours. But we had to celebrate and rejoice, for this brother of yours was dead and has begun to live,** and was lost and has been found."*

The father in the story represents God, the older son represents Judah (who is one of the sons of Jacob the and elder brother to Joseph), and the younger son, the prodigal, represents Israel. Remember, that, regarding tribal/two house identity over the generations, Joseph = Ephraim = Israel:

*"Behold, I am bringing them from the north country, And I will gather them <u>from the remote parts of the earth</u> ... I will lead them; I will make them walk by streams of waters, On a straight path in which they will not stumble; **For I am a father to Israel, And Ephraim is My firstborn**"* (Jeremiah 31:8-9).

[Don't get confused by this "firstborn" reference, because it is used here essentially as a legal title. Ephraim (second in birth order of Joseph's sons) is Joseph's heir, the (actual) firstborn of Jacob/Israel's favored wife Rachel and thus owns the firstborn birthright, while Joseph's elder brother Judah (fourth son of Jacob by Leah whose older brothers were disqualified by sin) is the de-facto "firstborn" son of the less-favored wife Leah, and owns the scepter birthright, so that it is his bloodline that produces Hebrew royalty, including Jesus Christ, the King of Kings.]

The prodigal son, having squandered his inheritance and finding himself destitute among the pigs (unclean Gentiles), comes to his senses and decides to repent and return to his father.

What is the inheritance that he squandered? Specifically, his inheritance included political power and authority among the twelve tribes equivalent to that of Judah, and ownership of much more land in the territory of Israel than Judah owned: two-twelfths of the land being the "double portion" for Joseph as firstborn son, which was in turn a part of the ten-twelfths of the land which was the collective wealth of the ten tribes of the house of Israel.

But his inheritance also included the broader birthright promise given by God to Abraham: the promise of many nations and vast numbers of descendants. He squandered that first by committing idolatry/adultery against God – earning the consequence of "divorce" – then, while in "the wilderness," by intermarrying with the pagan Gentiles so that the seed of the house of Israel was dispersed throughout the entire world, both geographically *and genetically*.

Upon his return he begs forgiveness and the father restores him:

*"And the son said to him, 'Father, I have sinned against heaven and in your sight; I am no longer worthy to be called your son.' But the father said to his slaves, 'Quickly **bring out the best robe and put it on him, and put a ring on his hand and sandals on his feet**; and bring the fattened calf, kill it, and let us eat and celebrate; **for this son of mine was dead and has come to life again; he was lost and has been found**'* " (Luke 15:21-24).

The robe, ring and sandals are clear biblical emblems of restoration, and an unmistakable reference to the house of Israel (Joseph). [Which explains our choice of artwork for the front cover.]

While Joseph is clearly associated with perhaps the most famous robe or "outer garment" in the Bible -- the coat of many colors -- the robe and ring are actually a more direct reference to Joseph's restoration from an Egyptian dungeons and elevation to power by Pharaoh after Joseph had interpreted the king's dreams in Genesis 41:41-42:

"Pharaoh said to Joseph, 'Behold, I have set you over all the land of Egypt.' **Pharaoh took off his signet ring from his hand, and put it on Joseph's hand, and arrayed him in robes of fine linen,** *and put a gold chain about his neck."*

The sandals are a reference to the transfer of property and represent the restoration of land and property to the son (Israel).

"Now this was the custom in former times in Israel concerning the redemption and the exchange of land to confirm any matter: a man removed his sandal and gave it to another; and this was the manner of attestation in Israel" (Ruth 4:7).

[Interestingly, this verse in Ruth is part of the same paragraph in which the two houses are identified -- uniquely in all of Scripture -- by association with Rachel and Leah. Remember that the story of Ruth centers on her redemption by Boaz, perhaps the best model of the "kinsman redeemer" (a type of Christ) in all the Bible. Upon his redemption of Ruth *"All the people who were in the court, and the elders, said, 'We are witnesses.* **May the Lord make the woman who is coming into your home like Rachel and Leah, both of whom built the house of Israel'** *"* (Ruth 4:11). Boaz and Ruth begat Obed, progenitor of Jesus. Clearly, this is an example of "house of Israel" meaning all Hebrews because Boaz was Judean.]

Famously, in the Parable of the Prodigal Son, the older son was not happy with his brother's restoration. This reflects the "sibling rivalry" that exists between Judah and Israel during the age of the Gentiles but ends in the Millennial Kingdom.

"There was continual warfare between Rehoboam and Jeroboam," the Scripture reports in 2 Chronicles 12:15 beginning immediately after the division of the Davidic kingdom, Judah's and Ephraim's rivalry would wax and wane over the centuries, and will continue until the second coming of Christ to restore David's throne on the far superior foundation of His authority as King of Kings.

"Then it will happen on that day that the Lord Will again recover the second time with His hand The remnant of His people, who will remain, From Assyria, Egypt, Pathros, Cush, Elam, Shinar, Hamath, And from the islands of the sea. And He will lift up a standard for the nations And assemble the banished ones of Israel, And will gather the dispersed of Judah From the four corners of the earth. **Then the jealousy of Ephraim will depart, And those who harass Judah will be cut off; Ephraim will not be jealous of Judah, And Judah will not harass Ephraim"** (Isaiah 11:11-13).

Note the "banished" status of Israel v. the "dispersed" status of Judah in the passage above, a reminder that the "marriage" relationship of Judah and God was never broken.

Thus in the parable the elder son Judah appeals to the fact of his longstanding (relatively better) loyalty compared to the prodigal son as a justification for his anger toward Israel.

Significantly, the setting of this parable is the Holy Land, where modernly the house of Judah has been formally gathering at least since the Balfour Declaration of 1917, and at a much faster pace since the establishment of the State of Israel in 1948. Also, as many people from the house of Israel (Christians) have settled there as the Jews reluctantly allow.

Validation by Isaiah

There is no book of the Old Testament more rich in prophecy about the coming of the Messiah and its association with the reunification of the two houses than Isaiah. Who could forget the beautiful bitter-sweet poetry of Isaiah 53, filled with specific details of the sacrifice and sorrows of Christ? But how many readers of Isaiah recognize the Two House teaching in the scriptural context? In the broadest sense, this context includes all of Chapters 40-66, but the immediate context of Chapters 50-53 is most clear and relevant.

Isaiah 50:1 begins the theme by posing the rhetorical question *"Thus says the LORD, 'Where is the certificate of divorce by which I have sent your mother away?' "* and continues with the reason for the divorce: *"... for your iniquities you [the prodigal son] have sold yourself, and for your transgressions your mother [the house of Israel] has been put away.' "* The rest of Chapters 50 through 51 then restates the theme of restoration at God's initiative despite the righteousness of his anger, just as in Hosea 1-3.

Isaiah 52 then discusses the redemption of Jerusalem at the first coming of Christ to the House of Israel. Importantly, while the historic context in which Isaiah writes is the captivity of the newly-exiled house of Judah in Babylon, the subject of *this* passage is the long-exiled House of Israel among whom Isaiah lived, a fact shown in 52:4 *"My people went down at first into Egypt to dwell there [history most closely associated with Joseph — patriarch of the House of Israel], then the Assyrians [not the Babylonians] oppressed them without cause."*

The reference to *"My Servant"* in 52:13 begins the story of the Messiah in Jerusalem, in His role as the suffering servant who *"was bruised for our iniquities [that justified our divorce]. The chastisement for our peace was upon Him. And by His stripes we are healed. All we like sheep [the "lost sheep of the house of Israel" per Matthew 15:24] have gone astray...and the Lord has laid on Him the iniquity of us all"* (Isaiah 53:5-60).

Our study will now take us to the prophecies of Jeremiah and Ezekiel for the more specific explanation of God's plan for the restoration of Israel to Himself, and to the New Testament to see its fulfillment.

CHAPTER EIGHT:

THE REMARRIAGE
OF ISRAEL TO GOD

The prophet Jeremiah lived more than a century after Hosea, and his primary focus was on the imminent desolation of Judah in 586 BC, just as Hosea's focus was on the imminent desolation of Israel in 722 BC. However, Jeremiah also prophesied about Israel, and provides additional detail about Israel's divorce and restoration.

THE DIVORCE CONUNDRUM

In Jeremiah 3, a chapter devoted almost exclusively to the house of Israel, God first states His law forbidding remarriage in the form of a rhetorical question:

"*God says, 'If a husband divorces his wife And she goes from him And belongs to another man, Will he still return to her? Will not that land be completely polluted?'* " (Jeremiah 3:1).

But a few verses later, in a prophecy about the future restoration of the two houses to the land, He identifies Himself as divorced Israel's husband

" '*Return, faithless people,' declares the Lord, 'for I am your husband. I will choose you—one from a town and two from a clan—and bring you to Zion…At that time they will call Jerusalem The Throne of the Lord, and all nations will gather in Jerusalem to honor the name of the Lord. No longer will they follow the stubbornness of their evil hearts. In those days the people of Judah will join the people of Israel, and together they will come from a northern land to the land I gave your ancestors as an inheritance'* " (Jeremiah 3:14-18).

How can this be? The answer is in the death and resurrection of God Himself, in the form of Christ, the Messiah. The married wife Israel is divorced by her husband, who then dies, resurrects and ascends to Heaven. He is transformed into a "new" persona whom the house of Israel is free to marry without defiling the land. And whomever accepts the resurrected Christ as Savior becomes a member of the Bride of Christ. At Christ's second coming the bride will be fully restored to the status of wife at the Wedding Feast of the Lamb. Thus, God redeems Israel without breaking His own law, and in the process creates a way of salvation for the Gentiles.

The prophecy of Jeremiah 16: 14-16 reveals how this will be accomplished:

" 'Therefore behold, days are coming,' declares the LORD, 'when it will no longer be said, 'As the LORD lives, who brought up the sons of Israel out of the land of Egypt,' but, 'As the LORD lives, who brought up the sons of Israel from the land of the north and from all the countries where He had banished them.' For I will restore them to their own land which I gave to their fathers. **Behold, I am going to send for many fishermen,' declares the LORD, 'and they will fish for them; and afterwards I will send for many hunters, and they will hunt them from every mountain and every hill and from the clefts of the rocks.'**"

First, note the second witness of this prophecy in Jeremiah 23:3-8, cited in the previous chapter, in which the subject is more clearly identified as the house of Israel. "*So behold...Instead, they will say, 'As surely as the LORD lives, who brought and led the descendants of the <u>house of Israel</u> from the land of the north and from all the other countries to which I had banished them.'*"

Importantly, these parallel passages prophesy about both the first and second coming of Christ, leading up to the Millennial Kingdom, but the Jeremiah 16 version identifies the *instruments* by which He will accomplish the first and second ingathering of the scattered Israelites. Remember that fishers <u>lure</u> their prey ("*I will allure her…in the wilderness,*" Hosea 2:14), while hunters <u>drive</u> their prey (Isaiah 13:19, cited below).

In His first coming He will send out fishers:

"*Now as Jesus was walking by the Sea of Galilee, He saw two brothers, Simon who was called Peter, and Andrew his brother, casting a net into the sea; **for they were fishermen**. And He said to them, '**Follow Me, and I will make you fishers of men**.' Immediately they left their nets and followed Him. Going on from there He saw two other brothers, James the son of Zebedee, and John his brother, in the boat with Zebedee their father, mending their nets; and He called them. Immediately they left the boat and their father, and followed Him*" (Matthew 4:18-22).

It is not mere coincidence that Jesus chose fishermen as His first disciples, nor that He defined their role as "fishers of men." It is a clear reference to and fulfillment of the prophecy of Jeremiah.

And who did He send these fishers of men to fish for? He made it clear: "*Go not into the way of the Gentiles, and into any city of the Samaritans enter ye not: But go rather to the lost sheep of the house of Israel.*" (Matthew 10:5-6). (We will shortly address how their mission was expanded to others but first let's finish unpacking the prophecy.)

In preparation for His second coming He will send out hunters. This is described in Isaiah 13:9-19:

"*See, the day of the Lord is coming —a cruel day, with wrath and fierce anger— to make the land desolate and destroy the sinners within it. The stars of heaven and their constellations will not show their light. The rising sun will be darkened and the moon will not give its light. I will punish the world for its evil, the wicked for their sins. I will put an end to the arrogance of the haughty and will humble the pride of the ruthless. I will make people* *scarcer than pure gold, more rare than the gold of Ophir. Therefore I will make the heavens tremble; and the earth will shake from its place at the wrath of the Lord Almighty, in the day of his burning anger. **Like a hunted gazelle, like sheep without a shepherd, they will all return to their own people, they will flee to their native land**.*"

Cross reference this to the Olivet Discourse by Jesus in Matthew 24 for its place in the end times chronology (sun and moon darkened, etc.), and then align the reference in Jeremiah 16:16 regarding "clefts of the rocks" with the sixth[th] seal of Revelation 6:12-17, especially verses 15-16:

"*I looked when He broke the sixth seal, and there was a great earthquake; and the sun became black as sackcloth made of hair, and the whole moon became like blood; and the stars of the sky fell to the earth, **as a fig tree casts its unripe figs** when shaken by a great wind. The sky was split apart like a scroll when it is rolled up; and every mountain and island were moved out of their places.* **Then the kings of the earth and the great men and the commanders and the rich and the strong and every slave and free man, hid themselves in the caves and <u>among the rocks</u> of the mountains**; *and they said to the mountains and to the rocks, 'Fall on us and hide us from the presence of Him who sits on the throne, and from the wrath of the Lamb; for the great day of their wrath has come, and who is able to stand?'* "

Interestingly, this also correlates with the prophecy of Christ the soon-coming Bridegroom in the Song of Solomon, particularly 2:10-17:

"*My beloved responded and said to me, 'Arise, my darling, my beautiful one, And come along....The time has arrived for pruning the vines...**The fig tree has ripened its figs**...*

*...<u>**my dove**</u>, **in the clefts of the rock**, In the secret place of the steep pathway, Let me see your form, Let me hear your voice; For your voice is sweet, And your form is lovely...*

*My beloved is mine, and I am his...Turn, my beloved, and **be like a gazelle**...*"

Note the symbolism linking this to related passages from other prophecies: the "*gazelle*" (Isaiah 13:14) and the "*clefts of the rocks*" (Revelation 6:15; Isaiah 2:21).

Especially intriguing is the reference to the fig tree (symbol of Judah, e.g. Jeremiah 24 and Matthew 21:19) which is shown just putting forth leaves at the start of the last pre-millennial generation (Matthew 24:32-34) but later at the close of that generation, as the Bridegroom nears, the fig tree is ready to bear ripened fruit. However, the *un*ripened figs, like the unprepared virgins at the wedding feast of Matthew 25:10, are cast to the ground and "left behind" as the Bride is being resurrected and raptured (Revelation 6:13; Matthew 24:40-41).

Most importantly to our study, however, is the question of who is "hunted" during this period. That brings us to Isaiah 2:5-21:

"Come, <u>house of Jacob</u>, and let us walk in the light of the LORD…For the LORD of hosts will have a day of reckoning……Men will go into…the caverns of the rocks and the clefts of the cliffs Before the terror of the LORD and the splendor of His majesty, When He arises to make the earth tremble."

The hunted are clearly all people, not just the house of Israel. A reference to the house of Jacob here is a reference to all of the Hebrews. But, the Revelation 6:12-17 iteration shows that ALL the still-unsaved peoples of the world are included in the prophecy (v. 15). And the reference to the dove in rock clefts in the Song of Solomon iteration suggests that even in that late hour many will accept Christ and receive the Holy Spirit (dove) by which God will know them.

This hunting period appears to begin in the very last days prior to Christ's return but to also encompass the Ten Days of Wrath following the resurrection and rapture of the believers.

The hunters would seem to be the demon-possessed wicked men who hate and blaspheme God. I believe they are described in Revelation 16:9-12, during the Days of Wrath (bowl judgments), but that their rebellion against God and hatred of men begins much earlier. The hunter metaphor is found in numerous biblical passages:

First in Genesis 10:9 by reference to the Antichrist figure, Nimrod, *"a mighty hunter before the Lord."*

Then in Jeremiah 5:20…26 in reference to the victimization of Judah; *"Declare this in the house of Jacob And proclaim it in Judah….For wicked men are found among My people, They watch like fowlers lying in wait; They set a trap, They catch men."*

And then in Ezekiel 19:1-6, describing evil Judean kings Jehoahaz and Jehoiakim in identical language:

"As for you, take up a lamentation for the princes of Israel and say, 'What was your mother? A lioness among lions! She lay down among young lions, She reared her cubs. **'When she brought up one of her cubs [Jehoahaz], He became a lion, And <u>he learned to tear his prey; He devoured men</u>.** *Then nations heard about him; He was captured in their pit, And they brought him with hooks To the land of Egypt.* **'When she saw, as she waited, That her hope was lost, She took another of her cubs [Jehoiakim] And made him a young lion. And he walked about among the lions; He became a young lion, <u>He learned to tear his prey; He devoured men</u>.**"*

Note here that the "princes of Israel" in this context are Judean, not princes of the house of Israel. Could Jacob have seen a dangerous element in the posterity of his son Judah as he prophesied over him in Genesis 49:9? *"Judah is a lion's whelp; From the prey, my son, you have gone."* Could the "hunters" be wicked Jews such as George Soros and his ilk who wield such extraordinary power among the globalist elites in government policy, mass media and banking? Taking the speculation further, could these people be "*those of the synagogue of Satan, who say that they are Jews and are not*" (Revelation 3:9)? Importantly, such people are obviously not representative of all Jews but are merely the Judean version of the same challenge Christians face of "*tares among the wheat.*"

In contrast to all of these references to the hunters, Jesus Christ the Messiah is praised in the magnificent Psalm 91 as the one who delivers His own from the hunter's trap (v.2-4): "*I will say of the LORD, He is my refuge and my fortress: my God; in him will I trust. <u>Surely he shall deliver thee from the snare of the fowler</u>, and from the noisome pestilence. He shall cover thee with his feathers, and under his wings shalt thou trust….*" [Note also the special implication for the house of Judah in this Psalm – foreshadowing Christ's allusion to Himself as a mother hen and the Jews as chicks in Matthew 23:37-39.]

Likewise, Psalm 124, especially verses 6-8, offers praise to God for deliverance from the hunter. "*Blessed be the LORD, who hath not given us as a prey to their teeth. <u>Our soul is escaped as a bird out of the snare of the fowlers: the snare is broken, and we are escaped</u>. Our help is in the name of the LORD, who made heaven and earth.*"

Lastly, look how all of the above themes are encapsulated in Hosea 10:11: "*Ephraim is a trained heifer that loves to thresh; so I will put a yoke on her fair neck. I will drive Ephraim, Judah must plow, and Jacob must break up the ground.*" Notice the association of Ephraim with the "wheat" of Christianity and the last days threshing process, and the fact that God "*drives*" Ephraim, while already compliant Judah is shown in the same yoke (the two together as "*Jacob*"), plowing (the Holy Land).

THE EXPANSION OF THE HOUSE OF ISRAEL

As we have previously noted, God has always welcomed non-Hebrews into the house of Jacob, and in that sense His people have always been a "mixed multitude," as the nation was described in Exodus 12:38.

It should therefore be no surprise that God's plan for the salvation of the Gentiles would involve His invitation to all people in the world to enter into the household of Israel on the same terms that He invited back the "lost sheep" of Israel -- the "natural branches" of the olive tree of Romans 11. That divine system for redemption and restoration is in fact the plan of salvation that we Christians have always understood in other terms.

Importantly, since Judah was never divorced by God, it has always been possible for any person to approach God through the house of Judah, even in the age of the Gentiles. But that is an exceptionally hard and unnecessary road compared to the astonishing freedom and blessing anyone can have in Christ by simply believing and abiding in Him. And most importantly, **those of the household of Judah must still accept Christ before they can complete their journey to**

God, and that won't occur until the close of the age of the Gentiles (Romans 11:25-26). As Jesus said, "*I am the way, the truth, and the life, <u>no one</u> may come to the Father except by me*" (John 14:6).

In short, when Christ came to redeem the house of Israel, he opened the door to everyone: Romans 10:9-13:

"*That if thou will confess with thy mouth the Lord Jesus, and will believe in thine heart that God hath raised him from the dead, thou shalt be saved. For with the heart man believeth unto righteousness; and with the mouth confession is made unto salvation. For the scripture saith, Whosoever believeth on him shall not be ashamed. For there is no difference between the Jew and the Greek: for the same Lord over all is rich unto all that call upon him.* For <u>whosoever</u> shall call upon the name of the Lord shall be saved.*"

(In light of our study it would seem that the reason for the requirement to believe that Jesus rose from the dead was perhaps not limited to acknowledging His power over death, but was also an attitudinal legal prerequisite for Israelites. If they did not acknowledge that the husband had passed through death, thus nullifying the restriction in both Deuteronomy 24:1-4 and Matthew 5:32, they would be seen as condoning the illegal "remarriage" of divorced Israel to God).

Nevertheless, the invitation went first to the Hebrews of Israel, then to rest of the world, including both the Hebrews of Judah and to non-Hebrews.

THE TWELVE, THE SEVENTY, AND THE CHURCH

- **The Twelve**

We have already discussed the Lord's sending out of His twelve disciples exclusively to the lost sheep of the house of Israel. He made clear that this was His own exclusive mission as well in Matthew 15:21-24:

"*Jesus went away from there, and withdrew into the district of Tyre and Sidon. And a Canaanite woman from that region came out and began to cry out, saying, 'Have mercy on me, Lord, Son of David; my daughter is cruelly demon-possessed.' But He did not answer her a word. And His disciples came and implored Him, saying, 'Send her away, because she keeps shouting at us.'* **But He answered and said, 'I was sent only to the lost sheep of the house of Israel.'** *But she came and began to bow down before Him, saying, 'Lord, help me!' And He answered and said, 'It is not good to take the children's bread and throw it to the dogs.' But she said, 'Yes, Lord; but even the dogs feed on the crumbs which fall from their masters' table.' Then Jesus said to her, 'O woman, your faith is great; it shall be done for you as you wish.' And her daughter was healed at once.*"

Yet, even as He limited the first stage of His ministry to a specific population in this exchange with the Canaanite woman, the context clearly foreshadows the salvation of the Gentiles.

- **The Seventy**

Some time later, Jesus sent out seventy disciples with a different, broader mandate: *"Now after this the Lord appointed seventy others, and sent them in pairs ahead of Him to every city and place where He Himself was going to come"* (Luke 10:1).

This time He sent them to the cities he intended to minister in. The number seventy (or seventy-two in some translations) is a reference to the Table of Nations in Genesis 10 and 11 -- the list of nations established by the immediate descendants of Noah -- which symbolically represent all the nations of the world. In that sense, the sending of the seventy implies an invitation to salvation sent out to all the world.

The Gospel of Luke does not list those cities, indicating only that *"He was passing through from one city and village to another, teaching and proceeding on His way to Jerusalem"* (Luke 13:22). In other words, He passed through Galilee and Samaria (Luke 17:11) to Judea. Several of the cities are identified in Matthew, beginning in Chapter 19: *"When Jesus had finished these words He departed from Galilee, and came into the region of Judea beyond the Jordan"* (19:1). They include Jerusalem (20:17), Jericho (20:29), Bethphage (21:1) and Bethany (26:6) all of which were in Judea.

So, while the invitation to salvation in Christ was extended beyond the ethnic boundaries of the house of Israel, the emphasis remained for a time on the Hebrews of both houses.

Indeed, as we have shown in a prior chapter, this remained the emphasis of Jesus until His ascension and then remained the emphasis of the apostles for another 3 ½ years until the martyrdom of Steven and anointing of Paul as the apostle to the Gentiles.

"He came to His own [house of Jacob], and those who were His own did not receive Him. But as many as received Him, to them He gave the <u>right to become</u> children of God [house of Israel], even to those who believe in His name, who were born, not of blood, nor of the will of the flesh, nor of the will of man, but of God" (John 1:11-13).

Because they (the house of Judah as a whole) did not receive Him, Jesus pronounced judgment on the house of Judah in Matthew 23:37-39. Steven delivered the final recitation of the charges and pronouncement of the sentence in Acts 7:1-53 (and, being a type of Christ, symbolically received the death sentence upon himself in 7:54-60). And Paul then received his own Holy Spirit-issued mantle of authority through which he was empowered to explain how and why salvation was extended to non-Hebrews – teachings that run through all of his writings.

• **The Church**

Again, it is Jesus who sets the agenda to be followed by the church in due season:

"*[G]o and make disciples of <u>all nations</u>, baptizing them in the name of the Father and of the Son and of the Holy Spirit, and teaching them to obey everything I have commanded you. And surely I am with you always, to the very end of the age*" (Matthew 28:19-20).

This is His final command to the church, and His declaration of the fulfillment of the Father's promise to Abraham that "*through your seed shall ALL the families of the earth be blessed*" (Genesis 22:18).

Yet the starting date for this agenda awaits the anointing of Paul, after which the church begins to harvest souls outside of the house of Jacob (Acts 10).

Paul explains God's plan in Romans 9-11, a prophetically-rich portion of scripture which is greatly illuminated by an understanding of the Two House prophecy.

This is also the appropriate point to address some of the erroneous, anti-Semitic doctrines that sprang up (but significantly diverged) from the sound, pro-Semitic Two House teaching of writers such as J.H. Allen. Invariably, these doctrines purported to vest in their adherents the status of "the true Israel" while excluding all Hebrews and/or "the Jews," and/or "Blacks, and/or "Whites." Often, the foundation stone of these doctrines is the idea that salvation is exclusive to Israel per Matthew 10 and 15, and then "Israel" is interpreted to be the believers in the particular doctrine. The "Christian Identity" and "Black Israel" adherents are two such groups.

A Two House analysis of Paul's treatise on Israel clears away the confusion. By use of contextual clues it is relatively easy to see how Paul distinguishes the house of Jacob (both houses together), the house of Judah and the house of Israel in telling the story of salvation.

He begins with the house of Jacob:

9:3-5 "*For I could wish that I myself were accursed, separated from Christ for the sake of my brethren, my kinsmen according to the flesh, who are Israelites, to whom belongs [1] the adoption as sons, [2] and the glory [3] and the covenants [4] and the giving of the Law [5] and the temple service [6] and the promises, whose are the fathers, and from whom is the Christ according to the flesh, who is over all, God blessed forever. Amen.*"

"*My brethren according to the flesh*" for whom Paul prays, are defined by the six enumerated criteria that together identify them unmistakably as the entire house of Jacob (all twelve tribes). The "fathers" are then expressly identified as Abraham, Isaac and Jacob in verses 6-23.

Importantly, Paul differentiates race from grace by saying, "*they are not all Israel who are descended from Israel...but the children of the promise are regarded as descendants*" (v.8). In other words, that even among the descendants of Jacob, only those who are *called* are His *"vessels of mercy."* It is the *"election of grace"* (Romans 11:5).

Those being *called* by God are *"even us, whom He also called, not from among the Jews only, but also from among the Gentiles"* (9:24).

And by "Gentiles" in this narrow context He means the house of Israel:

"I will call those who were Not My People, 'My People,' and her who was Not Beloved, 'Beloved.' And it shall be that in the place where it was said to them, 'You are not My people, there they shall be called Sons of the Living God" (Hosea 1:10, quoted in Romans 9:25-26).

We have already seen in our study that this passage addresses the house of Israel exclusively and unmistakably, but that the house of Israel in the New Testament context means everyone who receives Christ. By definition then, the Jews who accept Christ, like Paul himself (of the Judean Tribe of Benjamin), are no longer of the house of Judah but of the house of Israel, spiritually speaking.

So is the house of Judah excluded? Or as Paul stated it in Romans 11:1 *"I say then, God has not rejected His people, has He?* -- meaning the members of the house of Jacob who have not yet accepted Christ. This includes especially the house of Judah which retains a special relationship with God through Moses *"For they [Jews] have a zeal for God, but not according to knowledge. For not knowing about God's righteousness and seeking to establish their own, they did not subject themselves to the righteousness of God. For Christ is the end of the law for righteousness to everyone who believes. For Moses writes that the man who practices the righteousness which is based on law shall live by that righteousness"* (Romans10:2-5).

The far superior path is the way of grace created by Jesus Christ at His first advent (Romans 10:6-13), but God remains long-suffering toward the Jews, saying, *"All the day long I have stretched out My hands to a disobedient and obstinate people"* (10:21)…[and yet, just two verses later, He confirms through Paul that] *"God has not rejected His people whom He foreknew"* (11:2).

The entire eleventh chapter of Romans is then devoted to the fate of the remainder of the house of Jacob who have yet to receive Christ but will do so when *"the fullness of the Gentiles has come in, and so all Israel will be saved"* (v.26a).

When does this occur in the last days timeline? When…*"the Deliverer will come from Zion, He will remove ungodliness from Jacob"* (11:26b, quoting Isaiah 59:20). That event is described most clearly in Zechariah 14:1-5 and Revelation 19:11-21, but its *effect* is best stated in Zechariah 12:10:

"I will pour out on the house of David and on the inhabitants of Jerusalem, the Spirit of grace and of supplication, so that they will look on Me whom they have pierced; and they will mourn for Him, as one mourns for an only son, and they will weep bitterly over Him like the bitter weeping over a firstborn."

The Jews will finally recognize their Messiah and be forgiven their sins.

But in conclusion, to reiterate and confirm the greater point of this section -- that the plan of salvation for the house of Israel also opened the door of salvation to the non-Hebrew Gentiles -- we turn to a small portion of Paul's beautifully-reasoned Letter to the Galatians, called by many in the church today the *Magna Carta* of Christian Liberty.

"*Know ye therefore that they which are of faith, the same are the children of Abraham.* **And the scripture, _foreseeing that God would justify the heathen through faith_, preached before the gospel unto Abraham, saying, 'In thee shall <u>all</u> nations be blessed.'** *So then they which be of faith are blessed with faithful Abraham....Now to Abraham and his seed were the promises made. He saith not, And to seeds, as of many; but as of one, And to thy seed, which is Christ....[Thus] We are all the children of God by faith in Christ Jesus. For as many of you as have been baptized into Christ have put on Christ. There is neither Jew nor Greek, there is neither bond nor free, there is neither male nor female: for ye are all one in Christ Jesus. And if ye be Christ's, then are ye Abraham's seed, and heirs according to the promise*" (Galatians 3:7-29).

CHAPTER NINE:

THE RETURN TO THE LAND

DID ISRAEL RETURN FROM BABYLON WITH JUDAH?

It is commonly taught in modern churches that the house of Israel returned to the Holy Land with the house of Judah at the end of the Babylonian exile, but that is largely untrue.

There were, of course, individual members of all twelve tribes in both houses, and some trickled back to the Holy Land over the centuries. The Apostle Paul notes their presence in his testimony to Herod Agrippa in Acts 26:6-7: "*And now I am standing trial for the hope of the promise made by God to our fathers; the promise to which our twelve tribes hope to attain, as they earnestly serve God night and day.*"

However, it was common knowledge in the days of the early church that the large majority of Israelites never returned to the Holy Land. The historian Flavius Josephus records this fact in *Antiquities of the Jews* (11:133, 93 AD): "the ten tribes are beyond the Euphrates till now, and are an immense multitude and not to be estimated in numbers." And the Apostle James begins his epistle: "*James, a bond-servant of God and of the Lord Jesus Christ, to the twelve tribes who are <u>dispersed abroad</u>: Greetings*" (James 1:1).

1 Chronicles was written more than a century after Ezra and Nehemiah led the newly freed Jews to Jerusalem from Babylon, and it states that Israel remained in exile "*to this day*." The context from which this is drawn is a commentary on the genealogy of Reuben, which was the first of the ten tribes captured and relocated by the Assyrians along with Gad and Manasseh long before 722 BC. While this particular passage is silent on the other tribes of the Kingdom of Israel, there is no indication anywhere in Scripture that the other seven did not remain with these three. They are nearly always addressed as a single entity.

Let's look at the context of 1 Chronicles 5:23-26, because it also acknowledges another important factor in determining the fate of the Israelites:

"*Now **the sons of the half-tribe of Manasseh** lived in the land; from Bashan to Baal-hermon and Senir and Mount Hermon they were numerous. **These were the heads of their fathers' households**, even **Epher, Ishi, Eliel, Azriel, Jeremiah, Hodaviah and Jahdiel, mighty men of valor, famous men, heads of their fathers' households**. But they acted treacherously against the God of their fathers and played the harlot after the gods of the peoples of the land, whom God had destroyed before them. So the God of*

*Israel stirred up the spirit of Pul, king of Assyria, even the spirit of **Tilgath-pilneser king of Assyria, and he carried them away into exile, namely the Reubenites, the Gadites and the half-tribe of Manasseh, and brought them to Halah, Habor, Hara and to the river of Gozan, <u>to this day</u>.**"*

Note carefully the governmental system implied by the identification of the tribal leaders in this manner. These were the important oligarchs or warlords of the tribe of Manasseh, and it is safe to say that no matter how many members may have repatriated themselves back in the Holy Land, the legal and practical "ownership" and identity of the tribe of Manasseh was vested in these patriarchal leaders.

Let's now consider the matter of tribal identity in relation to the chronology of events relating to the removal of Israel and Judah from the Holy Land (dates are approximate).

*   United Monarchy of Israel divided into Kingdoms of Judah and Israel 930 BC.
*   Neo-Assyrian Empire established 911 BC.
*   Assyria conquers and relocates Israel north of the Euphrates 740-722 BC.
*   Babylon conquers Assyria 627-605 BC.
*   Babylon conquers and takes Judah captive 605-586 BC.
*   King Cyrus of Persia conquers Babylon 539 BC.
*   Cyrus issues decree freeing Jews 538 BC.
*   Hebrew temple reconstruction completed 516 BC.
*   1 Chronicles written probably between 400–250 BC.
*   Epistle of James written 49 AD.
*   Antiquities of the Jews written by Josephus 93 AD.

Importantly, from its very first days in 930 BC, the newly established kingdom of Israel departed from Torah-based worship and temple sacrifice, under its first king, Jeroboam:

*"Jeroboam thought to himself, 'The kingdom will now likely revert to the house of David. If these people go up to offer sacrifices at the temple of the Lord in Jerusalem, they will again give their allegiance to their lord, Rehoboam king of Judah. They will kill me and return to King Rehoboam.' After seeking advice, **the king made two golden calves. He said to the people, 'It is too much for you to go up to Jerusalem. Here are your gods, Israel, who brought you up out of Egypt.'** One he set up in Bethel, and the other in Dan. And this thing became a sin; the people came to worship the one at Bethel and went as far as Dan to worship the other. **Jeroboam built shrines on high places and appointed priests from all sorts of people, even though they were not Levites.** He instituted a festival on the fifteenth day of the eighth month, like the festival held in Judah, and offered sacrifices on the altar. This he did in Bethel, sacrificing to the calves he had made. And at Bethel he also installed priests at the high places he had made"* (1 Kings 12:28-32).

Naturally, this did not sit well with Torah-faithful Hebrews of the northern tribes:

"When Rehoboam arrived in Jerusalem, he mustered Judah and Benjamin—a hundred and eighty thousand able young men—to go to war against Israel and to regain the kingdom for Rehoboam. But this word of the Lord came to Shemaiah the man of God: ...This is what the Lord says: Do not go up to fight against your fellow Israelites. Go home, every one of you, for this is my doing.' So they obeyed the words of the Lord and turned back from marching against Jeroboam...,[However], **The priests and Levites from all their districts throughout Israel sided with [Rehoboam]. The Levites even abandoned their pasturelands and property and came to Judah and Jerusalem, because Jeroboam and his sons had rejected them as priests of the Lord when he appointed his own priests for the high places and for the goat and calf idols he had made.** ***Those from every tribe of Israel who set their hearts on seeking the Lord, the God of Israel, followed the Levites to Jerusalem to offer sacrifices to the Lord, the God of their ancestors.*** *They strengthened the kingdom of Judah and supported Rehoboam"* (2 Chronicles 11:1-17).

This had the effect of further alienating Israel from Judaism and the Torah. With the Torah-faithful (*of every tribe*) gone back to Judea, the idolatrous Israelites grew ever more entrenched in their rebellion, eventually succumbing even to outright Baal worship under Ahab and Jezebel. Israel never returned to God and was therefore "divorced" by Him. The Assyrian conquest was Israel's punishment by God's design.

That process lasted fully 208 years, but was only the beginning. It would be over 135 more years before the whole of Judah began its own exile in Babylon, and around 65 after that before the Jews returned to Jerusalem to rebuild the temple. That's around 400 total years that the Israelites had embraced paganism and rejected Judaism and temple worship. It would be illogical to assume that Israel would suddenly choose to resubmit to Judaism and to the Levites and relocate to Jerusalem.

The Bible says that the house of Israel does eventually return, in the last days and in association with the second coming of Christ and His establishment of the Millennial Kingdom, but not half a millennium before Christ's first coming, and not under the auspices of the house of Judah.

Contrast that history of the Israelites with the experience of the Judeans. The Jews' exile was only 70 years – of which just 52 years involved actual captivity in Babylon by those captured in 586 BC when the temple and the old city of Jerusalem were destroyed. Other Jews who had been taken in earlier raids, such as Daniel, had been there longer – since 605 BC in his case, but still this was the blink of an eye compared to the Israelite experience. And, of course, Jerusalem was the Jews' natural home and national capital, which was not true of the Israelites.

Moreover, all the families who returned to Jerusalem from Babylon are clearly identified in Ezra and Nehemiah as Judeans.

"Then the heads of fathers' households of Judah and Benjamin [the two tribes of the house of Judah] and the priests and the Levites [who had defected en-masse to Judah after Jeroboam's rejection of Temple worship] arose,

even everyone whose spirit God had stirred to go up and rebuild the house of the LORD which is in Jerusalem" (Ezra 1:5).

"These are the people of the province who came up from the captivity of the exiles whom Nebuchadnezzar the king of Babylon had carried away, and who **returned to Jerusalem and Judah, <u>each to his city</u>**" (Nehemiah 7:6).

As we have acknowledged, some Israelites of the ten Tribes did return to the Holy Land over the years, but the Bible makes clear they were relatively few in number: *"though your people, O Israel, may be like the sand of the sea, Only a remnant within them will return"* (Isaiah 10:20-22). Only in conjunction with the second coming of Christ will the ten Tribes themselves return in large numbers.

Again, note the phrase *"heads of fathers' households of Judah and Benjamin"* in Ezra 1:5, making clear that Hebrew tribal identity is still vested in the ruling families or oligarchy, not the general population. No similar recognition of the leadership of any of the ten tribes in the Holy Land is found in Scripture following their exile, even centuries later at the time of Jesus' earthy ministry. In those days He referred to the Israelites collectively as *"the lost sheep of the house of Israel."* And (unlike Judah) the part of the Holy Land most of them lived in was called "Galilee of the Gentiles," not by the names of any of the ten tribes.

Even in Galilee, however, the majority of the Hebrews were not Israelites but Judeans. Following is an excellent summary of the evidence from a Christian Holy Land travel website:

> "Archaeological research now reveals no human occupation of the Galilee during the sixth and seventh centuries BCE. A few scattered, small settlements began to appear in following centuries, mostly military outposts and a few small farming communities which sent their harvests to the coastal cities. The same conclusions can be drawn from the excavations of major sites as well. So Galilee remains essentially empty for more than half a millennium following the Assyrian invasions.
>
> The archaeological evidence reveals a sudden change about the start of the first century BC. Over a period of a couple decades, dozens of new villages appear. This indicates that a new, rather large, population comes into Galilee. The trend continues for the next half century or so, with many new settlements appearing and then growing larger.
>
> Who were these new inhabitants? These new archaeological findings indicate that they were transplanted Judeans. The ancient historian Josephus relates how Alexander Jannaeus, the King of Israel from 102 to 76 BC, extended the northern boundary of his Judean-centered country into Galilee during his reign using military means.

The archaeology reveals that the new inhabitants were Judeans. First, the currency of the region is now that of the Judean Janneaus and his successors; it is not that of the coastal cities or of Damascus further north in Syria. Second, excavated village areas reveal the same interest in religious purity common among Judeans, with ritual baths cut out of the bedrock and houses that contained stone bowls, cups and plates that were impervious to impurity. Third, the Galileans followed a Judean diet in that they did not eat pork; no pig bones are found in the garbage dumps.

So the archaeological research of recent decades now shows that the Galilean population of Jesus' time were descendants of Judean immigrants of a century or so earlier."⁹

Neither were the people called "Samaritans" Israelites either. It was the practice of the Assyrians to displace conquered peoples and repopulate their lands with conquered people from other lands, thus limiting the potential for rebellion against Assyrian control. They did this in Israel, removing all Israelites from the territory and repopulating the southern half of it, later known as Samaria, leaving the Galilean region largely unpopulated:

"*The king of Assyria brought men from Babylon and from Cuthah and from Avva and from Hamath and Sepharvaim, and settled them in the cities of Samaria <u>in place of the sons of Israel</u>. So they possessed Samaria and lived in its cities. At the beginning of their living there, they did not fear the LORD; therefore the LORD sent lions among them which killed some of them. So they spoke to the king of Assyria, saying, 'The nations whom you have carried away into exile in the cities of Samaria do not know the custom of the god of the land; so he has sent lions among them, and behold, they kill them because they do not know the custom of the god of the land.' Then the king of Assyria commanded, saying, "Take there one of the priests whom you carried away into exile and let him go and live there; and let him teach them the custom of the god of the land." So one of the priests whom they had carried away into exile from Samaria came and lived at Bethel, and taught them how they should fear the LORD. But every nation still made gods of its own and put them in the houses of the high places which the people of Samaria had made, every nation in their cities in which they lived.....They feared the LORD and [also] served their own gods according to the custom of the nations from among whom they had been carried away into exile*" (2 Kings 17:24-33).

So the Samaritans were non-Hebrews who had adopted the corrupt form of Hebrew worship invented by Jeroboam. They were neither ethnically, nor spiritually the descendants of Jacob, but occupied roughly half of the former territory of the Northern Kingdom of Israel.

IF NOT AFTER THE BABYLONIAN EXILE THEN WHEN?

First we will consider Isaiah's prophecy and commentary regarding the removal of the house of Israel from the Holy Land.

Isaiah Chapter 11 contains one of the most recognized and quoted descriptions of the coming Millennial Kingdom when Christ will rule the earth from Jerusalem as the King of Kings. That thousand-year reign will be the glorious crescendo of the creation story, the Sabbath "day" when:

"The wolf also shall dwell with the lamb, and the leopard shall lie down with the kid; and the calf and the young lion and the fatling together; and a little child shall lead them. And the cow and the bear shall feed; their young ones shall lie down together: and the lion shall eat straw like the ox. And the sucking child shall play on the hole of the asp, and the weaned child shall put his hand on the cockatrice's den. They shall not hurt nor destroy in all my holy mountain: for the earth shall be full of the knowledge of the LORD, as the waters cover the sea. And in that day there shall be a root of Jesse, which shall stand for an ensign of the people; to it shall the Gentiles seek: and his rest shall be glorious" (verses 6-10).

Yet, while that is the happy ending to the prophecy given to Isaiah, the beginning is a tale of rebellion against God by the entire house of Jacob, and bitter conflict between the houses of Judah and Israel. And interspersed throughout are glimpses of the Messiah whose first and second coming will be intimately connected with the rivalry and reunion of the two houses.

The first four chapters of Isaiah are addressed alternately to Judah (1:1, 2:1, 3:1, 4:3) and to all of Jacob (2:5) in the form of chastisement, but in Chapter 5 the waywardness of the house of Israel and its imminent banishment from the presence of God (by the hand of the Assyrians) begins to be invoked as a special warning to the house of Judah:

*"**And now, O inhabitants of Jerusalem and men of Judah, Judge between Me and My vineyard.** What more was there to do for My vineyard that I have not done in it? Why, when I expected it to produce good grapes did it produce worthless ones? So now let Me tell you what I am going to do to My vineyard: I will remove its hedge and it will be consumed; I will break down its wall and it will become trampled ground. I will lay it waste...**For the vineyard of the LORD of hosts is the house of Israel**"* (Isaiah 5:3-7).

Then in Chapter 7 comes the prophecy of the Messiah in the midst of a literal war between Israel and Judah. It is delivered to Ahaz, King of Judah in the depths of his despair about the military alliance of Israel and Assyria which has attacked Jerusalem:

*"Now it came about in the days of Ahaz...king of Judah, that Rezin the king of Aram and **Pekah...king of Israel, went up to Jerusalem to wage war against it**, but could not conquer it. When it was reported to the house of David, saying, 'The Arameans have camped in Ephraim,' his heart and the hearts of his people shook as the trees of the forest shake with the wind. Then the LORD said to Isaiah, 'Go out now to meet Ahaz...and say to him, 'Take care and be calm, have no fear and do not be fainthearted...[their plan against you] shall not stand nor shall it come to pass...**within another 65 years Ephraim [the house of Israel] will be shattered, so that it is no longer a people...If you will not believe, you surely shall not last**"* (Isaiah 7:1-9).

All looks lost to Ahaz, but God wants to show him that this war and the lasting hostility that it will engender between the two houses is part of a much, much bigger plan for the salvation of the world. Note here the apparent double meaning of the last phrase, *"If you will not believe, you surely shall not last"*: to Ahaz an exhortation not to shrink from a battle God intends him to win, but at the same time to the reader a proclamation of the key to salvation that is repeated continuously through the New Testament -- the concept of *abiding in Christ* (e.g. John 15:6). It is the phrase in the text that abruptly segues from history to prophecy, that pivots from the house of Israel in one of its darkest hours of sin, to the coming sunrise of the Messiah that will illuminate the path of Israel out of the wilderness and back to the Holy Land:

"Then the LORD spoke again to Ahaz, saying, 'Ask a sign for yourself from the LORD your God; make it deep as Sheol or high as heaven. 'But Ahaz said, 'I will not ask, nor will I test the LORD!' Then [Isaiah] said, 'Listen now, O house of David! [Judah], Is it too slight a thing for you to try the patience of men, that you will try the patience of my God as well? Therefore **the Lord Himself will give you a sign: Behold, a virgin will be with child and bear a son, and she will call His name Immanuel'** *"* (Isaiah 7:10-14) …

…*"there will be no more gloom for her who was in anguish; in earlier times He treated the land of Zebulun and the land of Naphtali with contempt [territory of the house and kingdom of Israel], but later on He shall make it glorious, by the way of the sea,* **on the other side of Jordan, Galilee of the Gentiles. The people who walk in darkness Will see a great light…For a child will be born to us, a son will be given to us; And the government will rest on His shoulders; And His name will be called Wonderful Counselor, Mighty God, Eternal Father, Prince of Peace. There will be no end to the increase of His government or of peace, On the throne of David and over his kingdom, To establish it and to uphold it with justice and righteousness From then on and forevermore"** (Isaiah 9:1-7).

Both by key prophetic clues and by contextual arrangement Isaiah clearly associates the coming of the Messiah with the house of Israel.

How will this plan of salvation come about? The explanation begins with the very next verse:

"The zeal of the LORD of hosts will accomplish this. The Lord sends a message against Jacob, And it falls on Israel. And all the people know it, That is, Ephraim and the inhabitants of Samaria…So the LORD cuts off head and tail from Israel" (Isaiah 9:7d-14).

It is accomplished through the divorce and subsequent allurement of the house of Israel.

ISRAEL'S FIRST AND SECOND RETURN TO THE LAND

- ### The First Return

Thus far in this book we have made mention of just the second of two waves of returning Northern Kingdom Israelites to the Holy Land, because that is the most significant of the two in that it metaphorically encompasses the house of Israel as a whole. However, Isaiah testifies of the return of a small number of Israelites following the fall of Assyria but preceding the first coming of Christ.

"Now in that day the remnant of Israel, and those of the house of Jacob who have escaped, will never again rely on the one who struck them [Assyria], but will truly rely on the LORD, the Holy One of Israel. **A remnant will return, the remnant of Jacob, to the mighty God.** <u>**For though your people, O Israel, may be like the sand of the sea, Only a remnant within them will return**</u>*"* (Isaiah 10:20-22).

We have already seen these returnees mentioned in Isaiah 9:1-2: *"in…* **the land of Zebulun and the land of Naphtali***…[known in the time of Jesus as]* **Galilee of the Gentiles***. The people who walk in darkness will see a great light."*

This is why there were "lost sheep" of Israel in Galilee at the time of Christ, and why during the same general time period the Apostle Paul could testify truthfully to King Herod Agrippa in Acts 26:6-7 that *"I stand on trial because of my hope in the promise that God made to our fathers,* **the promise our** <u>**twelve tribes**</u> **are hoping to realize as they earnestly serve God day and night***."* There was a remnant of all the tribes in the land, some under the auspices of the house of Judah and its system of synagogue worship (including some members of the ten northern tribes who had long before defected to Judea immediately after the formation of the kingdom of Israel – 2 Chronicles 11:16), and others who were "lost" in paganism of various sorts. But it was only a remnant.

- ### The Second Return

"And it shall come to pass in that day, that **the Lord shall set his hand again** <u>**the second time**</u> **to recover the remnant of his people***, which shall be left, from Assyria, and from Egypt, and from Pathros, and from Cush, and from Elam, and from Shinar, and from Hamath, and from the islands of the sea. And* **he shall set up an ensign for the nations, and shall assemble the** <u>**outcasts**</u> **of Israel, and gather together the** <u>**dispersed**</u> **of Judah from the four corners of the earth.** <u>*The envy also of Ephraim shall depart, and the adversaries of Judah shall be cut off: Ephraim shall not envy Judah, and Judah shall not vex Ephraim*</u>*"* (Isaiah 11:11-13).

The story of the reunion and return of the two houses is told and retold in many of the Old Testament prophecies.

Hosea 1:10-11: *"Yet the time will come when Israel's people will be like the sands of the seashore—too many to count! Then, at the place where they were told, 'You are not my people,' it will be said, 'You are children of the living God.' Then the people of Judah and Israel will unite together. They will choose one leader for themselves, and they will return from exile together."*

Jeremiah 3:18: *"In those days the house of Judah will walk with the house of Israel, and they will come together from the land of the north to the land that I gave your fathers as an inheritance."*

Jeremiah 31:7: *"For thus says the LORD, 'Sing aloud with gladness for Jacob, And shout among the chiefs of the nations; Proclaim, give praise and say, 'O LORD, save Your people, The remnant of Israel.' 'Behold, I am bringing them from the north country, And I will gather them from the remote parts of the earth, Among them the blind and the lame, The woman with child and she who is in labor with child, together; A great company, they will return here. With weeping they will come, And by supplication I will lead them; I will make them walk by streams of waters, On a straight path in which they will not stumble; For I am a father to Israel, And Ephraim is My firstborn.'"*

THREE PARABLES ABOUT THE RETURN

The most detailed and direct telling of the story of the reunion and return of the Two Houses is found in Ezekiel Chapter 37. Like the parables of the Lost Sheep, the Lost Coin, and the Prodigal Son told by Jesus in Luke 15, three aspects of a larger integrated message are presented in parable form. These are the allegories of the Dry Bones, the Two Sticks, the Davidic Kingdom. Importantly, these convey virtually the same message as the Parable of the Prodigal Son, but include more end-time symbolism.

THE DRAMA OF THE DRY BONES -- EZEKIEL 37:1-14

"The hand of the LORD was upon me, and He brought me out by the Spirit of the LORD and set me down in the middle of the valley; and it was full of bones. He caused me to pass among them round about, and behold, there were very many on the surface of the valley; and lo, they were very dry... He said to me, 'Prophesy over these bones and say to them, 'O dry bones, hear the word of the LORD.' Thus says the Lord GOD to these bones, 'Behold, I will cause breath to enter you that you may come to life. I will put sinews on you, make flesh grow back on you, cover you with skin and put breath in you that you may come alive; and you will know that I am the LORD.... 'Thus says the Lord GOD, **"Come from the <u>four winds</u>, [Matt 24, Isaiah 11:13] O breath, and breathe on these slain, that they come to life.' So I prophesied as He commanded me, and the breath came into them, and they came to life and stood on their feet, <u>an exceedingly great army</u>.**" [Host of heaven narrative in Revelation 19:11-21].

"Then He said to me, 'Son of man, **these bones are the whole <u>house of Israel</u>**; *behold, they say, "Our bones are dried up and our hope has perished. We are completely cut off." Therefore prophesy and say to them, "Thus says*

the Lord GOD, 'Behold, I will open your graves and cause you to come up out of your graves, My people; and I will bring you into the land of Israel. Then you will know that I am the LORD, when I have opened your graves and caused you to come up out of your graves, My people. I will put My Spirit within you and you will come to life, and I will place you on your own land. Then you will know that I, the LORD, have spoken and done it," declares the LORD' " (Ezekiel 37:11-14).

There are multiple layers of meaning in this allegory related to our study. First we must recognize that this is NOT a reference to the Jews returning to the Holy Land in the 20th century as is so often preached by people who don't know the Two House teaching. The scripture expressly identifies the dry bones as the house of Israel, not the house of Judah -- and to eliminate all doubt about it, the two houses are unmistakably distinguished from each other just a few verses later in God's prophetic account to Ezekiel.

This first portion of the three is about the house of Israel, the "prodigal son," being brought back to life after being "dead" to the Father due to the "divorce" and banishment of Israel of the adulterous wife. "*This son of mine was dead and has come to life again*" (Luke 15:24).

It is also a teaching on the association of the house of Israel with Christianity. The promise that: "*My people [invoking Hosea 1:10-11];* **I will put My Spirit within you and you will come to life**" is the very essence of the gospel message of the New Testament. "**Even when we were dead in our trespasses,** *Because of His great love for us,* **God, who is rich in mercy, made us alive with Christ.** *It is by grace you have been saved!*" (Ephesians 2:5) and "*Now it is God who establishes both us and you in Christ.* **He anointed us, placed His seal on us, and put His Spirit in our hearts as a pledge of what is to come**" (2 Corinthians 1:21-22).

Furthermore, it is a teaching distinguishing the first and second coming of Christ, and foreshadowing the resurrection and rapture at the second coming. In the first part of the narrative, the dry bones are lying on the surface of the ground (verse 10) -- the abandoned dead in the land of desolation. Upon the first coming of Christ, those who receive Him are only figuratively/spiritually dead and simply come to life and figuratively/spiritually stand on their feet.

But notice that in the second iteration of the same resurrection theme in the same Dry Bones prophecy (verse 12), the people are *actually* dead, and raised up from graves. This is what occurs at the second coming: "*The Lord Himself will descend from heaven with a loud command, with the voice of the archangel, and with the trumpet of God, and the dead in Christ will be the first to rise*" (1 Thessalonians 4:16). "*In a moment, in the twinkling of an eye, at the last trumpet; for the trumpet will sound, and the dead will be raised imperishable, and we will be changed*" (1 Corinthians 15:52). In that process they are assembled from the four winds

(Matthew 24:31), and will soon thereafter accompany the glorious return of the King of Kings as part of <u>an exceedingly great army</u> (Revelation 19:14).

So there are two returns to the land in the prophecy of the Dry Bones: a physical return to the land of Israel by the Christians of the house of Israel in the days leading to the second coming of Christ, and a second return in the glorified bodies we receive at the resurrection and rapture.

The second parable of Ezekiel 37 addresses that first return.

THE DEPICTION OF THE TWO STICKS -- EZEKIEL 37:15-23

"*The word of the LORD came again to me saying, 'And you, son of man,* **take for yourself one stick and write on it, 'For Judah and for the sons of Israel, his companions'; then take another stick and write on it, 'For Joseph, the stick of Ephraim and all the house of Israel, his companions.' Then join them for yourself one to another into one stick, that they may become one in your hand.** *When the sons of your people speak to you saying, 'Will you not declare to us what you mean by these?' say to them, 'Thus says the Lord GOD, "Behold, I will take the stick of Joseph, which is in the hand of Ephraim, and the tribes of Israel, his companions; and I will put them with it, with the stick of Judah, and make them one stick, and they will be one in My hand.' The sticks on which you write will be in your hand before their eyes. Say to them, 'Thus says the Lord GOD,* **'Behold, I will take the sons of Israel from among the nations where they have gone, and I will gather them from every side and bring them into their own land; and I will make them one nation in the land, on the mountains of Israel; and one king will be king for all of them; and they will no longer be two nations and no longer be divided into two kingdoms.** *They will no longer defile themselves with their idols, or with their detestable things, or with any of their transgressions; but I will deliver them from all their dwelling places in which they have sinned, and will cleanse them. And they will be My people, and I will be their God.*"

Two things are clear from the context: 1) that "sons of Israel" in this passage means any descendants of Jacob/Israel from any tribe, but 2) the house of Judah and house of Israel are distinct from each other as separate bases for Hebrew identity.

So the designation of the first stick: "*Judah and… the sons of Israel, his companions*" indicates that the "companions" of Judah includes members of the twelve tribes who are not technically Judeans nor Israelites of the house of Israel. They are the Hebrews from any tribe who adhere to Judaism.

However, the designation of the second stick "For…*Ephraim and all the house of Israel, his companions*" is inclusive of <u>only</u> the members of the house of Israel. This would seem to confirm that membership of the house of Israel is defined by and synonymous with membership in the Body of Christ. They are people from every tribe, tongue and nation, made "children of Abraham" by faith in Christ (Galatians 3:27-29).

All the "sons of Israel" (of both houses) will eventually, in the unfolding of end-time events, have one king, Yeshua Hamashiach (Jesus Christ).

THE FORETELLING OF THE DAVIDIC KINGDOM -- EZEKIEL 37:24-28

"My servant David will be king over them, and they will all have one shepherd; and they will walk in My ordinances and keep My statutes and observe them. They will live on the land that I gave to Jacob My servant, in which your fathers lived; and they will live on it, they, and their sons and their sons' sons, forever; and David My servant will be their prince forever. I will make a covenant of peace with them; it will be an everlasting covenant with them. And I will place them and multiply them, and will set My sanctuary in their midst forever. My dwelling place also will be with them; and I will be their God, and they will be My people. And the nations will know that I am the LORD who sanctifies Israel, when My sanctuary is in their midst forever."

This is the picture of the Millennial Kingdom, when Christ will rule from Jerusalem on the throne of David, over the unified house of all Israel (Israel and Judah). The Millennial Kingdom is the thousand-year "Sabbath day" of the Creation story and the model for the eternal spiritual heaven that will begin after the Great White Throne Judgment (Revelation 20:11-22:21).

Jews and Christians will live side-by-side in the Holy Land, when "*Ephraim shall not envy Judah, and Judah shall not vex Ephraim*" (Isaiah 11:13).

Cessation of hostility between Judah and Israel will mean that Christians will be welcomed to live in modern Israel in the waning days of the age of the Gentiles. That is not yet true today, as Israeli citizenship for immigrants is limited to Jews, but as the enmity of the world grows against both Christians and Jews, there will (we assume) be a reconciliation born of natural alliance. It would also seem to be a natural outcome of the growing awareness of the Two House teaching among both Jews and Christians that friendship between members of the two houses in God's plan.

CHAPTER TEN:

UNTIL SHILOH COMES

THE TWO-HOUSE PROPHECY OF JACOB

Genesis Chapter 49 contains the prophecies of Jacob over his sons Judah and Joseph (Israel), and is rich in symbolism that is helpful for interpretation of scriptural passages with Two House implications. We will consider the symbolism of the vine and the colt, as well as the implications of the Messiah being identified with Shiloh.

"The scepter will not depart from Judah, nor the ruler's staff from between his feet, until Shiloh comes and the obedience of the nations shall be his. He will tether his donkey to a vine, his colt to the choicest branch; he will wash his garments in wine, his robes in the blood of grapes" (Genesis 49:10-11).

"Joseph is a fruitful vine, a fruitful vine near a spring, whose branches climb over a wall" (Genesis 49:22). Alternately, this same verse is translated *"Joseph is a wild colt, a wild colt near a spring, a wild donkey on a terraced hill."*

THE VINE OF THE HOUSE OF ISRAEL

Just as the house of Judah is represented in scripture by the fig tree, the house of Israel (Joseph), is represented by the vine in Genesis 49. We find additional support for this in Isaiah 5:3-7:

"And now, O inhabitants of Jerusalem and men of Judah, Judge between Me and My vineyard......For the vineyard of the LORD of hosts is the house of Israel."

Now let's consider that Judah's sin in following Israel's example links Judah to the vine as well. Judah chose to follow the example of the vine and:

"Therefore this is what the Sovereign Lord says: As I have given the wood of the vine among the trees of the forest as fuel for the fire, so will I treat the people living in Jerusalem. I will set my face against them. Although they have come out of the fire, the fire will yet consume them. And when I set my face against them, you will know that I am the Lord. I will make the land desolate because they have been unfaithful, declares the Sovereign Lord" (Ezekiel 15: 6-8).

But just as Judah was defiled by following the example of Israel, he is redeemed through the same association. Jesus the Judean *"will tether his donkey to a vine, his colt to the choicest branch,"* meaning that He becomes intimately related to Israel as His bride, and in His role as Israel's redeemer becomes the rescuer of Judah as well: *"he will wash his garments in wine, his robes in the blood of grapes"* an unmistakable reference to His return as conquering king in Revelation 19, and the winepress of His wrath toward His enemies (the event at the close of the Ten Days of Awe/Wrath which causes the Jews to finally recognize Him as their Messiah).

Importantly, while God's vine is Israel, Satan's vine is Sodom. These vines produce the wicked grapes (men) whose blood marks the robes of the Messiah.

"For their rock is not like our Rock, as even our enemies concede. Their vine comes from the vine of Sodom and from the fields of Gomorrah. Their grapes are filled with poison, and their clusters with bitterness. Their wine is the venom of serpents, the deadly poison of cobras" (Deuteronomy 32:31-33).

Throughout the Bible, but especially after the Messiah has conquered His adversaries, and His Millennial Kingdom has begun, the vine and the fig tree are used as symbols of the harmony of the two houses.

1 Kings 4:25: *"So Judah and Israel lived in safety, every man under his vine and his fig tree."*

Zech 3:9-10: *"and I will remove the iniquity of that land in one day. In that day, saith the LORD of hosts, shall ye call every man his neighbour under the vine and under the fig tree."*

Micah 4:1-4: *"But in the last days it shall come to pass, that the mountain of the house of the LORD shall be established in the top of the mountains, and it shall be exalted above the hills; and people shall flow unto it. And many nations shall come, and say, Come, and let us go up to the mountain of the LORD, and to the house of the God of Jacob; and he will teach us of his ways, and we will walk in his paths: for the law shall go forth of Zion, and the word of the LORD from Jerusalem. And he shall judge among many people, and rebuke strong nations afar off; and they shall beat their swords into plowshares, and their spears into pruninghooks: nation shall not lift up a sword against nation, neither shall they learn war any more. **But they shall sit every man under his vine and under his fig tree; and none shall make them afraid: for the mouth of the LORD of hosts hath spoken it**."*

Shiloh Then and Now: This is a photo of an original water-color painting purchased by the author on his first trip to Israel in 2006 from a local artist in Shiloh, in the contested West Bank territory.

THE SIGNIFICANCE OF SHILOH

"The scepter will not depart from Judah, nor the ruler's staff from between his feet, until Shiloh comes and the obedience of the nations shall be his" (Genesis 49:10).

The leadership of the Hebrews will remain the purview of the tribe and house of Judah *"until Shiloh comes."* The context also makes clear that "Shiloh" is a reference to Jesus Christ, a Judean, and that His reign is yet a future one (since the obedience of the nations is not yet His). But the reference to Christ as "Shiloh" is unique in all of scripture, thus indicating a very special significance. Many Bible students have been baffled by this passage, but the analysis is quite simple when the Two House teaching is considered.

Shiloh was the home of God's tabernacle in the territory of Ephraim, when Joshua the Ephraimite was the Judge and leader of the Hebrews. We believe its significance is as a symbol of the authority of the house of Israel in contrast to the authority of the house of Judah (in whose territory was the first and second temple to God). When Jesus comes as "Shiloh," He comes as the Judean king of both the house of Israel and house of Judah, and high priest of a tabernacle whose authority precedes and is superior to that of the (future) third temple in Jerusalem (defiled by the Antichrist's "abomination of desolation").

TABERNACLE V. TEMPLE

Just as God's preferred system of leadership for the Hebrews was the rule of (Mosaic) law under the guidance of judges raised up during times of crisis, not kings (1 Samuel 7:4-7), His choice of dwelling place was the Tabernacle, not the Temple. The Tabernacle was ordained by God Himself while the Hebrews were under the leadership of Moses:

"And let them make me a sanctuary; that I may dwell among them. According to all that I shew thee, after the pattern of the tabernacle, and the pattern of all the instruments thereof, even so shall ye make it" (Exodus 25:8-9).

But building the temple was the choice of David the king, many years later:

"And it came to pass, when the king sat in his house, and the LORD had given him rest round about from all his enemies; That the king said unto Nathan the prophet, See now, I dwell in an house of cedar, but the ark of God dwelleth within curtains...And it came to pass that night, that the word of the LORD came unto Nathan, saying, Go and tell my servant David, Thus saith the LORD, **Shalt thou build me an house for me to dwell in?** *Whereas I have not dwelt in any house since the time that I brought up the children of Israel out of Egypt, even to this day, but have walked in a tent and in a tabernacle.* **In all the places wherein I have walked with all the children of Israel spake I a word with any of the tribes of Israel, whom I commanded to feed my people Israel, saying, Why build ye not me an house of cedar?"** (2 Samuel 7:1-7).

Yet, just as God allowed the people to reject His system of judges and replace it with their own system of kings, He allowed David's son Solomon to build the temple (2 Samuel 7:12-13). Thus, the replacement of the tabernacle with the temple is another example of God's mercy in indulging human will that departs from His own. And, just as the City of Jerusalem is synonymous with the temple, the town of Shiloh is synonymous with the tabernacle.

Importantly, the town of Shiloh was in the territory of Ephraim and was the resting place of the tabernacle of God (Joshua 18:1) until, under High Priest Eli, the people returned to idolatry and God *"forsook the tabernacle of Shiloh, the tent which he placed among men; And delivered his strength into captivity, and his glory into the enemy's hand"* (Psalms 78:55-61). The incident in which the Ark of the Covenant was captured by the Philistines is described in 1 Samuel 4.

As we know, the temple was in the territory of the tribe of Judah. It likewise was destroyed as a consequence of idolatry. Jeremiah Chapter 7 showcases God's warning of judgment against the temple, in which He invokes Shiloh as the example:

"The word that came to Jeremiah from the LORD, saying, 'Stand in the gate of the LORD'S house and proclaim there this word and say, 'Hear the word of the LORD, all you of Judah, who enter by these gates to worship the LORD!' Thus says the LORD of hosts, the God of Israel, 'Amend your ways and your deeds, and I will let you dwell in this place. Do not trust in deceptive words, saying, 'This is the temple of the LORD, the temple of the

LORD, the temple of the LORD.' ... Behold, you are trusting in deceptive words to no avail. Will you steal, murder, and commit adultery and swear falsely, and offer sacrifices to Baal and walk after other gods that you have not known, then come and stand before Me in this house, which is called by My name, and say, 'We are delivered!'—that you may do all these abominations? **Has this house, which is called by My name, become a den of robbers in your sight?** *Behold, I, even I, have seen it," declares the LORD.*

"But go now to My place which was in Shiloh, where I made My name dwell at the first, and see what I did to it because of the wickedness of My people Israel. And now, because you have done all these things,' declares the LORD...... 'therefore, I will do to the house which is called by My name, in which you trust, and to the place which I gave you and your fathers, as I did to Shiloh. I will cast you out of My sight, as I have cast out all your brothers, all the offspring of Ephraim' " (Jeremiah 7:1-15).

SHILOH AS A SYMBOL OF CHRIST THE JUDGE

As we proceed with this aspect of our study, we will find that Matthew 21 contains a wealth of essential information. Take special note of the common symbolism in Matthew 21 and Jacob's prophecies in Genesis 49.

First, we must remember that God's warning delivered by Jeremiah referred to the First Temple, invoking the specter of the tabernacle at Shiloh as the example of the consequence the people faced for idolatry. In like manner, centuries later during His first advent, Jesus Christ warned of the destruction of the second temple and invoked the first temple as the example.

"And Jesus went into the temple of God, and cast out all them that sold and bought in the temple, and overthrew the tables of the moneychangers, and the seats of them that sold doves, **And said unto them, It is written, My house shall be called the house of prayer; but ye have made it a den of thieves** *[quoting Jeremiah 7:11]....Now in the morning as he returned into the city, he hungered. And when he saw a fig tree in the way, he came to it, and found nothing thereon, but leaves only, and said unto it, Let no fruit grow on thee henceforward for ever. And presently the fig tree withered away"* (Matthew 21:12-19).

Note that Jesus specifically cites Jeremiah so as to leave no doubt as to the parallel to the first temple and its defilement. But note also the parallel symbolism of Ephraim (the vine) and Judah (the fig tree). Where Jeremiah 7:15 warns *"I will cast you out of My sight, as I have cast out all your brothers, all the offspring of Ephraim [the vine],"* Jesus curses the fig tree (Judah) in Matthew 21:19.

Compare the specific language of Jeremiah 7:

*"[T]herefore, **I will do to the house which is called by My name**, in which you trust, and to the place which I gave you and your fathers, **as I did to Shiloh**. I will cast you out of My sight, **as I have cast out all your brothers, all the offspring of Ephraim,'** "*

with that of Matthew 23:37-39:

*"**Jerusalem, Jerusalem**, who kills the prophets and stones those who are sent to her! How often I wanted to gather your children together, the way a hen gathers her chicks under her wings, and you were unwilling. '**Behold, your house is being left to you desolate! For I say to you, from now on you will not see Me until you say, 'Blessed is He who comes in the name of the Lord'**.'"*

The house of Judah, the fig tree symbolically cursed in Matthew 21:19, was *actually* cursed in Matthew 23, and in God's perfect timing suffering attack by the hand of General Titus of Rome in 70AD, and by a subsequent greater Roman attack in 135AD, it was made as desolate as Shiloh.

SHILOH AS A SYMBOL OF CHRIST THE KING

Note carefully here that immediately preceding the above passage about the cleansing of the temple in Matthew 21, is the passage detailing the triumphal entry of Jesus into Jerusalem.

*"And when they drew nigh unto Jerusalem, and were come to Bethphage, unto the mount of Olives, **then sent Jesus two disciples, Saying unto them, Go into the village over against you, and straightway ye shall find an ass tied, and a colt with her: loose them, and bring them unto me.** And if any man say ought unto you, ye shall say, The Lord hath need of them; and straightway he will send them. <u>**All this was done, that it might be fulfilled which was spoken by the prophet, saying, Tell ye the daughter of Sion, Behold, thy King cometh unto thee, meek, and sitting upon an ass, and a colt the foal of an ass**</u>. And the disciples went, and did as Jesus commanded them, **And brought the ass, and the colt, and put on them their clothes, and they set him thereon**. And a very great multitude spread their garments in the way; others cut down branches from the trees, and strawed them in the way. And the multitudes that went before, and that followed, cried, saying, Hosanna to the Son of David: Blessed is he that cometh in the name of the Lord; Hosanna in the highest"* (Matthew 21:1-9).

The prophet being cited here is not Jacob, who in Genesis 19:10-11 had said to Judah that his line would hold the royal throne *"until Shiloh comes and the obedience of the nations shall be his. **He will tether his donkey to a vine, his colt to the choicest branch**."* The prophet was Zechariah, expanding upon Jacob's prophecy:

"*Rejoice greatly, O daughter of Zion; shout, O daughter of Jerusalem:* **behold, thy King cometh unto thee: he is just, and having salvation; lowly, and riding upon an ass, and upon a colt the foal of an ass.** *And I will cut off the chariot from Ephraim [Israel], and the horse from Jerusalem [Judah], and the battle bow shall be cut off: and he shall speak peace unto the heathen: and his dominion shall be from sea even to sea, and from the river even to the ends of the earth....*

"*And the LORD shall be <u>seen over them</u>, and his arrow shall <u>go forth as the lightning</u>: and the Lord GOD shall <u>blow the trumpet</u>, and shall go with whirlwinds of the south. <u>The LORD of hosts shall defend them; and they shall devour</u>, and subdue with sling stones; and they shall drink, and make a noise as through wine; and they shall be <u>filled like bowls</u>, and as the corners of the altar. And the LORD their <u>God shall save them in that day as the flock of his people</u>: for they shall be as the stones of a crown, lifted up as an ensign upon his land...*

"**And I will <u>strengthen</u> the <u>house of Judah</u>, and I will <u>save</u> the <u>house of Joseph</u>, and I will bring them again to place them; for I have mercy upon them: and they shall be as though I had not cast them off: for I am the LORD their God, and will hear them**" (Zechariah 9:9-10:6)

Do you see the richness of this teaching about the first and second coming of Christ and their intimate association with the Two Houses? The first portion links the triumphal entry of Jesus into Jerusalem to Jacob's prophecy and to Shiloh. The second portion evokes multiple symbols of the second coming of Christ as conquering king from the Olivet Discourse and Revelation. The third portion links the reconciliation of the Two Houses to the Millennial Kingdom and identifies it as the purpose and goal of the second coming.

What is the purpose of the ass and colt symbolism? It is to identify Christ as Shiloh, and with the two Houses.

SHILOH AS A SYMBOL OF THE RETURN TO THE LAND

"*Then the whole congregation of the sons of Israel assembled themselves at Shiloh, and set up the tent of meeting there; and the land was subdued before them. There remained among the sons of Israel seven tribes who had not divided their inheritance.... They shall divide it into seven portions; Judah shall stay in its territory on the south, and the house of Joseph shall stay in their territory on the north....So the men went and passed through the land, and described it by cities in seven divisions in a book; and they came to Joshua to the camp at Shiloh.* **And Joshua cast lots for them in Shiloh before the LORD, and there Joshua divided the land to the sons of Israel [Jacob] according to their divisions**" (Joshua 18:1-10).

"*When Shiloh comes*," and the Millennial Kingdom is established, His tasks will include the restoration of the land to the tribes. As detailed in Ezekiel 48, the allocation of the territories to the tribes differs markedly from that under Joshua, but for the purposes of this study that fact only underscores the issue of authority and it's association with Shiloh. For, as we learned at the start of this section, God has made clear "*I am a father to Israel, And Ephraim is My firstborn*" (Jeremiah 31:9).

The division of the land is the task of the firstborn: the task of Joshua, the Ephramite leader of the twelve tribes, in Shiloh of the territory of Ephraim.

Yet, as King over both houses, the Messiah will at this time also ascend the throne of David, for, as God promised at the time of Solomon's betrayal *"I will humble David's descendants because of this, but not forever"* (1 Kings 11:39).

This is the site of the tabernacle/tent of meeting at Shiloh. The stone walls in the foreground form a corner of the original enclosure, while the naturally terraced hill rising behind (and curving behind the photographer out of sight) suggest seating accommodations for massive crowds of people overlooking the site.

CONCLUSION TO SECTION TWO

We have shown in this section just how central the Two House teaching is to understanding Bible history and prophecy. With this awareness, the Bible student is equipped to recognize how the teachings of Old and New Testaments intertwine and illuminate God's plan for humanity. We can also perceive the events and chronology of the last days in ways not otherwise possible.

In the light of this teaching, the prophecy of the Prodigal Son has profound implications for our personal theology. It is life-changing to know that the elder son, the house of Judah, was never "divorced" by God despite its extreme rebellion, and that God has a special dispensation for the Jews separate from the Christians (but not from Christ) -- and that Christianity IS the house of Israel, extending the invitation to salvation to "all the families of the earth" through grace by faith -- and that this division and restoration of the two Hebrew houses is the very purpose and plan of the Gospel of Jesus Christ!

But it is also greatly disruptive to a number of long-held assumptions in mainstream Christian tradition. Just summarizing these facts outside of the carefully reasoned totality of the study we have just completed could easily cause division through misunderstanding. But our love of truth must be stronger than our desire for the comfort of tradition, and if it is we can be set free from the expectations of men and work more closely with the Holy Spirit in the process of our sanctification and in our preparation for our soon-coming co-regency with Yeshua in His Millennial Kingdom.

SECTION THREE

WHAT COMES NEXT?

An Assessment of the Imminency of the Close of the Age Based upon the Extent of Lawlessness and Insanity in American Society

Introduction to Section Three

Author's Note: In the previous sections, the style of this book has been objective, scholarly and heavily Scripture-based. It has emphasized doctrine and theology using careful reasoning from the biblical world-view. This final section will have a somewhat different style. It will continue to be heavily Scripture-based in matters related to doctrine and theology, but it will also take on the challenge of making tentative predictions about the future based upon cultural and political factors and social trends in the church and the world. For this task I will draw upon my personal experience and insights as a long-time lawyer, pastor and "culture warrior" and offer some subjective perspectives and conclusions in the first person. Some of this will be more in the editorial style, and some in the style of personal testimony.

A Word to the Wise and the Wise-Guys

Human nature virtually guarantees that many people interested enough in the subject of prophecy to pick up a book like this will turn first to this section. Some will be most interested in whether I agree with their denominational position on the tribulation -- whether I am pre-trib, post-trib or mid-trib -- and the most zealous of these will be ready to toss the book aside if I do not agree with them. Some will be more interested in whether I have set a date for the rapture. Still others will simply want to skip ahead to find out what my conclusions are without having to consider the strength of my reasoning.

But this book is not about re-stating or defending any of the traditional views on prophecy. It is not about date-setting, nor numerical calculations of times and dates and calendars. It does not *prophesy* anything (as that term is commonly understood) – except that God's plan will unfold as He chooses.

This book is instead written to define and articulate the biblical worldview as understood from the Hebrew cultural perspective of the apostles, especially as that worldview applies to the study of prophecy. And the value of its conclusions is in some ways less important than in the reasoning process I used to get there, because my greater goal is to promote critical thinking through active engagement with biblical teachings and concepts.

To the religious tribalists encamped on various positions regarding the tribulation, I challenge you to set aside any denominational training you may have received and give honest consideration to a very different set of presuppositions and conclusions. You will find some agreement and some disagreement with each of the traditional camps, but they will be presented within an alternative paradigm in which many of the factors are re-aligned.

To those who want to know if I have set a date for the rapture, the answer is yes and no, but you'll need to read the book to know what I mean by that.

To those wanting to skip to the conclusions without learning the reasoning process, please know that the conclusions are scattered throughout the book in the context of the arguments they are based upon. This section is not a summary of what came before, but a separate discussion about how the last days *may* unfold based upon current events and trends.

Thus Sayeth the Lord?

What you will notice in this section (and throughout the book) is that I do not claim "Thus sayeth the Lord" for any of my assertions (other than citing Scripture itself).

I have just offered a prediction that many people would start reading this book here, to "cut to the bottom line." Importantly, that assertion is not "prophecy," but an example of both inductive and deductive reasoning, and this distinction should be kept in mind as you read this book. Indeed, the equating of "prophecy" exclusively with "predicting the future" is a significant but common error in Christendom.

Yes, prophecy can include predictions, but the primary Hebrew word for prophet is *Nabi* (naw bee), meaning "one from whom the truth of God bubbles up" like a spring of living water. Two other Hebrew words translated to prophet in English are *Roeh* which means "seer of visions" and *Hozeh* which means a "seer" who is also a musician (as in the School of the Prophets – the *Nabiim* – in 1 Samuel 19:18-23). The Greek word *prophétés* means "interpreter of God's will."

To falsely claim to speak for the Lord in a prophetic manner, when you're really speaking from your own imagination or for your own purposes (well-intentioned or not) is actually a capital offense under the Mosaic code (Deuteronomy 18:20). So anyone attempting even to *explain* Bible prophecy (let alone proclaiming "Thus sayeth the Lord" on a matter of special revelation) does so subject to an exacting spiritual principle. As James the Just, the brother of Jesus, whom we believe was the first Bishop of Jerusalem warned in James 3:1 *"Let not many of you become teachers, my brethren, knowing that as such we will incur a stricter judgment."*

Thus, carefully grounding ones beliefs in Scripture and setting forth one's reasoning process, while maintaining scrupulous personal dedication to knowing and abiding in the objective truth of God (and not any human-created doctrine or denominational perspective) is of paramount importance.

That having been said… what comes next?

CHAPTER ELEVEN

THE LAW OF CUMULATIVE SIN

THE LAW OF CUMULATIVE SIN

Throughout the Bible we see evidence of a fundamental law that governs God's creation regarding the cumulative effect of human sin, especially upon the Holy Land, but on the entire earth as well, and, indeed all of creation (Romans 8:22). It is a corollary to the law of Sabbath which requires every seventh day (and year) to be a "Sabbath" or rest period: not primarily for the people, but *for the land.*

As one of the original laws of creation (Genesis 2:1-3), the law of Sabbath pre-dates but is an essential tenet of the Mosaic Code in Leviticus 23:3 and 25:1-12 which chapters establish God's worship-based time and order-keeping system of feasts and *shemitahs* (time cycles of sevens) for what would eventually become known as Judeo-Christian civilization.

The law of Cumulative Sin is most clearly recognized in its regulation of punishment for violating the law of Sabbath, as detailed in Leviticus 26, the entirety of which is devoted to this topic.

Leviticus 26:2-13 first restates the law of Sabbath and the promise of blessing for keeping it: "*You must keep My Sabbaths and have reverence for My sanctuary. I am the LORD. If you follow My statutes and carefully keep My commandments, I will give you rains in their season, and the land will yield its produce, and the trees of the field will bear their fruit. Your threshing will continue until the grape harvest, and the grape harvest will continue until sowing time; you will have your fill of food to eat and will dwell securely in your land...*"

Leviticus 26:14-39 then details a series of escalating punishments that grow more severe at each level of ongoing lack of repentance, ending with the final consequence: expulsion from the land (desolation). "*If, however, you fail to obey Me and to carry out all these commandments, and if you reject My statutes, despise My ordinances, and neglect to carry out all My commandments, and so break My covenant, then this is what I will do to you... But if in spite of all this you do not obey Me, but continue to walk in hostility toward Me, then I will walk in fury against you, and I, even I, will punish you sevenfold for your sins. You will eat the flesh of your own sons and daughters. I will destroy your high places, cut down your incense altars, and heap your lifeless bodies on the lifeless remains of your idols; and My soul will despise you....I will scatter you among the nations and will draw out a sword after you as your land becomes desolate and your cities are laid waste....Those of you who survive in the lands of your enemies will waste away in their iniquity and will decay in the sins of their fathers."*

Importantly, Leviticus 26:34 clarifies the primary purpose of the desolation: "*Then the land shall enjoy its Sabbaths all the days it lies desolate, while you are in the land of your enemies. At that time the land will rest and enjoy its Sabbaths. As long as it lies desolate, the land will have the rest it did not receive during the Sabbaths when you lived in it.*"

And finally, Leviticus 26:40-46 states that if the people finally repent after being removed from the land, they will be spared from total destruction by God, but will still be required pay for their sins through captivity until the land has been cleansed of the consequences of their sins. "*But if they will confess their iniquity and that of their fathers in the unfaithfulness that they practiced against Me...then I will remember My covenant with Jacob and My covenant with Isaac and My covenant with Abraham, **and I will remember the land. For the land will be abandoned by them, and it will enjoy its Sabbaths by lying desolate without them. And they will pay the penalty for their iniquity,** because they rejected My ordinances and abhorred My statutes. Yet in spite of this, when they are in the land of their enemies, I will not reject or despise them so as to destroy them.*"[10]

Leviticus 26 was prophetic of the desolation of first Israel and then Judah, with, for example, the very specific and horrific consequence of cannibalism recorded in Samaria, the capital city of Israel in 2 Kings 6:28-29 and in Jerusalem, capital of Judah, in Lamentations 4:10. And it was prophetic regarding the remedy of the desolation of both Israel and Judah for the sake of the land as best recognized regarding Judah in 2 Chronicles *36:21 "So the land enjoyed its Sabbath rest all the days of the desolation, until seventy years were completed, in fulfillment of the word of the LORD through Jeremiah.*"

The law of Cumulative Sin can be seen throughout the Bible as a law binding upon all people, not just the Hebrews. For example, when God promised the Holy Land to Abraham's descendants (through Jacob's line), He told Abraham "In the fourth generation your descendants will return here, for the iniquity of the Amorites is not yet complete" (Genesis:15:16). The accumulation of the Amorites' sin would not rise to the level of justifying God's wrath until that future time.

The growth of sin in a tribe or nation follows the same sequence as in an individual, as described in James 1:13-15: "*When tempted, no one should say, 'God is tempting me.' For God cannot be tempted by evil, nor does He tempt anyone. But each one is tempted when by his own evil desires he is lured away and enticed. Then **after desire has conceived, it gives birth to sin; and sin, when it is full-grown, gives birth to*** *death*." It is the fruit of choices made by people and nations which ripens over the course of a season, until the time of harvest.

In the case of the Amorites (Canaanites), that harvest of death/desolation of the land is described in Leviticus 18:24-28 "*Do not defile yourselves by any of these practices, for by all these things the nations I am driving out before you have defiled themselves. Even the land has become defiled, so I am punishing it for its sin [primarily incest, child-killing, homosexuality and bestiality], and the land will vomit out its inhabitants. But you are to keep My statutes and ordinances, and you must not commit any of these abominations —neither your native-born nor the foreigner who lives among you. For the men who were in the land before you committed all these abominations, and the land has become defiled. So if you defile the land, it will vomit you out as it spewed out the nations before you.*"

Regarding the final judgment on the sin accumulated during the Age of the Gentiles which will likely soon be unleashed as an early event of the thousand-year Day of the Lord, John writes in Revelation 14:18-19 "*Still another angel, <u>with authority over the fire</u>, came from the altar and called out in a loud voice to the angel with the sharp sickle,* '**Swing your sharp sickle and gather the clusters of grapes from the vine of the earth, because its grapes are ripe. So the angel swung his sickle over the earth and gathered the grapes of the earth, and he threw them into the great winepress of God's wrath.**"

Importantly, the preceding passage invokes both the "angel with authority over the fire" and the symbol of the "grapes of wrath" – a clear association with Sodom per Jude 1:7 "*just as Sodom and Gomorrah and the cities around them, since they in the same way as these angels indulged in sexual perversion and went after strange flesh, are exhibited as an example in undergoing the punishment of eternal fire.*" And per Deuteronomy 32:32-33 "*from the vine of Sodom and from the fields of Gomorrah. Their grapes are poisonous; their clusters are bitter. Their wine is the venom of serpents, the deadly poison of cobras.*"

THE TWO CATEGORIES OF SIN THAT ACCUMULATE

"Oh, Lord GOD, when You pour out Your wrath on Jerusalem, will You destroy the entire remnant of Israel?" He replied, *"The iniquity of the house of Israel and Judah is exceedingly great. The land is __full of bloodshed__, and the city is __full of perversity__. For they say, 'The LORD has forsaken the land; the LORD does not see.' But as for Me, I will not look on them with pity, nor will I spare them. I will bring their deeds down upon their own heads"* Ezekiel 9:9.

In Yeshua's Sermon on the Mount, He highlighted two sins for special notice -- murder and adultery -- emphasizing the deeper spiritual principle behind the letter of the law. *"You have heard that it was said to the ancients, 'Do not murder' and 'Anyone who murders will be subject to judgment.' But I tell you that anyone who is angry with his brother will be subject to judgment....You have heard that it was said, 'Do not commit adultery.' But I tell you that anyone who looks at a woman to lust after her has already committed adultery with her in his heart."* It happens that these two sins represent the two categories of law-breaking that are most closely associated in Scripture to the law of Cumulative Sin: murder being associated with **blood-guilt**, and adultery being representative of all forms **sexual perversion** and the spiritual equivalent of idolatry.

- **Blood-Guilt:**

The spilling of innocent blood is the first category of sin that accumulates in the land until it is full, triggering wrath.

One example is especially pertinent here, that of God's curse on Edom in Ezekiel 35:5-15 *"Because you harbored an ancient hatred and delivered the Israelites over to the sword in the time of their disaster at the final stage of their punishment, therefore as surely as I live, declares the Lord GOD, I will give you over to bloodshed and it will pursue you. Since you did not hate bloodshed, it will pursue you....As you rejoiced when the inheritance of the house of Israel became desolate, so will I do to you. You will become a desolation, O Mount Seir, and so will all of Edom. Then they will know that I am the LORD."* It must be remembered here that <u>the Edomites are the descendants of Esau, Jacob's brother</u>, giving special meaning to this prophecy in light of Yeshua's extended comments on murder *"But I tell you that anyone who is angry with his brother will be subject to judgment....But anyone who says, 'You fool!' will be subject to the fire of hell"* (Matthew 5:22).

Bloodguilt was such an important issue to the Hebrews under the Torah that any unsolved murder that occurred near the border of two towns required an investigation to determine which town bore the bloodguilt, and thus the responsibility to atone for it (Deuteronomy 21:1). Known murderers were required under the law to be hunted down by the avengers of blood, per Numbers 35:19 *"The avenger of blood is to put the murderer to death; when he finds him, he is to kill him."*

The principle of blood guilt was so well understood by Christendom prior to the present generation that it featured prominently in one of the most famous of all political speeches in American history: Abraham Lincoln's second inaugural address delivered shortly before his assassination. It is engraved on the Lincoln Memorial in Washington, D.C., containing, in pertinent part, these words:

> "If we shall suppose that American slavery is one of those offenses which in the providence of God must needs come but which having continued through His appointed time He now wills to remove....Fondly do we hope ~ fervently do we pray ~ that this mighty scourge of war may speedily pass away. Yet, if God wills that it continue until all the wealth piled by the bondsman's two hundred and fifty years of unrequited toil shall be sunk and until every drop of blood drawn with the lash shall be paid by another drawn with the sword as was said three thousand years ago so still it must be said 'the judgments of the Lord are true and righteous altogether.' "

If that was true of innocent blood spilled from slaves, what are the implications from the slaughter of millions of unborn children? And how much of that blood does it take for the cup of wrath to be filled to overflowing?

- **Sexual Perversion**

The second category of cumulative sin is sexual perversion, and we have already noted above both the biblical emphasis on homosexuality as the form of deviance most severely condemned by God, and the fact that its normalization in society is the most clearly identified harbinger of God's wrath in Scripture, from Genesis to Revelation – each time being the last "straw that breaks the camel's back" as it were. Thus, we will devote the next segment to address that phenomenon in modern society, as a gauge of how close to judgment we may be.

The Point of No Return

While the law of Cumulative Sin covered sins beyond Sabbath-breaking, especially regarding the Gentiles, there were only two remedies seen for it in the Old Testament, the primary one being Sabbath-keeping by the Hebrews (obedience). Sabbath-keeping was, essentially, the pressure-release valve that prevented the accumulation of sin from reaching the point of triggering wrath. The other remedy was total sincere repentance (sacrifice) per 2 Chronicles 7:14 "*If my people who are called by My name humble themselves, and pray and seek My face, and turn from their wicked ways, then I will hear from heaven, and I will forgive their sin and will heal their land*." However, those remedies were only available prior to the "point of no return." Once sin had accumulated to the point of triggering God's wrath, there was no remedy that would prevent the punishment from being paid by the guilty under Leviticus 26:40-45.

Yet, per that same passage (consistent with our analysis in Chapter Three), the punishment could be limited by repentance (even during the Ten Days of Awe/Wrath), preserving one's eternal relationship with God.

Thus, the willingness of people to repent is of paramount importance. And that willingness is heavily dependent upon their perception of reality, most especially the reality of God's existence and expectations. The goal of Satan and his followers, therefore, is to so thoroughly defile human society and culture with the lie and practice of self-indulgent "consequence-free" sin that people will scorn and reject repentance as a concept, let alone a necessity.

What then is the measure of imminency of God's wrath? It is the degree to which sorrow for sinfulness (the attitude the leads to repentance) is replaced by the *celebration* of sin (the very opposite of repentance). This is what Paul described in his summary of the cause and constitution of apostasy in Romans 1: "*And even as they did not like to retain God in their knowledge, God gave them over to a reprobate mind, to do those things which are not convenient; Being filled with all unrighteousness, fornication, wickedness, covetousness, maliciousness; full of envy, murder, debate, deceit, malignity; whisperers, Backbiters, haters of God, despiteful, proud, boasters, inventors of evil things, disobedient to parents, Without understanding, covenantbreakers, without natural affection, implacable, unmerciful:* **Who knowing the judgment of God, that they which commit such things are worthy of death, not only do the same, <u>but have pleasure in them that do them</u>**."

That highlighted final sentence of the chapter-long treatise defines the context or season in which wrath becomes imminent — when the attitude of the society as a whole becomes one of celebration of what God has condemned.

DO YOU CARE WHAT GOD SAYS?

A dangerous modern heresy called "gay theology" is infiltrating the Christian church at an alarming pace. Many believers, fearful of being called "haters," are trivializing the threat by calling homosexuality "just another sin."

But from Genesis to Revelation, the Bible teaches that homosexuality is NOT "just another sin." It is a symbol of extreme rebellion against God and harbinger of His wrath.

GENESIS 1:27, 2:24 God sets forth the exclusive "one flesh" paradigm for human sexuality: the lifelong, faithful union of one man and one woman created in His image for procreation.

GENESIS, 6–9; TALMUD, GENESIS RABBAH 26:5:4 After 1000 years of increasing sin, God pours out His wrath in the form of a global flood which the ancient Hebrew rabbis taught was triggered by homosexual and bestial "marriages."

GENESIS 9:13 After the flood, God creates the "bow" (rainbow) as the symbol of His authority over the earth. It is not mere "coincidence" that the "gay" movement hijacked this symbol.

GENESIS 9:24-25 Corrupted by the pre-flood homosexual culture, Noah's son Ham passes it to his son Canaan, who sexually molests his grandfather. "And Noah awoke from his wine, and knew what his younger son had done unto him. And he said, Cursed be Canaan."

GENESIS 10:19-20 Banished, Canaan and his descendants then brazenly colonize the Holy Land and introduce ritual demon worship involving child sacrifice and sexual perversion SEE ALSO LEV. 18 ESP. V. 21–28. They also establish the cities of Sodom and Gomorrah.

As portrayed in this stained glass, the rainbow was given by God as a sign of His covenant of grace... a symbol of Christ Himself.

GENESIS 19 God destroys Sodom and Gomorrah with fire and brimstone, foreshadowing the last-days destruction of the earth SEE ALSO 2 PETER 2:6, JUDE 1:7. The final insult to God is the attempted homosexual rape of the two angelic witnesses whom He sent to Sodom to confirm its wickedness V.4–5.

LEVITICUS 18 God identifies incest, homosexuality and bestiality as the sins which cause the land to "vomit out its inhabitants" V. 25. Even in this dark context homosexuality is singled out for special condemnation as "an abomination" V. 22.

JUDGES 19:15–30 ESP. V.22 Ala Sodom, the attempted homosexual rape of a Levite by the Benjamites of Gibeah leads to civil war among the Hebrew tribes.

1 KINGS 14 Solomon's reintroduction of Canaanite ritual child sacrifice and sexual perversion, including homosexuality, causes God to take the Kingdom of Israel away from him and divide it in two V. 5-13.

2 KINGS 23 Josiah is named as the most righteous of all the Kings V. 25 in part because he "broke down the houses of the Sodomites who were in the House of the Lord" V.7 – ending what Solomon had begun 300 years before.

DANIEL 11:21-39 The Antichrist figure Antiochus IV Epiphanes uses homosexuality to corrupt Hebrew male youth in his plan to turn the Jews away from God SEE ALSO 1 MACCABEES 1, ESP. V.14-16.

ROMANS 1 Homosexuality is singularly condemned as the sin associated with the "reprobate mind" and apostasy V.24-32.

1 CORINTHIANS 6 The apostle Paul warns that homosexuals cannot inherit the Kingdom of Heaven, but they can be saved and healed of homosexuality by Christ V.9-11.

1 TIMOTHY 1:9–10 Homosexuals are equated with murderers, slavers and perjurers.

2 PETER 2 Noah's flood and Sodom's incineration are invoked to warn against "destructive heresies" in the last days which are defined by "sensuality" and "the lust of defiling passions" V.10 a clear reference to homosexuality.

JUDE 1:7 Jude reaffirms that the purpose of Sodom's destruction was to warn of the consequences of unrighteousness, exemplified by "going after strange flesh."

REVELATION 6 God warns that the end-times Antichrist (a counterfeit version of the Messiah in Rev. 19:11-16) will ride forth on a white horse "conquering and to conquer" holding aloft a "bow" (likely God's symbol of authority, the rainbow) V.2.

REVELATION 11 Jerusalem is identified under the reign of the Antichrist as "symbolically... called Sodom and Egypt" V.7-8 meaning that it is known for homosexuality and pantheism.

For more information or to download a free book that explains these bullet points in a clear Biblical context visit http://www.scottlively.net/scott-lively-books/the-petros-prophecy/

The 'Red Line' of Righteousness

From the moment that society as a whole celebrates sin, God's wrath is fully justified, and it is only His bargain with Abraham about Sodom that determines the timing of its fulfilment through desolation. In Genesis 18:23-32, Abraham negotiated a stay of execution for Sodom (for Lot's sake) based upon the number of righteous people remaining among the wicked. He started with 50, and negotiated down to just 10.

Abraham pleaded: *"Far be it from You to do such a thing—to kill the righteous with the wicked, so that the righteous and the wicked are treated alike. Far be it from You! Will not the Judge of all the earth do what is right?"*

God's final "concession" (His own plan all along), was *"On account of the ten, I will not destroy it."* I believe this is the true spiritual origin of the concept of *minyan* in Jewish rabbinic tradition in which a minimum of ten men are necessary to establish a congregation/synagogue – although their own sources suggest the origin relates to the ten spies of Numbers 14:27. In any case, this "red line of righteousness," as it were, is the point of no return. Once the number of righteous men in a place drops below ten, the sword of justice falls.

This legal standard is also seen at work in the story of Noah's flood, when only eight righteous remained to enter the Ark. In the case of Sodom, only four were spared, one of whom, Lot's wife, looked back and was turned to a pillar of salt. The rest of his family, his married daughters and their husbands had succumbed to Sodomic "wokeness," which Lot was only spared from by virtue of being "grieved in his heart at the conduct of the wicked" that he nevertheless chose to put up with by keeping his home there (2 Peter 2:7-8).

The "fullness" of iniquity, then, has a clear basis of measurement, which in the case of our "last generation" means the wrath of God will not fall until the rapture/resurrection, when all the righteous will be called up for the Wedding Feast of the Lamb on the first of the Ten Days of Awe/Wrath – the Feast of Trumpets in whatever year God has scheduled that to occur.

But that is small comfort, because the Leviticus 26 rules of escalating punishment for disobedience still apply, the only hope being that repentance remains effective as a remedy to reverse the trend right up until the red line is crossed.

So where are we in the process of escalating pre-wrath punishment/tribulation?

THE EMERGING AGE OF APOSTASY

Here I will shift to a testimonial style as a first-person witness of the topics I will address.

I began writing this book just over a decade ago in 2011, at which time I had already devoted twenty years of my life to fighting the culture war as a front lines Christian social and political activist across the globe. It was not accidental (in God's plan) that the focus of my ministry was opposition to the so-called LGBT movement. The "sexual revolution" has always been led (sometimes from behind the scenes) by this small but powerful faction since it emerged in Germany in the 1860s. This sexual juggernaut is both the centerpiece of the globalist agenda (in the sociopolitical context), and the fulfilment of prophecy regarding the age of apostasy (in the religious/spiritual context).

Regarding the sociopolitical context, my first book (co-authored by Orthodox Holocaust researcher, Kevin Abrams), *The Pink Swastika: Homosexuality in the Nazi Party* (1995) details key aspects of that history and their effect on Germany. My fourth book *Redeeming the Rainbow: A Christian Response to the "Gay" Agenda* (2009), addressed the continuation of that history in the United States, which became the new center of LGBT-driven "sexual revolution" after Germany was defeated in WWII. In many ways, the German experience was the "dress-rehearsal" for the American saga of debauchery and deviance-created chaos we are living today.

In any case, for the first twenty years of my thirty year ministry, I was single focused on the sociopolitical battles – to such an extent that in 2014 the largest and most powerful LGBT organization in the world, the Human Rights Campaign, named me the top opponent of their agenda internationally, in a dossier funded by the billionaire "gay rights" activist Paul Singer. I have thus had a particularly crucial vantage point on geopolitics relative to the rise of apostasy, which, importantly, the Apostle Paul in Romans 1:18-32 (bolstered by 2 Timothy 3:1-9) describes as

1.   a spiritual phenomenon measured by cultural effects

2.   triggered by the widespread normalization of homosexuality.

So, when in 2011 the Lord turned my attention to prophecy as a parallel ministry track, I already had a unique understanding and perspective of the cause/effect relationship of LGBT activism to cultural chaos. That gave me special insights into end time prophecy, culminating in my sixth book *The Petros Prophecy: Simon Peter's Prophetic Warning About the Heresy of the Last Days* (2017). Significantly, that book began as a section of this book, but took on a life of its own through its identification of "gay theology" as a heresy which became increasingly conspicuous as the LGBT conquest of Christian churches and denominations escalated in conjunction with the legal, cultural and political imposition of "gay" marriage on the nation.

The most important references to homosexuality in the Bible are catalogued in the chart on page 172 which was created to support the claim of *The Petros Prophecy* that the sum of the parts revealing the mind of God on this issue is greater than the whole, showing that the social normalization of homosexual perversion has always been the chief harbinger of the wrath of God. The implications for that – in the context of our question "What Happens Next" – are both profound and disturbing.

THE LUCIFERIAN SCHEDULE FOR CHAOS FROM ORDER

The biblical Book of Genesis explains the order of God's creation from the establishment of time, space and matter (Genesis 1:1-19), to the introduction of living things by the order of their "kinds" (1:20-25) to the creation of humankind as a binary male/female pair created in His image (1:27), to the establishment of family from the "one-flesh" paradigm (2:24), to the establishment and refinement of human civilization as an interconnected network of families that over time formed tribes and nations with separate, often conflicting laws and interests. After several human societal failures, God chose Abraham as his agent to introduce a new covenant-based civilization in which the descendants of Abraham, Issac and Jacob would serve as examples of right and wrong, good and bad, based upon their compliance or noncompliance with His laws which He issued in stages as civilization was ready for them.

That is a short summary of the simple, satisfying and truthful story of the birth of civilization that American school-children were taught from the founding of our nation until the middle of the 20th Century, when the humanist religion of Marxism supplanted Christianity and children began being taught they were the arbitrary product of random chance, descended from pond scum by way of monkeys.

Over a few short decades, the benign social order that comported with the biblical model morphed into today's chaos of confusion and human misery we still call public schools (not to disparage the many good Christian and other morally-grounded teachers who serve as praiseworthy exceptions to the rule). The tradition of happy and innocent kindergartners sitting around a beloved teacher to hear her read stories that blessed and inspired them has been replaced by the grotesque "Drag Queen Story Hour" in which adult men dressed as clownish caricatures of women introduce the children to LGBT political propaganda and teach them to parrot it. And parrot it they have, all the way into young adulthood, where the newest fad is "transitioning" to a different gender starting with puberty blocking chemicals and ending with transsexual surgery to permanently mutilate their bodies. All to fulfill the vision of "sexual freedom" they have been taught to cherish as the most important "human right" of all. All fully endorsed, supported and celebrated by the principalities and powers of the political left.

It is a collapse into social insanity so twisted and bizarre as to seem like some LSD-induced nightmare – but it is all too real. Just ask parent Rob Hoogland of British Columbia, Canada, who in 2021 served time in jail for trying to interfere with his minor daughter's choice to "transition" to the opposite sex after that choice had been endorsed by his government in defiance of his God-given parental rights.

The satanic agenda among humankind has always been to defile and destroy human beings, individually and collectively, because we are loved by God and made in His image. In the modern age he has worked to bring chaos from order through the so-called sexual revolution, and the cornerstone of his strategy has been the LGBT agenda, because the "sexual minorities" of that coalition have always had the greatest motivation to overthrow what cultural Marxism pioneer Herbert Marcuse called "the repressive order of procreative sexuality." And so from the rise of an organized "gay" movement in the late 1940s in the form of Harry Hay's Mattachine Society, to the sharp hard left turn to hard-core LGBT militancy in the Stonewall riots of 1969, to the Supreme Court's establishment of "gay" cultural supremacy over Christianity in the four landmark rulings of Justice Anthony Kennedy (1996–2015), the LGBT movement has driven the "progress" of social change.

If you look carefully at the history of the sexual revolution in America you can see that it has dismantled civilization in the reverse order to which God established it.

First came the attack on the rule of Bible-influenced law regarding natural-family centered society. That was a multi-faceted attack in the 1950s that was driven by Alfred Kinsey's fraudulent reports wildly exaggerating Americans' level of sexual deviance, the launch of the soft pornography industry by Hugh Hefner (who called himself "Kinsey's Pamphleteer"), and a new Hollywood genre of movies normalizing adultery and fornication featuring "in-the-closet" homosexuals such as Rock Hudson. That attack continued in the 1960s with the push for "contraception on demand" (to facilitate fornication as a cultural value), the push for abortion on demand (as a back-up to contraception), and the push for "no-fault divorce" laws (to neutralize the long-standing legal penalties for adultery).

Thus, the rule of God's law in sexual and family matters was effectively broken by the 1970s, with *Roe v Wade* in '73 being the Marxists' most prized conquest. Although they were largely unseen in this process, the LGBTs provided the army of activists pushing hetero-"sexual freedom" and absolute autonomy over one's body in sexual/reproductive matters as a necessary precursor to their own "liberation" and legitimization.

Second came the attack on the foundation of the family itself -- the "one-flesh paradigm" made from the two complimentary halves of humanity – per Genesis 2:24. This was the LGB phase – the normalization of lesbianism (L), male homosexuality (G), and bisexuality (B).

That campaign ran parallel to the attack on the rule of law but took center stage in 1969 with the Stonewall Riots, when the LGBTs dropped their pretense of seeking only what Harry Hay's partner Dale Jennings had called "the right to be left alone," and began fighting for total cultural control, starting with 200 of their groups publishing the (very aggressive) first written "Gay Agenda" in 1972. Next came the takeover of the American Psychiatric Association (APA) in 1973 to declassify homosexual deviance as a mental/behavioral disorder, followed by the slow but steady takeover of America's public education system to shape the future through the indoctrination of children. In the

1980s and 90s the overt promotion of LGBT propaganda to school-children was formalized in the "Safe Schools" "anti-bullying" campaigns that crushed all faculty and parental resistance like the *blitzkrieg* of Nazi tanks that rolled into Poland in 1939.

Both the school systems and the teachers' unions had long been conquered in the deep blue states (and the deep blue cities in the red states) by the time LGBT champion Barack Obama took the White House in 2008. He further solidified that control by creating the position of "Safe Schools Czar," manned by the pro-pederasty pioneer Kevin Jennings, founder of the Gay Lesbian Straight Teacher Network (GLSTN) which changed its name to Gay Lesbian Straight Education Network (GLSEN) both to obscure the activist role of the teachers, and to broaden its coalition of brain-washers to include school administrators. Jennings also launched the now nationwide network of "Gay-Straight Alliance" student clubs (which have never been anything other than LGBT recruiting and activism staging centers).

The third wave of attack, unfolding today, centers on the normalization of transgenderism – which in the spiritual perspective is to destroy the premise that human beings are indeed created male and female by God in His image. That is the purpose of the "non-binary" canard and the ever growing list of invented "genders" that children are encouraged to choose for themselves. It is not only preposterous but blasphemous.

Practically speaking, transgenderism means the end of the extended natural family as the acknowledged fabric of society. Already the English language is being reshaped to eliminate it, backed by the power of the state to punish dissent for "misgendering" people and banning words like "Mom" and "Dad." Every new category of "gender" to which children assign their loyalty becomes a new civil rights category with its own demands for accommodation – the collective effect of which is to make sexual identity arbitrary and meaningless. And, of course, every child who embraces transgender logic has essentially given themselves over to a "reprobate mind" with the possibility of never being restored to reason due to the effect that changes in our most fundamental sense of reality can have. It is literally (not figuratively) the choice of political-narrative-driven insanity over self-evident reality.

The transgender agenda also carries with it, like the soldiers in the belly of the Trojan Horse, both the elimination of parental rights, and the implicit normalization of pedophilia, by establishing the legal and cultural "right" of children to "sexual freedom" on their own terms. As noted above, the death of parental rights is the obvious consequence beginning to manifest. Less obvious is pedophilia – until you become aware of the euphemisms it hides behind: including "children's rights" (as in the global Treaty on the Rights of the Child, which the US has not signed...yet), and the phrase "intergenerational relationships" which has been a staple of Planned Parenthood's pro-LGBT propaganda to schoolchildren for well over a decade. Another name for "intergenerational relationships" which civilization has known for millennia is pederasty — the ancient core of male homosexual culture that the North American Man/Boy Love Association (NAMBLA) was formed to advocate for.

Fourth and finally, there is a second, hidden "T" behind transgenderism, which stands for transhumanism, the satanic attack on the order of creation itself as seen in God's division of animals into "kinds" and the distinction of human beings from the animals (Genesis 1:20-25).

Transhumanism is the philosophical and scientific movement to create a new, "higher" form of humans, created by us to be better than homo sapiens, through genetic modifications (including the blending of human and animal DNA), computer-based artificial intelligence, and physical augmentation of human bodies with robotic components. Once exclusively the realm of science fiction, it is the emerging next wave of human "evolution" that "transgenderism" is preparing the younger generations to accept as normal. It is the predictable maturation of "eugenics" that has entranced the global elites since the days of Charles Darwin and his nephew Francis Galton — and helps explain the mentality behind the tyrannical gene-therapy based mRNA global "vaccination" scheme we're presently suffering.

There would be nothing left of the biblical order in the aftermath of transhumanism. Satan's prophecy that we would become like gods for eating from the tree of the knowledge of good and evil (Genesis 3:1-7) would be fulfilled, and God's remedy of banishing us from the Garden of Eden (Genesis 3:22-24) to protect the tree of life would be thwarted (because the ultimate end goal of transhumanism is achieving immortality by our own hand). For this reason I believe God will soon intervene directly (Maranatha!) but until then we face very dark times.

All along it has been the public school system that has served as the engine of social transformation, and all along it has been the humanist doctrine of "sexual freedom" (in actuality sexual anarchy) that has served as the motivator for schoolchildren to first willingly comply and then become enthusiastic agents in its spread. The schools have become, emphatically, temples of humanism and the children acolytes of their anti-biblical doctrines.

To reiterate, I have been a frontlines Christian social and political activist for more than thirty years, in dozens of countries across five continents, as a pastor, lawyer, writer, public speaker, and human rights consultant. Nearly my entire adult life has been devoted to fighting the LGBT agenda and warning others about it. I have suffered extreme persecution for it, but have been blessed by God far beyond the cost I've paid.

However, from the time I joined the pro-family movement in the late 1980s at the height of the Reagan Revolution until the present time, the LGBT war on Christianity has been one long losing battle for the pro-family side — a continuous rear-guard action -- punctuated by a few temporary victories that stalled but never reversed the trend. The entire elite strata of globalist power-brokers and puppet-masters, including our own Supreme Court, is arrayed against us, and they own all the key institutions of our society, including public education, and a growing swath of "Christendom."

The Luciferian schedule of deconstruction has taken Judeo-Christian civilization to the brink of collapse, ushering in a scene such as the days of Noah that Jesus warned against, and fostering a culture of lawlessness that suggests the imminency of the Antichrist's emergence as described in 2 Thessalonians 2:3-12.

THE BIBLICAL ORDER OF SEX AND CIVILATION IN THREE CHARTS

 Chart 1 — The Biblical Pattern Established, from Creation to the Flood

1 Human identity, family and civilation are rooted in the "one flesh" paradigm.

Adam and Eve are united, monogamous. Gen. 1:27, 2:24.

2 Satan's goal is the division of the one flesh and dissolution of the order of family and society; targeting the "weaker vessel" first. 1 Peter 3:7

Eve, then Adam, disobeys God They discover "nakedness" (sexual guilt) Gen. 3:6-7.

3 Disobedience causes family and societal division and disorder.

Cain kills Abel. Gen. 4:8.

4 God accomodates sin to preserve His plan but creates a way of redemption for people to choose.

Cain is protected by God from revenge. Gen. 4:15.

Abel is replaced by Seth: first priest of God. Gen. 4:26.

5 Rebellion increases over time, measured by the degree and extent of murder and sexual deviance.

Cain: first murder
↓
Lamech: first adulterer
↓
"Days of Noah:"
homosexual and bestial "marriage."

Jesus highlights two "progressive" sins...
murder: Matt 5:21-22
adultery: Matt 5:27-30*
↓
...and the sins of the "Days of Noah:"
Matt. 24:37 + Gen. 6:5 = extreme perversion.

6 Righteousness of the Sons of God is undermined by sexual temptation and "Foreign Wives."

Cain
↓
Daughters of men . Gen. 6:1.

Seth
↓
Sons of God. Gen. 6:2.

7 Murder and sexual sin work in tandem to corrupt the land.

Blood guilt: Gen. 4:10-11, Num. 35:33-34, Psalm 106:37-38.
Defilement: Gen. 6:11-12, Lev. 18:25.

8 When corruption of the land reaches an intolerable level, God "desolates" the land (removes the people) and starts over: Noah's Flood. Gen. 6-9.

"Do not defile yourselves by any of these [sexual sins listed in Lev. 18:1-23]; for by all these the nations which I am casting out before you have become defiled. For the land has become defiled, therefore I have brought its punishment upon it, so the land has spewed out its inhabitants." Lev. 18:24-25.

* "Adultery" is symbolic of all sexual sin, a violation of the marriage of God and His people, and synonymous with "idolatry" per Deut. 31:16, Hosea 1. Without sincere repentance it always progresses from bad to worse in biblical patterns: homosexuality, bestiality and child killing being the extreme...

SEX AND CIVILIZATION

Let me be clear at the start of this segment, that while I have full confidence in my assertions about the LGBT movement and agenda, as an expert in this field of study I do not place the majority of blame for our crisis of civilization on homosexual activists and their social-engineering allies. Yes, the LGBTs have been the point of the spear of the sexual revolution, but their numbers are so few relative to the heterosexual majority that the sexual anarchy they pushed for could never have advanced to this degree without being enthusiastically embrace by non-homosexuals. Just as when King Balak sent in the Moabite women to lead Hebrew men into debauchery and idolatry in Numbers 25, the ultimate responsibility lay with the people who succumbed to temptation – and both the defilers and the defiled were punished by God.

Every person is responsible for his own conduct, regardless of external influences – and it is our collective guilt in failing to follow God's instructions that will bring judgment upon us. That has always been true.

Civilization as we know it was made possible by sexual self-restraint through the institution of marriage. Sex is like fire – a great blessing when safely contained, a deadly curse when unleashed: the difference between a campfire and a wildfire. Indeed, the word "fornication," from the root for "furnace" means "to misuse the fire burning within you."

The natural order of sexuality is based upon the model of Genesis 1:27 and 2:24, the "one flesh" paradigm. God, who created the first marriage by creating Eve in the role of a wife, made human beings in His image as male and female, and established the principle of lifelong monogamy at the initiation of the male (*"therefore shall a man cleave unto his wife"*) as the foundation of human civilization. The Bible then offers a series of cautionary tales about deviations from the model:

- the association of sexual deviance (in this case bigamy) with murder in the story of Lamech, near descendent of Cain;

- the story of Ham re-initiating pre-flood sexual evil into the world through his son Canaan, who was banished by Noah and then established a sex and murder-based demonic religion;

- the story of Abraham's polygamy that produced the anti-Hebrew nation of Ishmael;

- the story of Sodom and Gomorrah;

- the story of Lot's incest with his daughters from which came the anti-Hebrew nations of Ammon and Moab;

THE BIBLICAL ORDER OF SEX AND CIVILATION IN THREE CHARTS

Chart 2 The Biblical Pattern Repeated, from the Flood to the Babylonian Exile

1 | God desolates and cleanses the Earth: great flood. | Righteous Noah, sons Shem, Ham, Japheth and wives.

2 | Son of Ham reintroduces pre-flood culture of sexual sin and is banished from Noah's presence. | "Sees nakedness" of Noah: i.e. sex with Noah's wife. (Lev. 20:11) or homosexual abuse as Rabbis taught.

3 | Canaan then colonizes the Holy Land and launches religious system to undermine godly order. | Canaanite religion centers on sexual perversion and child sacrafice. Lev. 18:24-28.

4 | War of good vs. evil resumes for the soul of humanity: evil increases rapidly.

Canaan nephew Nimrod establishes anti-Shemite empires in Babylon and Assyria. Gen. 10:10-11.	Shem: first post-flood priest of God. Gen. 9:26, 14:18-20. (Melchizedek?)
Sodom's King Bera ("King of Evil") competes with Melchizedek ("King of Peace") for Abraham's allegiance. Gen. 14:17-24.	Abraham affirms his allegiance to God and gives a tithe to Melchizedek Gen. 14:18-20. God then makes covenant with Abraham. Gen. 15:1-21.

5 | God chooses Abraham and Sarah to establish a new covenant-based social order for humanity.

Abraham's nephew Lot witnesses Sodom's incineration for homosexuality, then through incest with daughters produces Ammonite and Moabite nations: perpetual enemies of the Shemites (Semites).	God makes Abraham a set of firm promises: Gen. 12:2-3, 17:4-8, 22:16-18, including the Scepter Promise (line of kings incl. Messiah) and Birthright Promise (vast numbers and double portion of inheritance).

6 | By Sarah's request, Abraham commits adultery with Hagar, produces "wild donkey" Ishmael, the root of Islam.

Sexual sin now infects the chosen people and worsens over time despite righteous interludes.	Isaac and Rebecca choose monogamy and God's promises are reaffirmed to them. Gen. 26:3-5.
Grandson Jacob "The deceiver" adopts polygamy, bearing twelve sons by two wives (Leah and Rachel) and two concubines. Sex-related sin disqualifies Leah's sons Rueben, Levi and Simeon from leadership and "scepter," which defaults to Judah. Gen. 49:1-10.	After birth of Joseph to Rachel, corrupt Jacob becomes righteous Israel, receives God's promises (Gen. 35:9-13) but they are split between the house of Leah (Judah) and the house of Rachel (Israel). Ruth 4:11. Joseph/Ephraim has "birthright." Gen. 49:22-26, Jer. 31:9.

7 | The two houses become two kingdoms, Judah and Israel, and both eventually fall to Canaanite sexual sins.

After the people reject God's system of judges, Saul bcomes their King but turns wicked.	David anointed to replace Saul and establishes righteous and powerful united kingdom.
David succumbs to adultery with Bathsheba and murder of her husband, his loyal captain.	David repents and is restored. Psalm 51. God confirms the Scepter Promise to him. 2 Sam. 7:10-16.
Solomon, son of Bathsheba, becomes uber-polygamist with many "foreign wives," imports Canaanite worship lasting 300 years alongside Yahweh worhip. God punishes by splitting the kingdom. 1 Kings 11:1-13.	God sends a series of prophets to warn against adultery/idolatry. Some kings of Judah repent and restore godliness, including most righteous king Josiah under Jeremiah. 2 Kings 23:1-27.
No kings of Israel repent, Ahab and Jezebal are last straw, replacing God with Baal. 1 Kings 16:25-33.	Judah's last straw: King Manasseh replaces God with Baal, sacrifices own son. 2 Kings 21:1-15.

8 | God desolates/cleanses the land, removing first Israel (722BC) and then Judah (568BC) per His Lev. 18 warning.

"I then will destroy your high places, and cut down your incense altars...I will lay waste your cities as well and... make the land desolate so that your enemies who settle in it will be appalled over it... Then the land will enjoy its Sabbaths all the days of the desolation, whil you are in your enemies' land; then the land will rest and enjoy its Sabbaths." Lev. 26:30-34.

- the story of Balaam's weaponization of Moabite sexual rebellion as a strategy to weaken the Isralite society from within; and

- the consistent Old Testament narrative theme identifying adultery as synonymous with idolatry, best recognized in the story of Hosea and Gomer.

There are others, but this list suffices to prove the point.

In the three charts included in this segment, we show how the sins of sexual deviance and murder accumulate in the land leading to desolation by God. The first instance resulted in Noah's flood. The second instance resulted in the removal from the land of first the house and kingdom of Israel, and then the house and kingdom of Judah. The third instance is the coming desolation of the Gentiles as the final sequence of events preceding the Millennial Kingdom. Note that even as wickedness increases God always offers a path of redemption.

THE BIBLICAL ORDER OF SEX AND CIVILATION IN THREE CHARTS

Chart 3 The Biblical Pattern Completed, from the Exile to the Millennial Kingdom

1 Return of the house of Judah from Babylonian exile is fresh start.

One flesh restored, "foreign wives" put away, monogomy is new permanent norm. Ezr. 10:3-5.

2 Antichrist Antiochus IV is "Epiphanes" (the "manifest god") targets boys and women in strategy to undermine God's law and impose demonic polytheism.

Turns male youth to homosexuality, hangs slaughtered infants on necks of women who circumcize sons. Judah Maccabee delivers Jews, restores Law. Dan. 11, 1 Macc. 1:14-15, 60-61.

3 Herod the Great slaughters Maccabee royal family, then all infants Jesus' age in Nazareth.

Beguiled by wife, Herod Antipas beheads John the Baptist for confronting his adultery. Mk. 6.

4 Jesus does not overthrow Romans but offers way of salvation through faith. Affirms one flesh.

Says "Give unto Caesar what is Caesar's but to God what is God's"

First non-Hebrew converts were Samaritans confronted ovr culture of adultery. Jn. 4.

5 Apostle Paul warns sexual sin will steadily increase and produce apostasy in last days.

Paul: Romans 1: 18-32 and 2 Tim. 3:1-8 taken together define last days culture of perversion.

In contrast, church is compared to spotless bride prepared for her husband. Eph. 5:27.

6 Apostle Peter warns last days heresy will lure believers away from truth into rebellion.

Last days heresy identified with 1) days of Noah, 2) Sodom and Gomorrah, 3) life of Lot, 4) way of Balaam: i.e. Same sins outlined in Lev. 18, justified and condoned by false teachers. 2 Peter 2.

Many false prophets will arise and mislead many. Becuase lawlessness is increased, most people's love will grow cold. But the one who endures to the end will be saved. Matt. 24:11-13.

7 "...just like the Days of Noah" (Matt. 24:37), the defilement of sin overwhelms the land itself:

"For the anxious longing of the creation waits eagerly for the revealing of the sons of God. For the creation was subjected to futility, not willingly, but because of Him who subjected it, in hope that the creation itself also will be set free from its slavery to corruption into the freedom of the glory of the children of God. For we know that the whole creation groans and suffers the pains of childbirth together until now." Rom. 8:19-22.

8 In the final "desolation" the wicked and Satan are held in chains pending the final judgment, so the earth and the righteous can enjoy a thousand-year Sabbath in Christ's Millennial Kingdom. Rev. 20.

"Then the seventh angel sounded his trumpet, and loud voices called out in heaven: 'The kingdom of the world is now the kingdom of our Lord and of his Christ... The nations were enraged, and Your wrath has come. The time has come to judge the dead, and to reward Your servants... and to destroy those who destroy the earth.'" Rev. 11:15-18.

"He has kept [them] in eternal bonds under darkness for the judgment of the great day, just as Sodom and Gomorrah... since they in the same way as these indulged in gross immorality and went after strange flesh, are exhibited as an example in undergoing the punishment of eternal fire." Jude 1:6-7.

"The wicked will be destroyed, but those who wait on the Lord will inherit the land." Psalm 37:9.

-186-

CHAPTER TWELVE:

CONCLUSIONS AND PREDICTIONS

Much of end-time prophecy in the Bible is ambiguous, which explains why so many have been so wrong in their predictions over the centuries. "Wars and rumors of wars" could have applied to many periods of history. If you believe that the Daniel prophecy regarding a "king of the North" and "king of the South" refers to an end-time reiteration of the historically-fulfilled saga of Antiochus IV Epiphanes, there have been many candidates for these roles over the centuries. Even Jesus' warning that the very last days would be "*like the days of Noah*," is susceptible to speculation based on subjective perceptions.

The Revealed Antichrist Prerequisite

But some of the Bible prophecies are totally *un*ambiguous, meaning that none of the human guesses of the past were ever truly realistic because certain clearly stated prerequisites for the second coming had not been met. The most obvious of those prerequisites are stated plainly in 2 Thessalonians 2:1-12:

"*Now concerning the coming of our Lord Jesus Christ and our being gathered together to Him, we ask you, brothers, not to be easily disconcerted or alarmed by any spirit or message or letter seeming to be from us, alleging that the* **Day of the Lord** *has already come.* **Let no one deceive you in any way, for** it will not come until the rebellion occurs and the man of lawlessness—the son of destruction—is revealed. *He will oppose and exalt himself above every so-called god or object of worship. So* he will seat himself in the temple of God, proclaiming himself to be God. *Do you not remember that I told you these things while I was still with you?* **And you know what is now restraining him, so that he may be** revealed at the proper time. *For the mystery of lawlessness is already at work, but the one who now restrains it will continue until he is taken out of the way. And then the lawless one will be revealed, whom the Lord Jesus will slay with the breath of His mouth and annihilate by the majesty of His arrival*" (2 Thessalonians 2:1-7).

Remember, that the "*Day*" in question is the "*the Day of vengeance of our God*," mentioned in Isaiah 61:2 (and *many* other prophecies) refering to the 1000 year "day" of the millennial kingdom (which begins with events described in Revelation 19:11-21). It is prophesied in Hosea 6:1-2: "*Come, let's return to the LORD. For He has torn us, but He will heal us; He has wounded us, but He will bandage us. "He will* **revive us** **after** *two days; He will* **raise us up** **on** *the third day, That we may live before Him.*" The Millennial Kingdom is the 7th 1000 year "day," the Sabbath, in the pattern of sevens established at the creation.

The "*two days*" of Hosea 6 (the 5th and 6th days of Creation) are the 2000 year *Age of the Gentiles* (Romans 11:25), begun by Christ at His first advent.

The "third day" of Hosea 6:2 is the third of the "last days" referenced by Peter in Acts 2:14-21, specifically when he said "*this [outpouring of the Holy Spirit on Pentecost at the birth of the Christian church] is what has been spoken through the prophet Joel: 'and it shall be* **in the last days***, God says, 'that I will pour out my spirit on all mankind.'*"

Thus the imminent "*third day*" of Christianity in Hosea 6 is a reference to the 7th and final day of the Creation, "*the great and glorious* **day of the Lord***"* when Christ will *literally* rule on earth from Jerusalem on the Throne of David for one full millennial "day." "Literally" is the operative word here, meaning *actually* as opposed to figuratively or symbolically.

To take the Bible literally means to accept its claims at face value instead of treating them as figures of speech or symbolic metaphors, a form of interpretation known in theology as spiritualizing. However it is labeled, the practice amounts to denying the plain meaning of the words and their context.

The greatest error in studying prophecy is spiritualizing what the Bible itself purports to be literal. And there is no topic more erroneously spiritualized than the millennial kingdom. Unfortunately, the official doctrine of Roman Catholicism (and thus most of Christendom whose roots are in Roman Catholicism) is "amillennialism" (which denies there will be a millennial kingdom). And there are also "post-millennials," who claim the millennial kingdom came and went without the prophecies having been fulfilled – putting us into unlimited "overtime" to use a baseball metaphor).

But for those of us with a literalist Biblical worldview, when, for example, the Bible says in Revelation 20 that the saints will rule for 1000 years while Satan and the wicked are held in chains, we believe the Bible. And in working to discover other supporting passages we find that literal millennialism is a harmony sung throughout the Scriptures – as this book has shown.

The Hebrews in the Holy Land Prerequisite

As we have noted throughout this book, all Bible prophecies should be viewed from the perspective of Jerusalem, especially those set in the Holy Land. Most importantly, many prophesies show the Hebrews dwelling in the land at the rise of the Antichrist kingdom, which the story of the two witnesses (Revelation 11:1-14) makes very clear.

In 135 AD the Roman authorities permanently expelled the Jews from the Holy Land and renamed it Syriac Palestine. The Jews only began to return in number some eighteen centuries later in 1917 with the conquest of the Islamic Ottoman Turks by the Christian British Empire, and the issuance of the

"Balfour Declaration" inviting the Jews to repopulate the land. In 1948, upon the expiration of the British Mandate under international law, the Jewish leadership declared Israel, including West Jerusalem, to be a modern independent state. In 1967, Israel reclaimed East Jerusalem to unite the Holy City under Hebrew control.

But those facts did not fully meet the conditions for the return of Christ. Per 2 Thessalonians 2, the Antichrist must control Israel, and he must set up the Abomination of desolation in the "Holy Place" (which is most likely a reconstructed 3rd Temple). We're not there yet.

The Beginning of Birth Pains

And so it appears that we are between the proverbial rock and a hard place. A rise in apostasy is obviously upon us. The demonic realm is manifesting itself in the world in various ways. The law of Cumulative Sin is still at work and the "grapes of wrath" are rapidly ripening on the vine.

What comes next is the beginning of birth pains – a period of global chaos that sets the stage for the Antichrist kingdom. It could happen at any time, and be triggered by any number of events, but a new world war or global economic meltdown seem most likely.

But we also know that (with some exceptions) the events in God's schedule do not come with mechanical precision but are usually more organic and seasonal – transitioning from one phase to the next like blossom to fruit or spring to summer. We can thus read the signs of what's to come in the circumstances and events of today.

Jesus said "*Now learn this lesson from the fig tree: As soon as its branches become tender and sprout leaves, you know that summer is near. So also, when you see all these things, you will know that He is near, right at the door. Truly I tell you, this generation will not pass away until all these things have happened* (Matthew 24:32-34). We know for sure that the House of Judah is the fig tree. Its new life in the Holy Land seems best measured from 1917. And the the biblical lifespan of the generation born then (120 years per Genesis 6:3) ends in the year 2037. That would give us about 15 or 16 years for all of the final events of prophecy to occur IF these assumptions are accurate. That's my best guess, in any case.

Whether I am right or wrong in the specifics of my timeline, I believe He is coming soon. This book is my best effort at modeling and teaching the biblical worldview, which is the work I want Him to find me doing when He returns. I hope and pray it has helped you.

As a final help, I am closing this book with a second, larger sized set of our charts that some readers may have had difficulty reading. All of the charts and other resources related to this project are available at ScottLively.net. God bless you, and us all, as we await the return of the King.

YESHUA'S CHRONOLOGY OF END-TIME EVENTS IN MATTHEW 24-25

MILLENNIAL KINGDOM 1000 YEARS

DURATION

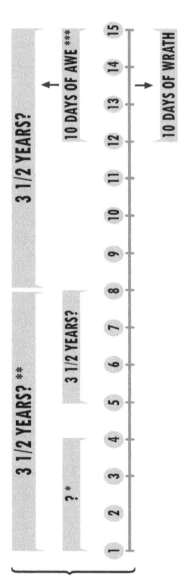

? * — 3 1/2 YEARS?

3 1/2 YEARS? **

3 1/2 YEARS?

1 2 3 4 5 6 7 8 9 10 11 12 13 14 15

10 DAYS OF AWE ***

10 DAYS OF WRATH

Jesus said "Not the end" but only "the beginnings of birth pangs." Duration is uncertain but we believe it is included in the first 3 1/2 years.

Seven year tribulation is speculative conclusion from just one verse, Daniel 9:27, projecting Daniel's 70th week into the last days. We tentatively agree but offer an alternative theory as well (Chapter 2).

These three events have a dual perspective, earthly and spiritual, showcasing the 10 Days of Awe that began with the Rapture on Yom-Teruah and end with Yom Kippur. The Matthew 25 emphasis is the perspective of the "Left Behind" on Earth.

SOURCE

MATTHEW 24: Twelve Events Leading to Rapture

1-4 False Christs, Wars, Earthquakes, Famine/Pestilence (v. 4-8).
5-7 Martyrdom/Apostasy, Gospel Preached Globally (v. 9-14).
8 Antichrist Revealed / Abomination of Desolation (v. 15-20).
9 Great Tribulation (v. 21-28), Cut Short for the Elect (v. 21).
10 Sun + Moon Darkened, Stars Fall to Earth (v. 29).
11 Return of Christ in the Clouds (v. 30).
12 Resurrection and Rapture (v. 22), 10 Days Before End (v. 21)

MATTHEW 25: Three Events Following the Rapture

13 Wedding Feast of the Lamb (v. 1-13).
14 Testing of the Works, Assignment of Rewards (v. 14-30).
15 Arrival of the King and Host of Heaven (v. 31a), Millennial Kingdom (v. 14-30).

YESHUA'S CHRONOLOGY OF END-TIME EVENTS
IN REVELATION 6-20 AS ALIGNED WITH MATTHEW 24-25

KEY: The Seven Seals: Seals 1-6 are chronological. Seal 7 contains and explains the chronology of the Seven Trumpets and Bowls.

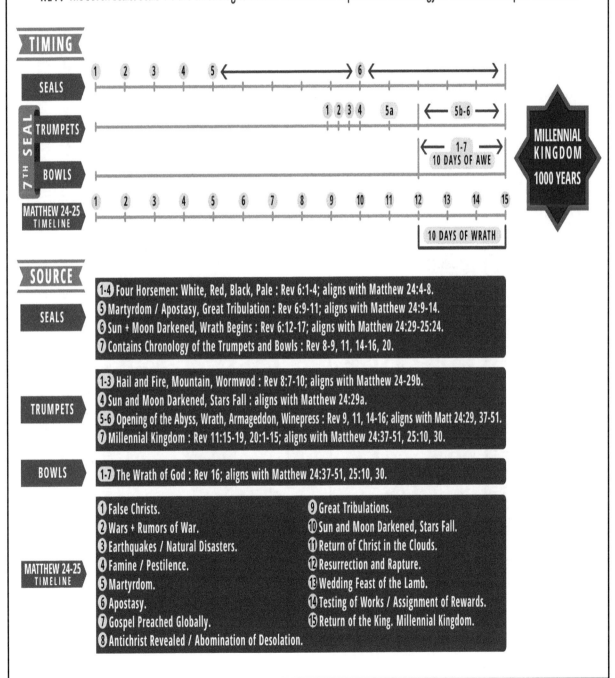

TIMING

SEALS

7TH SEAL — TRUMPETS — BOWLS

MATTHEW 24-25 TIMELINE

MILLENNIAL KINGDOM 1000 YEARS

1-7 10 DAYS OF AWE

10 DAYS OF WRATH

SOURCE

SEALS

1-4 Four Horsemen: White, Red, Black, Pale : Rev 6:1-4; aligns with Matthew 24:4-8.
5 Martyrdom / Apostasy, Great Tribulation : Rev 6:9-11; aligns with Matthew 24:9-14.
6 Sun + Moon Darkened, Wrath Begins : Rev 6:12-17; aligns with Matthew 24:29-25:24.
7 Contains Chronology of the Trumpets and Bowls : Rev 8-9, 11, 14-16, 20.

TRUMPETS

1-3 Hail and Fire, Mountain, Wormwod : Rev 8:7-10; aligns with Matthew 24-29b.
4 Sun and Moon Darkened, Stars Fall : aligns with Matthew 24:29a.
5-6 Opening of the Abyss, Wrath, Armageddon, Winepress : Rev 9, 11, 14-16; aligns with Matt 24:29, 37-51.
7 Millennial Kingdom : Rev 11:15-19, 20:1-15; aligns with Matthew 24:37-51, 25:10, 30.

BOWLS

1-7 The Wrath of God : Rev 16; aligns with Matthew 24:37-51, 25:10, 30.

MATTHEW 24-25 TIMELINE

1. False Christs.
2. Wars + Rumors of War.
3. Earthquakes / Natural Disasters.
4. Famine / Pestilence.
5. Martyrdom.
6. Apostasy.
7. Gospel Preached Globally.
8. Antichrist Revealed / Abomination of Desolation.
9. Great Tribulations.
10. Sun and Moon Darkened, Stars Fall.
11. Return of Christ in the Clouds.
12. Resurrection and Rapture.
13. Wedding Feast of the Lamb.
14. Testing of Works / Assignment of Rewards.
15. Return of the King. Millennial Kingdom.

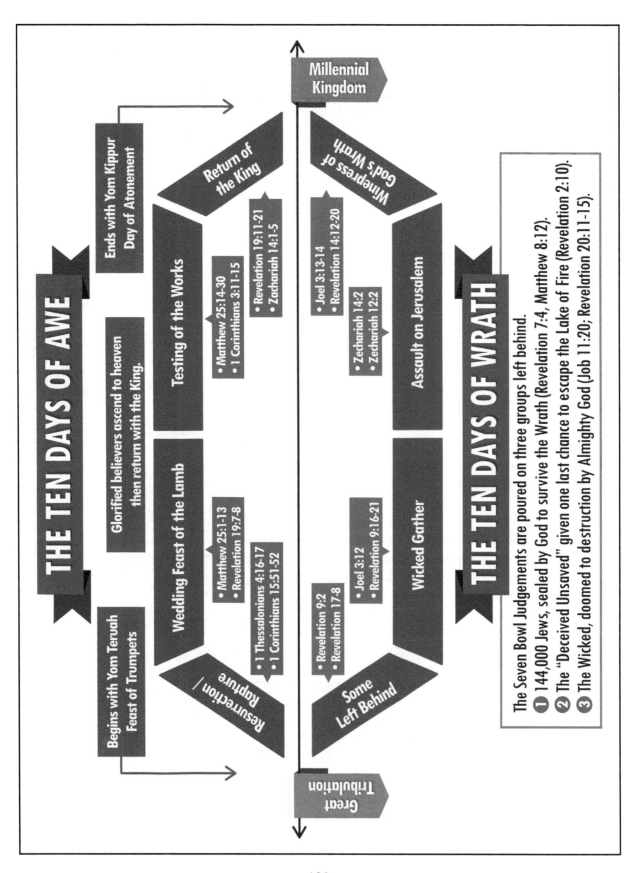

THE TEN DAYS OF AWE

Begins with Yom Teruah Feast of Trumpets

Ends with Yom Kippur Day of Atonement

Glorified believers ascend to heaven then return with the King.

Return of the King

Testing of the Works
- Matthew 25:14-30
- 1 Corinthians 3:11-15

Wedding Feast of the Lamb
- Matthew 25:1-13
- Revelation 19:7-8

Resurrection / Rapture
- 1 Thessalonians 4:16-17
- 1 Corinthians 15:51-52

Millennial Kingdom

Winepress of God's Wrath

- Revelation 19:11-21
- Zachariah 14:1-5

- Joel 3:13-14
- Revelation 14:12-20

- Zechariah 14:2
- Zechariah 12:2

Assault on Jerusalem

Wicked Gather

- Joel 3:12
- Revelation 9:16-21

- Revelation 9:2
- Revelation 17-8

Some Left Behind

Great Tribulation

THE TEN DAYS OF WRATH

The Seven Bowl Judgements are poured on three groups left behind.
1. 144,000 Jews, sealed by God to survive the Wrath (Revelation 7:4, Matthew 8:12).
2. The "Deceived Unsaved" given one last chance to escape the Lake of Fire (Revelation 2:10).
3. The Wicked, doomed to destruction by Almighty God (Job 11:20; Revelation 20:11-15).

THE LORD'S SUPPER AS A REHEARSAL FOR THE SECOND COMING

"For I received from the Lord what I also passed on to you: The Lord Jesus, on the night he was betrayed, took bread, and when he had given thanks, he broke it and said, "This is my body, which is for you; do this in remembrance of me." In the same way, after supper he took the cup, saying, "This cup is the new covenant in my blood; do this, whenever you drink it, in remembrance of me." For whenever you eat this bread and drink this cup, you proclaim the Lord's death until he comes."
- 1 Corinthians 11:23-26

"MY BODY"
Bread:
The Fall
Wheat Harvest

Rev. 14:15-16
"Then another angel came out of the temple, crying out in a loud voice to the One seated on the cloud, 'Swing Your sickle and reap, because the time has come to harvest; for the crop of the earth is ripe.' So...[He] swung His sickle over the earth, and the earth was harvested."

"MY BLOOD"
Wine:
The Grape Harvest

Rev. 14:17-18
"Then...another angel...called out...'Swing your sharp sickle and gather the clusters of grapes from the vine of the earth, because its grapes are ripe.' So the angel...gathered the grapes of the earth...and he threw them into the great winepress of God's wrath."

FEAST OF
TRUMPETS

10 DAYS OF AWE/WRATH

DAY OF
ATONEMENT

"Concerning the feasts of the LORD [*Moedim*] which ye shall proclaim to be holy convocations [*Miqra*], even these are my feasts [*Moedim*]" (Leviticus 23:1-2). The Hebrew word *moed* (plural *moedim*) means an appointed day or time. The word *Miqra* means rehearsal.

Facts to remember:
Both the fall wheat harvest and the grape harvest are celebrated in the fall pilgrimage of Tabernacles (*Sukkot*). The Bible associates the Wheat Harvest with the Resurrection and Rapture (Matt 13:24-30, Rev 14:15-16), and the Grape Harvest with the destruction of the wicked (Rev. 14:17-18, Joel 3:13). Tabernacles itself is symbolic of God dwelling with man: the Millennial Kingdom.

-193-

DECIPHERING THE REVELATION CHRONOLOGY

THREE KEY FACTS

1. Revelation is an expanded version of Yeshua's timeline in Matthew 24-25.

2. The story is told from four perspectives.

3. Passages from the heavenly perspective are not time bound and thus may be out of chronological sequence, but contains markers (symbols and phrases) that allow the events they describe to be plotted on the earthly timeline.

FOUR PERSPECTIVES

- A Earth seen from Earth.
- B Earth seen from Heaven.
- C Heaven seen from Earth.
- D Heaven seen from Heaven.

EVENTS OF REVELATION AS THEY APPEAR IN THE TEXT

1
CHAPTER 1:1-9
Introduction and Notice of John's Vision to the Seven Churches

2
CHAPTER 1:10-19
The Lord's Instruction to John about Conveying His Message

3
CHAPTER 2-3
Warnings: Some Will be "Left Behind" with One Last Chance

4
CHAPTER 4-5
Jesus Presented with Sealed Scroll in the Throne Room of Heaven

5
CHAPTER 6-7:8
Jesus Opens the Six Seals and Shields the 144K from Wrath

6
CHAPTER 7:9-8:4
Future Worship in Heaven of Those Now Suffering on Earth

7
CHAPTER 8:5-9:21
Seventh Seal Shown to Contain Seven Trumpets. Six now Sound

8
CHAPTER 10
John Receives and Seals Up Prophecy of Seven Thunders

9
CHAPTER 11:1-14
The Two Witnesses During the Kingdom of the Antichrist

10
CHAPTER 11:15-19
Seventh Trumpet Declares Start of the Millennial Kingdom

CHAPTER 12

11

Vision of Last Days as Displayed in Constellations of the Night Sky

CHAPTER 13

12

The Beast: Cryptic Description of the Antichrist and his Kingdom

CHAPTER 7:9-8:4

13

The Lamb and the 144,000 in the Throne Room of Heaven

CHAPTER 14:8-20

14

Five Angels, Five Events: Gospel Preached through Winepress

CHAPTER 15

15

Seven Angels Receive the Seven Bowls of Wrath

CHAPTER 16

16

The Pouring Out of the Bowls of Wrath on the Earth

CHAPTER 17

17

ProÀle and History of Babylon the Great

CHAPTER 18

18

Punishment of Babylon the Great Ending with Seventh Bowl

CHAPTER 19:1-10

19

Exultation in Heaven Over Babylon's Destruction

CHAPTER 19:11-16

20

The King of Kings Returns to Claim His Throne

CHAPTER 19:17-21

21

Defeat of the Wicked, the Beast and False Prophet

CHAPTER 20:1-10

22

Beginning and End of the Millennial Kingdom

CHAPTER 20:11-15

23

Great White Throne Judgement

CHAPTER 21-22:5

24

The New Heaven and Earth in Eternity

CHAPTER 22:6-21

25

Concluding Summary and Warnings

The Hebrew Feast Cycle in the Gospel of John

Facts to Remember

- The Jewish Religious Calendar Observed during Yeshua's Earthly Ministry Included Nine Holidays: the Seven Feasts of Leviticus 23, plus Hanukkah and Purim.

- The Original Seven Feasts were Divided into Three Mandatory Pilgrimages. 1. *Sukkot* (Tabernacles), 2. *Pesach* (Passover/Unleavened Bread), and 3. *Shavuot* (Pentecost).

- The Cycle Begins in the Fall with Rosh Hashana (New Year), the Feast of Trumpets.

- Each Holiday/Pilgrimage is Associated with Key Symbols and Images which Can Serve as Textual Landmarks.

Post-Torah Holidays

Hanukkah
- Satan / Antichrist
- Cleansing of the Temple
- Menorah / Light v. Darkness

Purim
- Conspiracy
- Murder
- Humility / Self-Sacrifice

Fall Pilgrimage

Tabernacles
- God Dwelling with Man
- Millennial Kingdom
- Heaven
- Water Ritual
- Celebration of Harvest Season

Atonement
- High Priest / Human Intermediary
- Judgment / Mercy
- Grape Harvest

Trumpets
- Birthday of Creation and Celebration
- Resurrection
- Fall Wheat Harvest

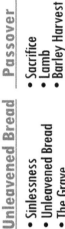

Spring Pilgrimage

Passover
- Sacrifice
- Lamb
- Barley Harvest

Unleavened Bread
- Sinlessness
- Unleavened Bread
- The Grave

First Fruits
- First of Many to Bear Fruit
- Deliverance from Grave
- Barley Harvest

Pentecost
- Holy Spirit
- Mountain Sojourn
- Leavened Bread
- Birth of the Church
- Spring Wheat Harvest

Summer Pilgrimage

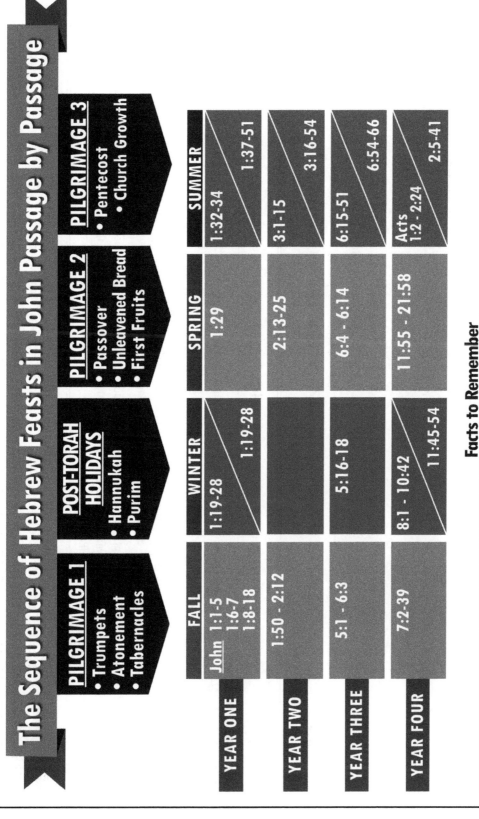

The Sequence of Hebrew Feasts in John Passage by Passage

	PILGRIMAGE 1	POST-TORAH HOLIDAYS	PILGRIMAGE 2	PILGRIMAGE 3
	• Trumpets • Atonement • Tabernacles	• Hannukah • Purim	• Passover • Unleavened Bread • First Fruits	• Pentecost • Church Growth
	FALL	WINTER	SPRING	SUMMER
YEAR ONE	John 1:1-5 1:6-7 1:8-18	1:19-28 1:19-28	1:29	1:32-34 1:37-51
YEAR TWO	1:50 - 2:12		2:13-25	3:1-15 3:16-54
YEAR THREE	5:1 - 6:3	5:16-18	6:4 - 6:14	6:15-51 6:54-66
YEAR FOUR	7:2-39	8:1 - 10:42 11:45-54	11:55 - 21:58	Acts 1:2 - 2:24 2:5-41

Facts to Remember

• Chapter One of John presents the nine holidays as a series of symbols, only the latter of which are part of the real-life timeline of Jesus' ministry.

• The cycle begins in the fall with Rosh Hashana (New Year), the Feast of Trumpets.

• The original seven feasts were divided into three mandatory pilgrimages. 1. *Sukkot* (Tabernacles), 2. *Pesach* (Passover/ Unleavened Bread), and 3. *Shavuot* (Pentecost).

• Each holiday/pilgrimage is associated with key symbols and images which can serve as textual landmarks.

LETTERS TO THE "LEFT BEHIND" - REVELATION 2-3

FEAST OF TRUMPETS
Resurrection and Rapture for the Righteous

DAY OF ATONEMENT
Return of the King to Reclaim the Earth

WHITE THRONE JUDGMENT
Final Resurrection
Revelation 20:11-15

TRIBULATION | TEN DAYS OF AWE | 1000 YR MILLENNIAL KINGDOM | HEAVEN

TRIBULATION | TEN DAYS OF WRATH | PRISON FOR SATAN AND THE WICKED | LAKE OF FIRE

TRUE CHRISTIANS Resurrected and raptured on Trumpets to join the Wedding Feast and return with the King on Atonement (Rev 19:11-21).

PSEUDO-CHRISTIANS Left behind in "outer darkness" with ten days to repent and gain Heaven if they "endure to the end" (see below).

THESE INCLUDE:
the "Saved by Works" people of Matthew 7:21-23. "I never knew you" (v. 23).
the "Unprepared Wedding Guests" of Matthew 22:1-13. "Outer darkness" (v. 13).
the "Foolish Virgins" of Matthew 25:8-12. "I don't know you" (v.12).
the "Worthless Servants" of Matthew 25:14-30. "Outer darkness" (v. 30).

All or most will die during the 10 Days of Wrath but those who repent and endure to the end without renouncing Christ will have their names written in the book of life (Rev 2:10-11) and earn rewards retroactive to the Day of Atonement (Rev 19:11-21) which they can claim in heaven after the final resurrection and the White Throne Judgment (Rev 20:12).

LETTER 1: EPHESUS Ephesus and Laodicea are bookends to the other letters with a common theme: If you repent before the rapture you will not face the wrath. Ephesus message: all 7 letters are for all believers (Rev 2: 7). Ephesus reward: Tree of Life (Rev 22:14).

LETTER 1: EPHESUS Ephesus and Laodicea are bookends to the other letters with a common theme: If you repent before the rapture you will not face the wrath. Ephesus message: all 7 letters are for all believers (Rev 2: 7). Ephesus reward: Tree of Life (Rev 22:14).

LETTER 2: SMYRNA

Smyrna message: if you do not repent, you will face the wrath for 10 days and will probably die.

However, if you repent during the 10 days and do not renounce Christ you will not face the second death, which is the lake of fire (Rev 20:14).

Smyrna reward: The crown of life (Rev 19:12).

LETTER 3: PERGAMUM

Pergamum message: Those who fail to repent during the 10 days will be numbered with the wicked and slain by Christ the returning King with "the sword of His mouth" (Rev 19:15).

Pergamum rewards: hidden manna (Rev 11:19). White stone with new name (Rev 19:12). (Per Roman custom, contest winners got this prize.)

LETTER 4: THYATIRA

Thyatira message: those who do not repent of adultery with Jezebel will face the wrath in which they will be judged by their deeds.

Those not aligned with Jezebel have no other duty but to endure through the Tribulation.

Thyatira reward: reign with Christ and wield "iron scepter" during Millennial Kingdom (Rev 19:15).

LETTER 5: SARDIS

Sardis message: many believe they are saved but aren't and will be left behind to face the wrath.

Those who repent during the wrath will not have their names blotted out of the book of life.

Sardis reward: wear white garments in eternity (Rev 7:9) (but not "walk with Him" during Millennial Kingdom (Rev 19:14)).

LETTER 6: PHILADELPHIA

Philadelphia message: those who have been faithful to Christ and do not deny His name will not face the wrath.

Those left behind who repent and endure during the wrath will be accepted into heaven.

Philadelphia Reward: bear the name of God and the new Jerusalem (Rev 21:1-21).

LETTER 7: LAODICEA If you repent before the rapture you will not face the wrath. Laodicea message: buy gold refined by fire (Rev 3: 18 & 1 Peter 1:7), white garments (Rev 3:18 & Rev 3:4) and eye salve, items associated with the righteous at the time of the rapture. Reward: to sit with Jesus on a throne (Rev 3:21 & Matt 19:28), a reference to the Millennial Kingdom.

THE BIBLICAL ORDER OF SEX AND CIVILATION IN THREE CHARTS

Chart ① The Biblical Pattern Established, from Creation to the Flood

1 Human identity, family and civilation are rooted in the "one flesh" paradigm.

> Adam and Eve are united, monogamous.
> Gen. 1:27, 2:24.

2 Satan's goal is the division of the one flesh and dissolution of the order of family and society; targeting the "weaker vessel" first. 1 Peter 3:7

> Eve, then Adam, disobeys God
> They discover "nakedness" (sexual guilt)
> Gen. 3:6-7.

3 Disobedience causes family and societal division and disorder.

> Cain kills Abel.
> Gen. 4:8.

4 God accomodates sin to preserve His plan but creates a way of redemption for people to choose.

> Abel is replaced by Seth: first priest of God.
> Gen. 4:26.

5 Rebellion increases over time, measured by the degree and extent of murder and sexual deviance.

> Cain: first murder
> ↓
> Lamech: first adulterer
> ↓
> "Days of Noah:"
> homosexual and bestial "marriage."

> Jesus highlights two "progressive" sins...
> murder: Matt 5:21-22
> adultery: Matt 5:27-30*
> ↓
> ...and the sins of the "Days of Noah:"
> Matt. 24:37 + Gen. 6:5 = extreme perversion.

6 Righteousness of the Sons of God is undermined by sexual temptation and "Foreign Wives."

Cain
↓
Daughters of men . Gen. 6:1.

Seth
↓
Sons of God. Gen. 6:2.

7 Murder and sexual sin work in tandem to corrupt the land.

Blood guilt: Gen. 4:10-11, Num. 35:33-34, Psalm 106:37-38.
Defilement: Gen. 6:11-12, Lev. 18:25.

8 When corruption of the land reaches an intolerable level, God "desolates" the land (removes the people) and starts over: Noah's Flood. Gen. 6-9.

"Do not defile yourselves by any of these [sexual sins listed in Lev. 18:1-23]; for by all these the nations which I am casting out before you have become defiled. For the land has become defiled, therefore I have brought its punishment upon it, so the land has spewed out its inhabitants." Lev. 18:24-25.

* "Adultery" is symbolic of all sexual sin, a violation of the marriage of God and His people, and synonymous with "idolatry" per Deut. 31:16, Hosea 1. Without sincere repentance it always progresses from bad to worse in biblical patterns: homosexuality, bestiality and child killing being the extreme...

THE BIBLICAL ORDER OF SEX AND CIVILATION IN THREE CHARTS

Chart 2 The Biblical Pattern Repeated, from the Flood to the Babylonian Exile

#		
1	God desolates and cleanses the Earth: great flood.	Righteous Noah, sons Shem, Ham, Japheth and wives.
2	Son of Ham reintroduces pre-flood culture of sexual sin and is banished from Noah's presence.	"Sees nakedness" of Noah: i.e. sex with Noah's wife. (Lev. 20:11) or homosexual abuse as Rabbis taught.
3	Canaan then colonizes the Holy Land and launches religious system to undermine godly order.	Canaanite religion centers on sexual perversion and child sacrafice. Lev. 18:24-28.
4	War of good vs. evil resumes for the soul of humanity: evil increases rapidly.	
	Canaan nephew Nimrod establishes anti-Shemite empires in Babylon and Assyria. Gen. 10:10-11.	Shem: firt post-flood priest of God. Gen. 9:26, 14:18-20. (Melchizedek?)
	Sodom's King Bera ("King of Evil") competes with Melchizedek ("King of Peace") for Abraham's allegiance. Gen. 14:17-24.	Abraham affirms his allegiance to God and gives a tithe to Melchizedek Gen. 14:18-20. God then makes covenant with Abraham. Gen. 15:1-21.
5	God chooses Abraham and Sarah to establish a new covenant-based social order for humanity.	
	Abraham's nephew Lot witnesses Sodom's incineration for homosexuality, then through incest with daughters produces Ammonite and Moabite nations: perpetual enemies of the Shemites (Semites).	God makes Abraham a set of firm promises: Gen. 12:2-3, 17:4-8, 22:16-18, including the Scepter Promise (line of kings incl. Messiah) and Birthright Promise (vast numbers and double portion of inheritance).
6	By Sarah's request, Abraham commits adultery with Hagar, produces "wild donkey" Ishmael, the root of Islam.	

Isaac and Rebecca choose monogamy and God's promises are reaffirmed to them. Gen. 26:3-5.

After birth of Joseph to Rachel, corrupt Jacob becomes righteous Israel, receives God's promises (Gen. 35:9-13) but they are split between the house of Leah (Judah) and the house of Rachel (Israel). Ruth 4:11. Joseph/Ephraim has "birthright." Gen. 49:22-26, Jer. 31:9.

7 The two houses become two kingdoms, Judah and Israel, and both eventually fall to Canaanite sexual sins.

David anointed to replace Saul and establishes righteous and powerful united kingdom.

David repents and is restored. Psalm 51. God confirms the Scepter Promise to him. 2 Sam. 7:10-16.

God sends a series of prophets to warn against adultery/idolatry. Some kings of Judah repent and restore godliness, including most righteous king Josiah under Jeremiah. 2 Kings 23:1-27.

Judah's last straw: King Manasseh replaces God with Baal, sacrifices own son. 2 Kings 21:1-15.

8 God desolates/cleanses the land, removing first Israel (722BC) and then Judah (568BC) per His Lev. 18 warning.

"I then will destroy your high places, and cut down your incense altars...I will lay waste your cities as well and... make the land desolate so that your enemies who settle in it will be appalled over it... Then the land will enjoy its Sabbaths all the days of the desolation, whil you are in your enemies' land; then the land will rest and enjoy its Sabbaths." Lev. 26:30-34.

Sexual sin now infects the chosen people and worsens over time despite righteous interludes.

Grandson Jacob "The deceiver" adopts polygamy, bearing twelve sons by two wives (Leah and Rachel) and two concubines. Sex-related sin disqualifies Leah's sons Rueben, Levi and Simeon from leadership and "scepter," which defaults to Judah. Gen. 49:1-10.

After the people reject God's system of judges, Saul bcomes their King but turns wicked.

David succumbs to adultery with Bathsheba and murder of her husband, his loyal captain.

Solomon, son of Bathsheba, becomes uber-polygamist with many "foreign wives," imports Canaanite worship lasting 300 years alongside Yahweh worhip. God punishes the kingdom by splitting the kingdom. 1 Kings 11:1-13.

No kings of Israel repent, Ahab and Jezebal are last straw, replacing God with Baal. 1 Kings 16:25-33.

THE BIBLICAL ORDER OF SEX AND CIVILATION IN THREE CHARTS

Chart 3 The Biblical Pattern Completed, from the Exile to the Millennial Kingdom

1 Return of the house of Judah from Babylonian exile is fresh start.

One flesh restored, "foreign wives" put away, monogomy is new permanent norm. Ezr. 10:3-5.

2 Antichrist Antiochus IV is "Epiphanes" (the "manifest god'") targets boys and women in strategy to undermine God's law and impose demonic polytheism.

Turns male youth to homosexuality, hangs slaughtered infants on necks of women who circumcize sons. Judah Maccabee delivers Jews, restores Law. Dan. 11, 1 Macc. 1:14-15, 60-61.

3 Herod the Great slaughters Maccabee royal family, then all infants Jesus' age in Nazareth.

Beguiled by wife, Herod Antipas beheads John the Baptist for confronting his adultery. Mk. 6.

4 Jesus does not overthrow Romans but offers way of salvation through faith. Affirms one flesh.

First non-Hebrew converts were Samaritans confronted ovr culture of adultery. Jn. 4.

5 Says "Give unto Caesar what is Caesar's but to God what is God's"

Apostle Paul warns sexual sin will steadily increase and produce apostasy in last days.

In contrast, church is compared to spotless bride prepared for her husband. Eph. 5:27.

Paul: Romans 1: 18-32 and 2 Tim. 3:1-8 taken together define last days culture of perversion.

6 Apostle Peter warns last days heresy will lure believers away from truth into rebellion.

Last days heresy identified with
1) days of Noah, 2) Sodom and Gomorrah, 3) life of Lot,
4) way of Balaam: i.e. Same sins outlined in Lev. 18, justified and condoned by false teachers. 2 Peter 2.

Many false prophets will arise and mislead many. Becuase lawlessness is increased, most people's love will grow cold. But the one who endures to the end will be saved. Matt. 24:11-13.

Last days heresy identified with
1) days of Noah, 2) Sodom and Gomorrah, 3) life of Lot,
4) way of Balaam: i.e. Same sins outlined in Lev. 18, justified
and condoned by false teachers. 2 Peter 2.

Many false prophets will arise and mislead many. Because lawlessness is increased, most people's love will grow cold. But the one who endures to the end will be saved. Matt. 24:11-13.

7 " . . . just like the Days of Noah" (Matt. 24:37), the defilement of sin overwhelms the land itself:

"For the anxious longing of the creation waits eagerly for the revealing of the sons of God. For the creation was subjected to futility, not willingly, but because of Him who subjected it, in hope that the creation itself also will be set free from its slavery to corruption into the freedom of the glory of the children of God. For we know that the whole creation groans and suffers the pains of childbirth together until now." Rom. 8:19-22.

8 In the final "desolation" the wicked and Satan are held in chains pending the final judgment, so the earth and the righteous can enjoy a thousand-year Sabbath in Christ's Millennial Kingdom. Rev. 20.

"Then the seventh angel sounded his trumpet, and loud voices called out in heaven: 'The kingdom of the world is now the kingdom of our Lord and of his Christ... The nations were enraged, and Your wrath has come. The time has come to judge the dead, and to reward Your servants... and to destroy those who destroy the earth.'" Rev. 11:15-18.

"He has kept [them] in eternal bonds under darkness for the judgment of the great day, just as Sodom and Gomorrah... since they in the same way as these indulged in gross immorality and went after strange flesh, are exhibited as an example in undergoing the punishment of eternal fire." Jude 1:6-7.

"The wicked will be destroyed, but those who wait on the Lord will inherit the land." Psalm 37:9.

END NOTES

[1] An excellent summary of the Feasts of the Lord may be found here: http://www.binarybees.biz/Feasts.htm

[2] There are numerous Messianic Jewish websites which address this point, one of which I found particularly useful: http://hatikva.org/no-man-knows-the-day-or-the-hour.html

[3] Philostratus, *The Life of Apollonius of Tyana* 6.29

[4] Philo of Alexandria, *On the Embassy to Gaius,* XXX, 203.

[5] We will address that topic more fully in due time but for those who would like to jump ahead, some key insights are provided in Zechariah 12 and 13 (esp 13:9), and Isaiah 59.

[6] (http://www.biblestudytools.com/dictionary/proselyte/).

[7] It is in my view no coincidence that the demonic guild called Freemasonry traces its origins to Solomon, and there is one very plausible school of thought that Solomon is the model of the end-time Antichrist -- and connected in some way with Freemasonry -- based 1 Kings 10:14-23. Irrespective of that, I am of the opinion that Solomon later repented and wrote the book of Ecclesiastes before his death, which likely explains why God never banished Solomon from His presence as He had done with Saul (2 Samuel 7:12-15).

[8] For information on Hebrew marriage rituals and symbolism see http://www.bible-history.com/links.php?cat=39&sub=400&cat_name=Manners+%26+Customs&subcat_name=Marriage+Customs

[9] http://www.travelujah.com/articles/entry/Who-were-the-Galileans-in-the-Days-of-Jesus-

[10] Note that this is the same legal principle that we see at work in the "second chance" available to the "left behind" as addressed in Chapter 3.

CPSIA information can be obtained
at www.ICGtesting.com
Printed in the USA
LVHW011102251121
704186LV00003B/15